The Great We-Set™

TacticalCivics.com

The

GREAT WE-SET™

How you can join Americans who are
taking America back one county at a time,
and enforcing the Constitution at last

David M. Zuniga

Founder, Tactical Civics™

Books by David M. Zuniga

This Bloodless Liberty

Fear The People (Fourth Edition)

Our First Right

(Book One) Tactical Civics™

(Book Two) Mission to America (Second Edition)

A Republic to Save: Essays in Tactical Civics™

Grand Jury Awake: Tactical Civics™ Primer on Grand Jury (2ⁿᵈ Ed)

Tactical Civics™ Ready Constitution

A Tax Honesty Primer

Tactical Civics™ for Church Leaders

Tactical Civics™ High School Edition (31-unit homeschool tutorial)

The Great We-Set™

No king but King Jesus

*Time to Start Over, America: Introducing American Militia 2.0™, Restoring Our
Founding Fathers' Law Enforcement, Riot & Border Control, and Social Glue*

Books in Process

Our Master and Idol No More

(Book Three) Engine of Change

(Book Four) The Banished Bureaucrat

(Book Five) The Greatest Awakening

*The Statesman's Manual: A Citizen-Statesman's Guide to Writing and Enacting
Legislation Conforming to the Constitution and Supporting the Rule of Law*

Dedication

The tombstone of a civilization is laid at that place where truth is
no longer defended because it cannot be known.

Honest, productive Americans are being crushed by our lawless
servants who think themselves our masters. This is God's
judgment for our faithlessness. We must repent.

I dedicate this work to every American
who loves Jesus Christ,
who is ready to know the truth,
and who to the last breath, will defend it.

You can't make this stuff up.

Like a Marvel Comics or James Bond script, the so-called *'Great Reset'* is a plan of billionaire globalists led by Klaus Schwab, who 50 years ago spawned a plan for world government, called the World Economic Forum...

For much more information on each of the subjects in the following brief chapters, read the appendices and *Tactical Civics™ High School Edition*.

Although reading to learn truth is important, we need to get into action *now*. Help launch your Tactical Civics™ chapter and become part of the solution, today – *then* begin doing the deeper reading.

CONTENTS

— CHAPTER 1 —
The Why

The most vital question in life's challenges and trials is always: *Why?*

Despite appearances, this is the *best* period in American history if a diligent remnant of America will repent. Repentance isn't words; it's *actions*. If you're in the remnant *you already feel it.* You've been waiting for this.

AmericaAgain! is a private, perpetual, charitable trust and member organization to glorify Jesus Christ by teaching, supporting, and organizing America's repentant remnant to enforce the Constitution for the first time and for the rest of history via Tactical Civics™, a repentant way of life on four pillars: Jesus Christ, the Constitution, Grand Jury, and Militia.

We don't accept elected public servants or public employees because in our Constitution, We The People create a sovereign-servant relationship between those who serve us and we who pay them for it:

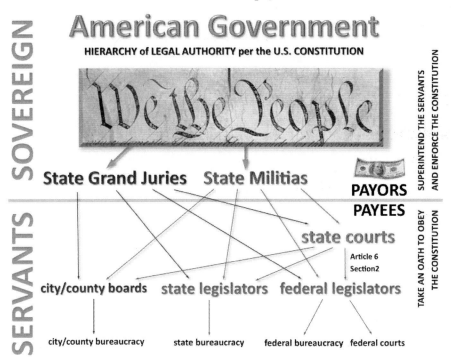

But since the generation of Lincoln, Marx, and Darwin, the hierarchy created by the We The People through our Constitution for public servants and employees has been flipped on its head – *hijacked.*

At every level from public school districts to congress, the presidency, and federal courts, those who are supposed to *serve* the People instead *rule* us and allow us no defense. Public employees at every level are briefed, trained, and supported by a powerful group of unions and organizations that supply and support teachers, school boards, mayors, county commissioners, 'law enforcement', judges, governors, state legislatures, and other public functionaries, training them in 'us-vs-them'. *And We The People pay for it.*

If you think I overstate the case, spend just one eye-opening Saturday visiting these nine websites of an industry made up of national unions who program, train, and support America's public employees to lord it over the People, extracting more money and 'compliance' from us. On a search engine, look up these unions to grasp how organized the predators and parasites are. All funded by your tax dollars. They are *very* organized, and we are not; and this is only a *partial* list...

- National Association of School Boards

- National Education Association

- AASA The School Superintendents' Association

- National League of Cities

- United States Conference of Mayors

- National Association of Counties

- County Judges & Commissioners' Association

- National Conference of State Legislatures

- American Federation of Government Employees

Is there a similar special-interest union for congress, presidents, and federal judges? Sure; Washington, D.C., the most powerful, ruthless, unaccountable, predatory, independent city-state in history.

You may think, *"Boy howdy...with all those organizations and their staffs training, briefing, and supporting over 20 million public employees and their bureaucratic staffers, how can Tactical Civics™ fight all of that?"*

Although Tactical Civics™ is the only action organization fighting on the People's side against the Deep Axis plus that huge industry of special interest unions, our mission is inspired by, and serves at the pleasure of, *The Creator of the Universe.*

Can regular, productive Americans join those training-and-support unions for public employees, bureaucrats, and politicians? No, we cannot.

So Tactical Civics™ is training productive, responsible citizens to finally fight back by putting our foot down with arrogant servants. Never-ending growth of public salaries, agencies, offices, programs, fleets, buildings, projects, junkets…that's Communism and Fascism, not our constitutional system of enumerated government powers.

American Communism exists in every school district, town, county, and state; *Americans are not allowed to own private property.* If you fail to pay taxes to the school district, city, and county you *will* lose your home, farm, shop or land, even if you paid off the note. We can *never* own private property in America because in Communism, *the takers are on top and the makers – the productive people – are on the bottom.* From cradle to grave.

Our mission teaches and organizes the People to finally arrest corrupt public servants and stop runaway government growth, beginning at the local and county levels. Tactical Civics™ is the *only* full-spectrum solution in America. No other effort even *remotely* approaches it. This way of life *can* restore our Republic, but it demands that we face the painful facts about public servants who put us in prison or take our wages or homes if we don't pay them. Who demand honor from us while treating us, their collective sovereign, as oxen. Who look down their protected-class noses at us, the *'general public', 'civilians', 'taxpayers',* or *'voters'.*

Does this offend you or a family member whose salary and pension come from productive America? You're not in the remnant. Moreover, the *sovereign* can be offended *too!* The arrogance and unaccountability of public unions and the powerful, daily-reinforced conflict of interests has driven America to *in-our-face* Communism including stolen elections, a fake president and his (April 2022) 'Ministry of Truth', just like an Orwell novel.

The sovereign-servant reversal in every public office, waiting line, and opulent school board chamber is driving Americans to despair. It's leading millions more into public jobs; more money and benefits for less work and accountability than in the productive sector. *It's time to end the hijacking.*

3

This is why we do not accept as members those who are elected to public offices or whose career or paychecks are earned 'below the line'.

You can't have it both ways: spend taxpayer money, but say you want to cut public excess and corruption. The layers of bureaucracy we suffer today, all funded by taxes extracted *against our will* and without our oversight or control is *not* the system of government intended by our Founders. It's the Old World all over again, right in God's face.

Those who tell us, "Drop the religion!" fail to understand that *America is under God's judgment and only repentance will lift His hand.* Those who tell us to accept public employees likewise don't understand a basic concept; they want *this* to be our system of government:

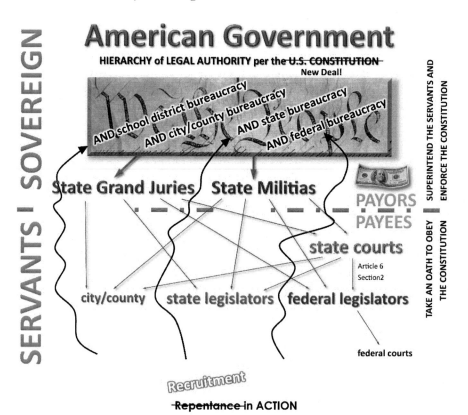

We understand that our daily stand for Jesus Christ as LORD and King will drive some people away, just as our bedrock policy of not accepting public employees or Muslims as members will drive some people away. But our 'red pill' mission is dedicated to truth. Enforcing constitutional and free market limits is our duty. *Law enforcement is not a popularity contest.*

4

In our Tactical Civics™ Training Center, we see five kinds of Americans; those who:

1) Immediately praise God and go to work for this is what they're seeking;

2) After months of detox, accept hard facts and finally take responsibility;

3) Are offended at our mention of Jesus, and leave;

4) Kick the tires, decide it's too much work, and leave;

5) Enter our Training Center with a *"Look at ME!"* social media act, start peddling their own brew, or start arguing with our mission's principles before even doing the reading, and are removed after several warnings.

America is not what we were a century ago. But *why?* And *how* do we repair these ruins? That's what I asked God while sitting by a fire in October, 2007 and the Lord answered my prayer with *great* specificity over many months. The hard, true lessons of Tactical Civics™ are the results of that answer. Like coming of age and having your grandparent sit you down and tell you all the shocking secrets of your family's past.

Once you know the hard facts of our past, you solve the 'mystery' of how America fell to this retrograde place. Some people accept responsibility in an hour or a day or a week. Others require months; but once they hear the truth, they can't un-hear it. By God's grace, Tactical Civics™ is for the repentant remnant who are *ready to face reality*.

This book is a brief version of a larger book, our 31-unit High School Tutorial. To drill down on each concept in this book, read that one. And don't let the high school label fool you; it's *advanced* material.

Our network of county chapters must grow to critical mass, and we must *focus*. This must begin at the state and county levels. We have the detailed plan and are building the leadership team, but restoration will not come until we have the numbers, members know the civics, and we implement our tactical plan in thousands of America's counties.

While we'll eventually need the numbers (half of 1% of county population is our long-term target) we must begin by seriously re-evaluating our lives. God sends the remnant; we don't pull you in or try to hook you. *If you don't feel led to it, you're not right for the mission. At least not yet.* Uncomfortable as it is, as 'missionaries to the Americans', our first step in this ministry and new way of life is our *own* sincere repentance.

And repentance is an *action* word.

— CHAPTER 2 —
Overview of federal government

The government of these fifty United States is based on a written Constitution which is only 4,400 words long; the shortest constitution in the world. It is also the oldest written constitution in effect in the world today. After the Constitutional Convention in Philadelphia, held from May-September 1787, the final Constitution was sent to the 13 states for ratification. Some textbooks claim that our Constitution for the United States was a 'compact' or a contract and the States were the parties to that contract. That is false, as evidenced by Article VI, Section 2 of the law itself, which states,

This Constitution, and the Laws of the United States which shall be made in Pursuance thereof; and all Treaties made, or which shall be made, under the Authority of the United States, shall be the supreme Law of the Land; and the Judges in every State shall be bound thereby, any Thing in the Constitution or Laws of any State to the Contrary notwithstanding.

Thus, the U.S. Constitution is not a compact or a contract. It is the highest and most authoritative *law* in these united States, by which We The People created, defined, and *severely limited* our federal servants in three branches.

Our federal servants and supposed representatives violate the highest law with impunity in D.C., far from their collective sovereign *We The People*, the only human power with authority to stop this crime spree.

The Constitution's five basic principles were once deeply ingrained in the minds of Americans but today have all given way to D.C. organized crime:

Popular Sovereignty: The source of governmental power lies with the People; we are collectively the sovereign over all government.

Limited Government: We The People create, define, and severely limit the powers and functions of our servants. It must obey its own laws and *only* do things that we authorize it to do, in the U.S. Constitution.

Separation of Powers: Our federal servant is divided into three branches so that no one branch has too much power.

Checks and Balances: To protect ourselves against corrupt servants, We The People establish *horizontal* checks and balances; each branch of our federal servant keeping the other two from becoming too powerful.

Federalism: Our federal servants have *only* the 17 powers granted to them by We The People, who reserve *all other conceivable powers* for ourselves and our state servants.

Some people include another supposed principle of federal government, *judicial review,* misrepresenting it as judicial *supremacy.* Yes, the power of 'judicial review' was created by chief justice John Marshall in a side note to his opinion in *Marbury v. Madison* in 1803. But law schools teach the lie that Marshall created a new governing power over presidents and Congress; the *opposite* of what Marshall wrote:

[T]*he Constitution of the United States confirms and strengthens the principle…that a law repugnant to the constitution is void; and that courts, as well as other departments, are bound by that instrument.*

[T]*he framers of the Constitution contemplated that instrument as a rule for the government of courts, as well as of the legislature.*

We The People in the U.S. Constitution stipulate and limit the powers of our servants, yet our highest law is *daily violated* by a massively corrupt politics industry; the Democrat and Republican machines, actors in theater to keep the People entertained as the industry cuts deals, trades favors, and *passes laws written by industry lawyers, not by legislators.* Yes: for generations, laws have been written by industry lawyers and only *sponsored* by legislators.

We *supposedly* elect a president via the Electoral College, one elector for each member of Congress. But in most states, Electoral College votes are 'thrown' by the dominant political machine to the candidate with the most votes; corrupt state legislatures and party machines destroyed the Electoral College. Corrupt party machines have been operating fraudulent elections for decades. Nobody can know how many politicians today are in office legitimately. As long as Dominion Voting Systems and other criminal enterprises are counting electronically, turnout will continue to drop in elections and the criminal fraud will repeat as in 2020.

Yet, despite the rampant corruption, *this is the most exciting time in two centuries of American history.* Why? Because elections and constitutional rule of law can be restored by an informed sovereign, We The People. We only need to *repent* and start enforcing it.

— CHAPTER 3 —

Tactical Civics™ Introduction

To control the Supreme Court we must first lay claim to the Constitution ourselves. That means publicly repudiating justices who say that they, not we, possess ultimate authority to say what the Constitution means…It means refusing to be deflected by arguments that constitutional law is too complex or difficult for ordinary citizens…the Supreme Court is not the highest authority in the land on constitutional law. We are.[1]

– Larry D. Kramer

Amen. This is the *best* time to be alive in American history. This book can be the most important thing you have ever read. It will debunk lies and teach you vital civics that schools and colleges leave out, giving you all you need to live a new way of life as we repair America's fallen walls, end D.C. organized crime, and begin to restore our civilization. Many excellent organizations *teach* the U.S. Constitution. This book trains you to *enforce* the Constitution and teach future generations to do the same. A whole new way of life. Yes, we have a lot to repair. But America was not destroyed in a year and it won't be restored overnight. As you learn how our government is designed to work and how simple it is to take responsibility, you'll wonder why it took us so long to do this.

We will astound ourselves (and the world) over the next generation if we can realize this is not about presidents. This restoration project is, and always has been, *up to us*. And as you will see, this is not politics. *It's life.*

After the COVID hoax and Election Steal 2020, can we end today's hijacking? Absolutely. In the Constitution, We the People create, define, and limit our federal servant, give them 17 duties, and give ourselves only one: *enforce it*. We the People alone have the authority to restore our rule of law. Born into this uniquely blessed civilization, our ancestors let it collapse. Not *once* have they ever *enforced* the Constitution.

---

[1] Dr. Kramer, at that time dean of Stanford Law School, on pages 247-248 of his groundbreaking book, *The People Themselves: Popular Constitutionalism and Judicial Review.*

'We the People' means only those Americans who choose to perform the duties that we confer on ourselves in our highest law. This remnant can do what a president cannot dream of doing. We must only graduate from fear, cynicism, Facebook rants, pointless rallies, and Fear Porn.

AmericaAgain! Trust is a charitable trust and member organization whose mission was developed by 45 volunteers over 66,000 hours in R&D since early 2008, and now run the TACTICAL CIVICS™ Training Center – not a social media hangout, but *action*. To restore America, our objectives in order are:

- Launch & build a TACTICAL CIVICS™ chapter in every county

- Support true county Grand Juries via our county ordinance

- Restore constitutional Militia via our county ordinance

- Finish ratifying the original First Right in our Bill of Rights

- Take Congress out of Washington D.C. forever

- Force through 18 other reform laws over time

- Launch the AmericaAgain! Indictment Engine™

Countless books, conferences, blogs, podcasts, radio shows, videos and declarations rehash the problem. But as you now see, Washington D.C. is earth's most corrupt city-state and federal judges will not help. We The People, through Grand Jury, Militia, and our State courts are *the only constitutional means* to finally end the hijacking that began with Lincoln.

We can never convert the masses, but as Margaret Meade said, *"Never doubt that a small group of thoughtful, committed citizens can change the world. Indeed, it is the only thing that ever has."* Most people are apathetic and will not change. That is no problem; as noted earlier, we only need about half of 1% of America to do this. But complaining daily in social media rants is exactly Einstein's definition of insanity: *"repeatedly doing the same thing and always expecting a different result"*.

As he walked out of the 1787 convention, Ben Franklin was asked by Lady Powell of Philadelphia, *"Doctor Franklin, what kind of government have you given us?"* He replied, *"A Republic, Madam, if you can keep it."*

We haven't kept it; we've been trained by government schools to look to politicians instead. Like Trump: his populist style was Andrew Jackson or Teddy Roosevelt; his hard-nosed business sense, Calvin Coolidge. His PR strategy and vocabulary were Cassius Clay, like a force of nature. Yet

Donald Trump was only one *effect* of the movement in America's heartland that included Moral Majority, Christian Coalition, the Constitution and Libertarian parties, Ron Paul Revolution, and the TEA Party. *The Deep Axis beat them all.*

With his huge ego and opulent lifestyle, Trump never appreciated that he was our *servant,* whose job was to obey the Constitution. When heartland America elected him, we did more than cast a ballot in one more election; we crossed partisan lines in 2016 and *much* bigger in 2020. But the Deep Axis set the trap years in advance: Russiagate, Shampeachment, BLAntifa riots, the COVID hoax, and the stolen 2020 election; all steps in the largest gaslighting operation in history. Trump was our servant, but his millions of fans wanted a savior instead. Many of his cabinet picks were terrible, and toward the end he embraced the COVID hoax and drove it to a whole new level with Pence, Fauci, Birx, and Big Pharma.

Moral and ethical life continues in America's 31,000 small towns and rural areas. In the 2016 election we defeated and shocked Progressives; we did it again in 2020, but the Deep Axis overthrew the government anyway. Now, after two generations running from a ruthless, small minority that fights dirty and plays only offense, we in the Remnant *now stay on offense.*

Tactical Civics™ rejects all the failed past ideas: an Article V convention, nullification, secession, the TEA Party, armed revolution, anarchy, PACs and think tanks, a shadow government, and a D.C. coup.

We also detox our civics terms. We always capitalize *State;* never capitalize *federal* or offices of our servants (mayor, governor, president, congressman, senator, judge), and we write *supreme Court* as the founders did.

Second, popular sovereignty is *collective,* not individual. We're not each a monarch as 'sovereign citizen' cultists claim. Popular constitutionalism is the *antithesis* of anarchy. Now, the ten words that we detox…

Nation: America is a constitutional republic; see the Constitution, Article IV, Section 4. A 'nation' is a population under a central government. These united States are a *republic*, not a nation.

Democracy: Calling America a democracy is as inaccurate as calling it monarchy. James Madison wrote: *"Democracies have ever been spectacles of turbulence and contention…and have in general been as short in their lives as they have been violent in their death."* Adams wrote: *"Democracy never lasts long. It soon wastes, exhausts, and murders itself. There never was a democracy yet that did not commit suicide."*

Government: Most people who say, *"I'm against the government!"* in truth are against organized crime. We The People are the highest level of government. So federal government is *only those who perform duties enumerated* in Article I, Section 8. Those who skim payroll accounts, counterfeit money, and open our borders are not government but *organized crime.*

Revolution: means overturning government. In our Constitution We The People create, define and severely limit government. The last thing we want to do is overturn it.

Grassroots: We The People are the highest level of government in our republic, not brainwashed *grassroots,* earthworms underfoot.

Voter: We constantly breathe and walk. Why don't we refer to ourselves as 'breathers' or 'walkers'? Don't say *voter;* it's not a noun. Voting is only a small part of our citizen power and duty.

Elected leaders: Have you ever been *led* by a politician? Statesmen *represent* sovereigns, they do not *lead* us.

Elected officials: If an office is nowhere authorized by us in the Constitution, a person cannot be an *official.* 'Public servant' is a fitting term if they are honest, or 'criminal' if they are not.

Constituent: This one is worse than *voter,* tiny citizens making up one politician. We don't *constitute* servants; we *oversee* them.

Tyranny: is a term used for a corrupt sovereign who becomes ruthless. Today, our servants are financial criminals, extortionists, defrauders, embezzlers, and shameless bureaucrats. This is not tyranny; it's longstanding *crime.*

Like ideas, words have consequences. Galileo said, *"All truths are easy to understand once they are discovered; the point is to discover them."* This new life includes responsible *action,* not more words; duty that our fathers shirked. Just one action at a time, we will recover our lives, property, liberty, civilization, and Christian witness. TACTICAL CIVICS™ is a new way of life for an American remnant as humanity finally learns to use the Internet for self-government. No other people can do this; our Constitution make us unique on earth. Just as one generation hijacked us, now by God's grace, our generation can end the long hijacking through a network of homes, churches, small businesses, shops, farms, ranches, VFW halls, constitutional Militia units, educated Grand Jury members, and others; Christians who will not run for the hills but will instead join us as we repair the ruins of our civilization.

— CHAPTER 4 —

Applying Romans 13 in America

Faced with corrupt and tyrannical government, too many Christians let criminals off the hook by using Romans 13, *"Let every soul be in subjection to the higher authorities, for there is no authority except from God, and those who exist are ordained by God…For the authority is not a terror to those who do good, but to those who do evil. Do you want to have no fear of the authority? Do that which is good, and you will have praise from the same…But if you do that which is evil, be afraid, for he does not bear the sword in vain. He is a minister of God, an avenger for wrath to him who does evil."*

How Christians Pervert This Scripture

Consider this in the context of our Republic; we are not ancient Rome under Caesars, so who are 'the higher authorities' in our system? See the first three words of our Constitution: *We the People* collectively are the highest authority! We are *over* the Constitution.

The first chief justice of the U.S. supreme Court, John Jay, wrote, *The People are Sovereign… (A)t the Revolution, the sovereignty devolved on the People and they are truly the sovereigns of the country… the Citizens of America are equal as fellow Citizens and as joint Tenants in the sovereignty.*

It's our power and duty to enforce the law when servants do that which is evil. Instead, our arrogant servants have trained *us* to fear *them*. We the People, the parents who gave birth to our government, must instill proper fear in criminal hearts. In Chapter 8, you learn how America's sovereigns will have our State Criminal Court 'bear the sword' against any member of congress or our state legislature who violates our highest law.

What's Wrong With This Picture?

Your servants control your life, property, and future. Making illegal 'laws' for us, congress exempts itself. They have been counterfeiting our money for 150 years. They invite millions of illegals over our border and force taxpayers to pay welfare, healthcare, incarceration, and 'free' government schooling costs so they can gain these illegals' votes and their industry puppeteers can gain the cheap labor. Meanwhile for their sovereigns, they track, record, and store our conversations, emails, travel and purchase records; they fine us for using our own land; regulate everything from lightbulbs to toilet flushes, and legitimize perversion as 'marriage' while muzzling our pulpits. Our abdication created the Caesar that threatens history's most blessed Christian civilization.

Repentance demands that we *never again* apply Romans 13 to our Republic as if we are ancient Rome. Repentance is an *action* word. Our book, *Tactical Civics™ for Church Leaders* teaches pastors how to teach citizens to finally perform our duties in the highest office in American government: enforcing the Constitution and glorifying Jesus Christ, as was once our way before a watching world.

— CHAPTER 5 —

Dishonest Abe, American Idol

Brace yourself. This chapter will shock you and make you angry. But as Christ taught, truth will set us free. Hard truths of history must be faced and lies hooted off the stage in our homes, churches, schools and colleges if we are to avoid the collapse in communist countries and across Europe.

Like so many Russians or Chinese, Americans have been lied to in schools. Even private, Christian, and *most homeschools.* One of the most destructive frauds in our culture is that Lincoln was a great president and a good man. In truth, *he was the most ruthless, destructive president in our history.*

Americans are ignorant of the affinity that Abraham Lincoln had for Karl Marx and his Communist system. Even as liberals have banished the Confederate flag, those who think Lincoln was a hero are as ignorant of our history as the average Russian citizen is of his.

If you think I exaggerate, the first resource I recommend is available at no cost. *Reading Karl Marx with Abraham Lincoln: Utopian Socialists, German Communists, and Other Republicans* is a 2011 article in *The International Socialist Review,* the communist news source of record, describing the mutual admiration between Marx and Lincoln.

The first book is *Forced Into Glory: Abraham Lincoln's White Dream* by Black scholar and author Lerone Bennett Jr. Impeccably documented with many original source quotes, Bennett paints Lincoln as the consummate White Supremacist and mendacious snake-in-the-grass.

The second book is *Lincoln's Marxists* by Al Benson and Walter Kennedy. Exposes the ties between Marxism, Lincoln's illegal new national army, and the new GOP that rose from the ashes of the Whig party. A second shocking exposé of our most execrable president.

The third book on Lincoln's character and lasting destruction is *Lincoln Unmasked: What You're Not Supposed to Know About Dishonest Abe*, by Thomas DiLorenzo. A shocking portrait of a tyrant, manipulator and opportunist.

The fourth book to banish idolatry of America's hijacker is *America's Caesar* by Greg Durand. With countless original source cites, Durand paints a picture of a nineteenth-century agnostic attorney of riverboat operators and railroad barons; whose only use for Jesus was to lure the masses. The most destructive man in history makes Clinton look like a saint.

The fifth book is *The Unpopular Mr. Lincoln,* by Larry Tagg, a compilation and analysis of public statements and articles during Lincoln's rule. According to his associates, the most despised president in our history.

The sixth book is *A Century of War* by John Denson. It provides copious original source documentation of Lincoln's Northern mercantilist handlers making him defy his cabinet to sucker the South into firing the first shots at Fort Sumter, where no one was killed or even wounded.

Don't take my word that our former idol was a monster; read any of those resources. Take the red pill to see that *we have work to do.* The programming of once-godly, productive, tough-minded folk began in the generation of Lincoln, Marx, and Darwin. Since that time we increasingly turned from God to accept every imaginable sin. The wages of rebellion is God's judgment. We wander in the desert, oblivious to where we have been and what happened there. Like dumbfounded hijack victims, we simply stare out the windows. Our only path back to sanity is *repentance.*

American Communism didn't begin with Obama. Read any of the books linked above and will see that it began with Lincoln. If you perform due diligence but still prefer to honor Lincoln, then don't just hate the Confederate flag; hate the U.S. Constitution too, as he did. And don't blame me for bringing you hard truth. Blame your teachers, whose comfortable traditions – whose *lies* – you prefer to liberty.

— CHAPTER 6 —

Split Them Up

We cover this material in much greater detail in Appendix A. This is the most powerful thing the People can do to stop D.C. organized crime.

To take Congress out of Washington D.C., we first need a tactical preliminary to change the makeup of Congress. By God's grace, the framers of the Constitution left us just the weapon we need: their first Article in the original Bill of Rights. The only one that has not been fully ratified, it has been gathering dust for over two centuries. So our first action project, called Our First Right, is designed to get our State legislatures to finish ratifying it. This was done before, by *just one man.*

The original First Amendment was designed to preclude exactly the corruption we have: multimillion dollar campaigns with congressmen reigning over 750,000 citizens that they can't know, much less represent.

Two years before the Bill of Rights was finalized, on the last day of the 1787 Constitutional Convention, Nathaniel Gorham made a motion to change one word in Article I, Section 2, Clause 4 of the new Constitution: "the number of Representatives shall not exceed one for every forty thousand" would now read, "…for every *thirty* thousand". Others seconded the motion, then George Washington rose to speak for the first and only time in the four month long convention, as James Madison describes on page 644 in *Records of the Federal Convention*:

When the President rose…he said that although his situation had hitherto restrained him from offering his sentiments…he could not forbear expressing his wish that the alteration proposed might take place… The smallness of the proportion of Representatives had been considered by many members of the Convention an insufficient security for the rights and interests of the People.

He acknowledged that it had always appeared to himself among the exceptionable parts of the plan…as late as the present moment was for admitting amendments, he thought this of so much consequence that it would give much satisfaction to see it adopted.

The delegates passed the change unanimously.

For the next two years the State legislatures deliberated about ratifying the new Constitution. On June 8, 1789 Madison's team introduced 39 amendments. On September 25, Congress did pass the Bill of Rights, but only twelve of the 39 articles of amendment, and sent them to the States for ratification. We were taught that the Bill of Rights had ten amendments; in truth, it had twelve. But the first two were not ratified by the necessary three-quarters of the States so they remained open in the States, gathering dust...*for two centuries.*

Then in 1983, University of Texas student Greg Watson ran a campaign to get 29 more State legislatures to ratify the original Second Amendment. It stipulated that if Congress gives itself a pay raise, it does not take effect until an election intervenes. After Watson had toiled away for almost ten years, in May 1992 the U.S. Archivist certified that three-fourths of the States had ratified and that 'Article the Second' of the Bill of Rights was now the 27th Amendment.

Every article in our Bill of Rights is ratified except the first and most important one. It has 11 ratification votes; it needs 38. So when we get 27 more State legislatures to ratify it, the original 'Article the First' will become the 28th Amendment. A college student got this done; so can we!

Since Congress already passed the Amendment, Washington D.C. can't stop us and no constitutional convention is needed. Our State legislatures have a duty to ratify our full Bill of Rights so that we can finally restore the People's House. Twelve state legislatures – CT, KY, MD, NH, NJ, NY, NC, PA, RI, SC, VT and VA – already voted to ratify it, but CT failed to turn in its paperwork. So we need 27 more states out of the 38 who have not acted on it, to just vote 'yes'.

Appendix B is the 28th Amendment Fact Sheet with history of the original First Amendment and Appendix C is the model Joint Resolution for your state legislature to hold its vote. We will not try this project until we have a few thousand county chapters, because D.C. organized crime will fight to the death to stop this reform and the one we describe in Chapter 7.

Our elected servants are *never* on your side, no matter *what* they say. Your state capitol is no better than Capitol Hill. Recall civics from Chapter 2; this is not more 'political activist' nonsense. Our First Right is the crucial first step in the most powerful self-government transformation in history.

— CHAPTER 7 —

Bring Them Home

"If we lose freedom here, there is no place to escape to. This is the last stand on Earth. And this idea that government is beholden to the people, that it has no other source of power except to sovereign people, is still the newest and most unique idea in all the long history of man's relation to man... Whether we believe in our capacity for self-government or whether we abandon the American Revolution and confess that a little intellectual elite in a far-distant capital can plan our lives for us better than we can plan them ourselves". (Ronald Reagan, Oct. 1964)

Washington D.C. is earth's most corrupt and powerful city-state, working for the 534 billionaires and every industry in America. Idealistic statesmen win office, move to D.C., receive orientation, then are surrounded by veteran staffers, other unelected D.C. bureaucrats, D.C. law firms, and single-issue lobbyists.

But Our First Right will transform congressional elections forever. After the States ratify the 28th Amendment, the next congressional election will be for 6,500+ representatives in compact, local congressional districts rather than 435 huge, gerrymandered fiefdoms for industry.

Like the British, too many Americans are unwilling to govern themselves and instead seek monarchs like Barack and Michelle or like Donald and Melania with opulent lifestyles, to rule over them. I liked the Trumps, but a gold-plated first couple made Americans gawk like Brits, and too many Americans already had celebrity fetishes. If we accept or even demand celebrity of our public servants, we have no right to oversee them, or even to vote. It's time to wake up, repent, and take our lives back. The world awaits such hope; a model of what can be done. It must begin with repentance, then duty.

Every two years, one out of 50,000 of us can take responsibility to represent the others, obeying and supporting the U.S. Constitution as the oath of office demands, and co-sponsoring our reform laws. There are hundreds of thousands of intelligent, patriotic Americans who will accept our challenge after we ratify the 28th Amendment. If you're honest and of average intelligence, you're superior to the average member of Congress today. It will be no sacrifice: half of a congressman's salary is $90,000 and you won't have to move to D.C. or keep a second home. The Founding Fathers' dream: in the People's House, statesmen serve for two or four years, then return to regular life. No get-rich career in politics, just citizen-statesmen representing self-governing citizens.

It requires plain fiscal discipline, to shut down unconstitutional agencies, bureaus and programs; impossible for a politician seeking a lifelong career, but a no-brainer for productive Americans. And no one expects perfection in a congressman; only honesty and common sense.

Why do we despise politicians? Because they lie, cut deals, and huddle with one another in a world of make-believe, spending our hard-earned money like drunken sailors at a magic ATM machine. Congress runs earth's most powerful city-state as organized crime, to benefit a long list of powerful industries and groups. We the People believe we can't win because we can't get to the billionaires, *but we only need to get their puppets,* the control mechanism of our Constitution. We take Congress out of that corrupt city-state to work from their communities!

That's our first proposed reform law, the *Bring Congress Home Act* (BCHA). Something like the 2013 resolution called HR287 to bring Congress home to work from their district offices via *telepresence,* which is common tech today. Thousands of participants can meet by desktop, laptop, tablet or even smart phone. The BCHA stipulates that all members of Congress will work full-time back home in one modest office each, with staff of two for a congressman or six for a senator; limited to two terms, congressmen making half their present salary since districts will be 1/14 as large, and no benefits or pensions. *Congress should be short-term public service, not a career.*

Our first 'big Congress' will do what all past ones have done: set up their office and staff in their district. But then instead of moving to D.C., they will simply meet at a large D.C. venue on January 3 (2025 or 2027, for instance) for one item only: enact the BCHA. The president signs it and makes history, then they go home to a lease office and telepresence system.

Despite their great wealth and power, Pharaohs did not have flush toilets, cars, or air conditioning. By the grace of God and over 66,000 hours of due diligence and R&D by 44 volunteers, in the fullness of time, man's inventions will again change the world. Tactical Civics™ with Our First Right and the Bring Congress Home Act will be the most powerful acts of popular constitutionalism since those shopkeepers and farmers changed the world in 1776.

It's time to *bring Congress home.*

— CHAPTER 8 —

True Law Enforcement

In the Tenth Amendment, we stipulate that the States and People retain all powers except the 17 that we delegate to Washington, DC. *It has no sovereignty in any other area of life or jurisdiction in any other area of the world.*

Read that paragraph again. Slowly. *Twice.*

By now you're aware that our servants have been perpetrating massive crimes for generations. In the book *Organized Crime: The Unvarnished Truth About Government,* Thomas DiLorenzo exposes a long list of D.C. crimes. Countless whistleblower books expose D.C. organized crime. *War is a Racket,* the 1935 classic by General Smedley Butler, and *Theft of The Nation,* a detailed 1969 survey by criminologist Donald Cressey, describe how local, state, and federal governments 50 years ago were already operating organized crime. The five-year crime spree (Russia hoax, Shampeachment, Plandemic, Election Steal 2020 and massive gaslighting covering it up) illustrates that D.C. organized crime and its minions in corrupt cities won't just disappear if we elect 'better' ones. *Elections will never arrest criminals.*

Investigative journalist Peter Dale Scott, over 50 years, has published 40 books including *American War Machine,* and *Drugs, Oil, and War* and his latest book, *The American Deep State.* We produced a 6-part podcast series in 2019-20 entitled *Who Killed America's Militia?* available in the Tactical Civics™ Training Center. In those nine hours of podcasts, we explain the who, what, when, where, and why of the FBI, CIA, DOJ and other lawless D.C. agencies who run interference for mafia, to make you believe that things will all be better if you just "trust the Plan".

AmericaAgain! is a perpetual charitable trust whose action mission, Tactical Civics™ recruits, educates, supplies, and tactically organizes Americans to enforce the U.S. Constitution by restoring Grand Jury and Militia in every county and eventually by using the Indictment Engine™, a mobile app whose algorithms assign felony indictment target value to every bent member of Congress. The Constitution has been violated for generations by our servants because We the People have never *enforced* it. From now on via State criminal courts, we will. The Supremacy Clause (Article VI, Section 2) stipulates that *the Constitution,* not federal government, is supreme. It says that State judges are bound by it, but that means bound to *enforce* it as well as obey it!

Our founders rejected titles of nobility for public servants, to erase all vestiges of aristocracy. The original program for attorneys was that they had no special schools; they simply read law until they could stand before the bar and be found competent to practice. The original principle for judges was that they not be lawyers like the mechanics practicing before them; just men who demonstrated wisdom and integrity. Today, judges make the People bow and scrape before them; yet by law we made them the servants of our servants! See Article III of the Constitution, We the People create a U.S. supreme Court, then allow Congress, which we created in Article I, to create its inferior federal courts. All we needed was a mechanism to help us exercise our lawful power. Now we have one, but these things won't happen on their own. *We have chores.*

How the App Will Operate

The Indictment Engine™ is actually a planned combination of a mobile app, Tactical Civics™ staff work, and peaceful, perpetual citizen action to superintend servants via *tactical force-massing.*

A county Grand Jury and Militia work to bring a criminal legislator under felony indictment in State criminal court on felony charges under the politician's *State* laws that coincide with the omission, commission, support for, or acquiescence in Congress' violating our highest law. The legal principle *qui tacit consentit* regards any accessory to a crime; 'silence implies consent'.

The Indictment Engine™ produces felony presentments beginning with financial crimes against residents of your State by a fellow resident of your State who *happens* to be a member of Congress or your State legislature. Each time we get a State Grand Jury to hand down a criminal indictment against a legislator for a State Penal Code offense, our plea bargain deal will be like the one offered by the Saxons to King Ethelred in 1014 A.D., or by the English barons to King John in the *Magna Carta* in 1215 A.D., or by Congress' IRS thugs to every 'Taxpayer'... *"Agree to our terms or go to prison with your assets seized."*

Those members of Congress not yet targeted will receive the same offer, but as an immunity deal. But before all of that, our Tactical Civics™ Good Guys campaign will offer every candidate and incumbent an opportunity to step away from D.C. organized crime before being targeted.

Grand Jury

This subject is covered in much more detail in our Field Handbook #2, *Grand Jury Awake*. But basically, when We The People finally enforce the U.S. Constitution, we cause public servants to "be in subjection to the higher authorities" and we also keep the Leviathan state from growing back like a cancer.

The Grand Jury can serve for months, but is not a full-time thing; sometimes only one day per week or less. It considers only capital cases and other 'infamous crimes' (like stealing an election). The Grand Jury can make its own presentments based on any information its members discover themselves, or that is brought to them. The Grand Jury does not rule on the law at issue, nor does it determine guilt or innocence; that's for the 12-person petit jury in a trial. The Grand Jury only decides whether to issue a bill of indictment for prosecutors to take the target to trial.

The Indictment Engine™ will produce presentments for Grand Juries, citing specific felony counts that the targeted legislator is conspiring to perpetrate by passing the legislation (s)he is sponsoring. The Indictment Engine™ will prepare a comprehensive presentment including the text of the filed bill, names and association(s) of the individuals or corporations that drafted the bill for the politician to sponsor, and the relevant State Penal Code sections that it violates, besides violating the Constitution. Alas, our presentments cannot also name as indicted co-conspirators the attorneys and individuals in the corporations that drafted the proposed bill, for that would make it a federal case.

Next, the Grand Jury hands down the bill of indictment. To assure the case is not hijacked by a corrupt or timid prosecutor, our members in that Tactical Civics™ chapter will put public pressure on the prosecutor's office. If they are corrupt, *they* will be the next Grand Jury target.

As you read the history of Grand Juries in America, you see We The People stopping organized crime in government, and that's how the People have done it since 997 AD!

American Militia 2.0™

At this point, another aspect of our Tactical Civics™ trifecta is vital: well-regulated Militia. See our book, *Time to Start Over, America* for much more on constitutional Militia.

Locally, we'll offer Tactical Civics™ Affiliate membership to retailers, professionals like doctors and lawyers, and others who want to support our mission. American Militia 2.0™ is our project to make Militia fun, cool, and popular again; as patriotic here as it is in Switzerland and valued as highly as your local Volunteer Fire Department. We The People have a constitutional duty! We already have the world's largest and most active firearms and shooting culture; now, we just add American Militia 2.0™.

Trump claimed to be a 'law and order' president amidst the massive lawlessness and violence across America, for he didn't understand that law enforcement is a local and state function, *not* the job of presidents. He obviously also was unaware that the 'Department of Justice' is an illegal agency that began a century ago when a part-time job for one man was created without constitutional authority. *The agency shouldn't even exist!*

Some Days, the World Just Changes

For 28 years, the Berlin Wall changed the world of all East Germans. But like communism itself, their ruthless artifice could only remain standing by force or fraud. *Then Ronald Reagan spoke six words.*

His challenge, *"Mr. Gorbachev, tear down this wall!"* sparked the imagination of Gorbachev and kindled East German hearts. The world changed back again. Tasting liberty, the German people destroyed and carried away every chunk of the Berlin Wall almost as quickly as the Soviet crew had erected it. God turned a page of history for Germans when Ronald Reagan spoke those six words, and despite today's fake 'administration', Psalm 94 holds:

The LORD will not cast off his people, neither will He forsake his inheritance. But judgment shall return unto righteousness: and all the upright in heart shall follow it. Who will rise up for me against the evildoers? or who will stand up for me against the workers of iniquity? Shall the throne of iniquity have fellowship with thee, which frames mischief by a law? They gather themselves together against the soul of the righteous, and condemn innocent blood. But the LORD is my defense and my God, the rock of my refuge. He shall bring upon them their own iniquity, and shall cut them off in their own wickedness; yea, the LORD our God shall cut them off.

Psalm 94 has always inspired us; we believe that God is raising a repentant Remnant to cut off those who 'frame mischief by a law'. We the People *can* enforce our U.S. Constitution from now on. Corrupt school district, city, county, state, and federal bureaucracies have greedily held their place as our taskmasters, as powerful guilds held Medieval Europe in serfdom…

Until they didn't.

— CHAPTER 9 —

America Again in 19 Steps

We the People intend to draft, refine, and push through the following 19 reform laws. This is only an overview; a summary text of the proposed laws appears in the AmericaAgain! Declaration (see Appendix F).

As a plea-bargaining package offered to any member of Congress criminally indicted using the AmericaAgain! Indictment Engine™ or as an immunity package for those who have not yet been targeted, we will allow them to agree in writing to co-sponsor these reforms and vote for them without amendment. Truly, the Great We-Set™.

1) Shut down D.C. organized crime by passing the *Bring Congress Home Act*.

2) End the imperial rule of federal courts by passing the *Constitutional Courts Act,* which will disallow any case involving abortion, euthanasia, marriage, sexual practices, healthcare, education, religious laws (e.g. sharia), or state voter ID laws, out of federal court jurisdiction. Outlaws 'administrative law', assuring that no administrative law 'judge' can bind any citizen; outlaws use of terms like 'court', 'order', 'subpoena', 'due process', 'the record' and other judicial terms by administrative bureaucrats.

3) The *Non-Enumerated Powers Sunset Act* creates a house standing committee and will fund/support a Citizens' Volunteer Research Service, with authority to review and de-fund any federal regulation, agency, bureau or program not within a power *specifically* enumerated by We The People in the U.S. Constitution. Will outlaw every alphabet-soup agency including DHS and all federal meddling in education, farming, and the environment (for the most part) as well as all foreign aid.

4) Outlaw back-door pork and tyranny by enacting the *Clean Bill Act,* outlawing any omnibus bill or the addition of riders, unrelated-issue amendments, and earmarks to legislation. Will also require that all filed bills to have names and contact information of every private-sector individual or entity who initiated, proposed, or drafted elements of the bill.

5) Secure our Border and civilization by enacting the *Secure Borders Act,* acknowledging each state's duty to field a Militia for border defense, calling for construction or completion of the border wall, and immediately de-funding and outlawing all agencies, bureaus, policies and programs that

encourage, facilitate or support illegal immigration. This legislation shall also bar from entry into the U.S. any adherent to sharia law, whether or not the person attempting to enter the U.S. is a resident of an officially Islamic state.

6) *End the 'Anchor Baby' tactic* by enacting as a federal statute Senate Joint Resolution 6 of the 111th Congress.

7) The *Congressional Anti-Corruption Act* provides first, SEC insider trading rules will apply to members of Congress. It will be a federal crime for a member of Congress, directly or through proxies, trusts, or other entities, to purchase or sell stock in any company materially affected by legislation of which the member of Congress may be reasonably expected to have knowledge. Secondly, no member of Congress can be a lobbyist for five years after leaving office and *for life*, no former member of Congress or staffer for a member of Congress can lobby for a foreign government. Thirdly, it will be a federal felony to require a member of Congress to raise money as prerequisite to leadership or committee assignment.

8) Restore Privacy by enacting the *Citizens' Privacy Act,* reiterating Fourth Amendment privacy of the People's persons, houses, papers, communications, vehicles, and effects from any government surveillance, seizure, detainment, or file storage by any method including drones, mini-drones, hidden cameras, etc. The law makes any such activity a federal offense unless preceded by issuance of a specific, bona fide judicial warrant issued upon probable cause. Repeals any parts of the FISA, RFPA, USA Patriot Act, NDAA, Intelligence Authorization Act of 2004 or any similar legislation present or future.

9) The *Religious Treason Act* will outlaw religious laws or subversive activities meant to incite violence in the name of a religion or any foreign interest operating in the U.S.; stipulates a 'three strikes' policy eventually outlawing Islam in this republic if its adherents perpetrate three terrorist attacks; and makes it a felony for an elected or appointed public servant to travel to a foreign country funded by a foreign government or a private foundation or lobby group on behalf of any foreign country, people or religion.

10) We will secure the Internet for citizen use by enacting the *Internet Liberty Act,* making it a felony to disable Internet service within the USA, or selectively ban or hamper any individual's free access to a public Internet service on the basis of that individual's political or religious position unless espousing or calling for violence.

11) The *Constitutional Supremacy Act* based on the 1953 Bricker Amendment, will stipulate that no treaty will be valid if it violates the U.S. Constitution; that all Senate votes for a treaty must be recorded; that no Continuity of Government (COG) order can violate or suspend the Constitution; that federal courts will have no jurisdiction in any matter arising under this legislation; will make it a felony for any individual or group to engage in or materially support actions that threaten the sovereignty of any of the States without the consent of the legislature(s) of every affected State.

12) The *American Sovereignty Restoration Act* of 2009 (HR 1146) of the first session of the 111th Congress will terminate authorization of funds for the U.N. and withdraw diplomatic immunity for U.N. employees or delegates.

13) The *Lawful Wars Act* will disallow foreign hostilities without a Declaration of War and proof to Congress that such mobilization is necessary to defend against demonstrable threat to the States.

14) We end federal grants to cities, counties, and States by enacting the *Federal Pork Sunset Act,* making all federal grants/aid to the States as block grants for three years, after which all federal aid or grants end, and any further federal payment to States, counties, or cities will be a federal crime.

15) We help restore the Citizen Militias of the States via the *Minuteman Act,* to help Americans in their own counties to "execute the Laws of the Union, suppress Insurrections, and repel Invasions". This law will repeal every federal statute, regulation, executive order or other directive including the National Firearms Act of 1934 and later variations and preempts every such measure present and future of any State, county or city that infringes on or burdens the right to purchase, keep, carry, transport, or sell firearms, ammo, and accoutrements suitable for Militia service or that interferes with lawful design, manufacture, repair, or sale/distribution of arms, ammunition, etc.

16) We enact the *Non-Conscription Act,* declaring that Congress, presidents, and federal courts have no authority to conscript Americans of any age into involuntary servitude for any purpose.

17) We restore sovereign State lands and foreign countries by enacting the *Return of Sovereign Lands Act,* stipulating that other than land for military installations, federal government has no constitutional power to claim or control any private land, water, timber, oil, gas or other natural resources in, on, or under any sovereign State, for any reason, under any conditions, without the *"Consent of the Legislature of the State in which the Same shall be"*.

Much more comprehensive than Utah HB142 passed in 2013, all federally held or controlled lands and natural resources within each sovereign State *and any foreign country* will revert within 36 months to full ownership and control of that sovereign State or country. Repeals all federal land-use regulations, national forest and park acts, and like federal controls, subject only to laws of the States.

18) We finally end the long rule of banksters, government- sponsored FED counterfeiting, the 'fractional reserve' loan fraud, and the gargantuan derivatives industry built on those frauds, with the *Lawful United States Money and Banking Act* with aspects of, but more comprehensive than HR 459, 833, 1094, 1095, 1098, 1496, 2768 and SB 202, restoring lawful gold and silver U.S. money, and outlawing the FED cartel and any privately-owned entity ever having control over production of, or determining the value of, U.S. money. For more on this, see Chapter 26.

19) We end secret intelligence agencies and projects that are nowhere authorized by the Constitution, enacting the *Intelligent Republic Act*, based loosely on the *Smart Nation Act* sponsored by Congressman Rob Simmons (R-CT), transitioning to Open Source Intelligence and outlawing any government program kept secret from Congress, which is clearly illegal.

— CHAPTER 10 —
Granite Dome Syndrome

This chapter is a few excerpts from the most popular talk I have delivered so far on our Sunday night conference calls. It's the best way I know to prepare you for this new way of life; by showing you how the hired help has twisted American civics, and our lives, all backwards and upside-down.

I'll discuss Granite Dome Syndrome, Moral Hazard, and our abdication of our sovereign prerogative that has resulted in full-blown Washington D.C. Communism and Fascism. I mean *literal* communism and fascism as Marx and Mussolini defined them.

Let me first define sovereign prerogative. *Sovereign* just means one who exercises the supreme, permanent authority. That's established in the opening three words of the supreme Law of our Land.

In its first important decision in 1793, *Chisolm v. Georgia,* the U.S. Supreme Court held that the *People* are the collective sovereigns in our form of government. *Prerogative* means the exclusive right and power to command, decide, rule, or judge. So this will be a key Tactical Civics lecture because it will give you civics knowledge that you won't hear anywhere else but that's vital for overcoming the psychological conditioning that you've suffered all your life.

So. First, *this* idea.

The power to *think* – to initiate and conduct those electrobiological processes called human thought – is the most profound gift that God gave mankind alone, among all species of His creatures on earth. With each passing year, our days and weeks and years seem to be more packed full of noise. Of *busy*-ness and amusements that you only realize at the *end* of life were a total waste. I want to challenge you to start doing things differently. And further, I want to challenge you to winsomely and in a friendly and helpful tone, also start influencing those around you to do the same: to just start *thinking* about things that matter in life, and to start immediately tuning out the worthless nonsense when you see or hear it.

Criminogenic government creates and maintains oxen: 'taxpayer', 'consumer', 'voter'. I've spoken before on these calls about public architecture – what I call *Granite Dome Syndrome*. I've explained to you what happens right in the first week after a legislator or even their staffers get an office space under a granite dome. You've seen the incredible scale and opulence of the state capitols and of Capitol Hill. Not only the sheer massiveness and celestial beauty of the frescoed rotundas and massive colonnades, but the dining rooms with gold-trimmed china and silverware. The overstuffed leather chairs. The tapestries and portraits and Persian rugs. This does for those public servants exactly what it would do to *you* if you suddenly were given a palatial mansion. You'd wake up every day and see all around you the fact that you're now *very* special in society.

And what does Granite Dome Syndrome do to the sovereign; the People? Well, it does the same thing as if you lived in a 70-year-old blighted tenement house and you walk into a marble-floored 20,000-square-foot, 14-bedroom mansion. You definitely are *not* going to be able to conceive of yourself as the boss of the person in that mansion, right? So Granite Dome Syndrome is a no-brainer, and we need to do something about it.

Until we do take them out of those palaces – by the way, I propose that you start calling your state house the *capitol palace* from now on. So at least when the snot-nosed legislative aide looks down his or her nose at you, you'll keep in mind that the young fool is the servant of your *servant*, and you're the *boss* of their boss!

Okay, now a *second* element: Moral Hazard. In economic theory, the principle called *Moral Hazard* holds that the larger a taxpayer population grows, the less each taxpayer will care about a given expense because it impacts each one so little. Central governments tend to be more corrupt and opulent as a function of population; the larger the victim pool, the less each victim feels the hit.

A *third* element of criminogenic tactics is *distance*. Our legislators live and work far from their communities. Their sovereign can't see who they're meeting with for breakfast, brunch, lunch, cocktails, or dinner. If you don't see their day-to-day shenanigans it's like it's not even happening.

A *fourth* element is *unaccountability*. What difference will it make when we pass the Bring Congress Home Act and not only bring them home and cut their salaries and limit their terms, but also demand annual audits of our servants' expenditures, posted on a public website? Isn't it *ridiculous* that we've never demanded this before? And why on earth do we not get to determine their salaries rather than *them* doing so themselves?

The *fifth* element, 'mass civics deception', is fraudulent labeling of the lawless form of government we've allowed to grow right inside the shell of our constitutionally-limited one. Washington D.C. Communism is never called by its accurate name, yet the D.C. government today meets all ten of Karl Marx's stated goals in *A Communist Manifesto*.

The same goes for Washington D.C. Fascism. Mussolini defined *fascism* as the alliance of central government with the corporations, to control the people in the service of the State. Ending D.C. Fascism is simple; after we strip them of their Granite Dome palace, we begin filling those legislators' seats ourselves, and we stipulate in law that legislation *must actually be written by legislators* and specifically *not* by industry.

When we break down the House districts into small, local ones and take Congress out of Washington D.C., then we can enforce Article I, Section 8, Clause 17 – that's where We The People grant Congress exclusive legislative jurisdiction over the District of Columbia. See how nice that will be when Congress isn't there anymore but all the D.C. *tentacles* remain there? The remnant can end Communism and Fascism *without firing a shot.*

You see how the American mind is conditioned, and why young people seek careers in politics? Political careerists *never* lose their granite dome, perks, and pay (better pay than private-sector jobs). And what about us? Well, if we oxen fail to pay property tax on our *paid-for* farm, home, or shop – we lose everything to the arrogant hired help when *the sheriff* sells it on the courthouse steps. So the *sixth* element of corrupt government is the *ad valorem* property tax scam, making us fear our servants just like the IRS.

That's the *predator* aspect of the crime spree; what about the *parasite* army? Well, that's the *seventh* element of criminogenic American government. *Criminogenic* means it teaches criminality by example…and that's precisely what government in D.C. and your state palace has done. It has taught your county, city, and school district bureaucrats and boards to be as criminal in their presumptions as Congress is, with its $22 trillion debt burden palmed off on *our* backs.

The parasite army is a huge catalyst, a multi-generational welfare horde including 30 million illegal aliens, riding coattails of our corrupt servants and 20 million public employees in agencies, bureaus and departments: 50 million people bleeding productive America!

Our First Right and the Bring Congress Home Act are our last serious line of defense against rogue states that declare themselves *sanctuaries.* From under those granite domes, the state governments of California, Colorado, Illinois, Massachusetts, New Mexico, Oregon and Vermont have declared their states *outlaw territories,* against law and against the interests of

31

productive citizens. Close behind are many cities and counties in Iowa, Pennsylvania and Washington State.

With state governments proclaiming rule of law dead, do you see how Obama's administration including 'Resident' Biden, Hillary's open corruption, Bernie Sanders' candidacy and George Soros' astroturf hordes forged a coordinated attack by American Communism against rule of law?

This public, shameless rebellion against Productive America is straight out of Saul Alinski's book. And they took notes from the long history of success in the infanticide and sexual perversion communities.

Tactical Civics™ is the answer, and sincere repentance is Step One. As we've explained, Americans have been taught to self-label as *taxpayer* and *voter* like farmers use the terms *ox* and *mule*.

The war, banking, and oil industries piled on because no conditioning tool works as well as the shock of war; a one-way ratchet against productive America. But with Tactical Civics™, though we're only a mustard seed today, the ox is *beginning* to despise the growing blue whale on its back.

There are still millions of complaining, fearful, angry, cynical Americans on social media who suffer from Granite Dome Syndrome without even knowing it. But now you know more about your mental and emotional condition than you did a few minutes ago. We are watching the noisy, messy, cursing, biting collapse of 160-year-old American Communism.

There are countless complainers and Fear Porn hawkers, who daily spew passion on social media, but have no solution. What good does it do to complain? Even if America *is* collapsing – at some point we'll have to clean up and restore normal life. So Tactical Civics™ has already *begun*.

We The People, just a remnant, doing our best to take America back with the only full-spectrum action plan in this republic. Of *course* it will be difficult and of *course* it will take years! Restoring rule of law in the largest free republic in history after criminals had generations to perfect their game; what would you *expect*?

Perform your own research to corroborate this book's assertions. The hard truth: we were lied to in school and college and have been propagandized by the servants whose salaries and benefits we pay. But now the good news: *this is the best time to be alive in America,* and God is blessing us yet again, if we in the responsible remnant will only do our duty.

— CHAPTER 11 —

What's Under the Hood

I'm often asked, "What are the subjects of our 19 reform laws?"

You can read the draft reform laws in our *AmericaAgain! Declaration*, Appendix F. For a simpler draft of the 19 reform laws, see the final lesson in the book, *Mission to America: A Seven-Week Crash Course in Tactical Civics™*. Some of it is hard reading, but our civilization has been transmogrified into a godless nightmare and crime spree over 160 years by powerful cartels; so We The People need to grow up, repent our dereliction of duty, and start doing our chores.

Below is an outline of our proposed Reform Law #2, as an example of the extent of the research and planning that our team invested over a decade, to bring this mission to Americans so that the remnant can introduce it and live it out in their own counties.

Reform Law #2, The Constitutional Courts Act

Section 1. A consensus exists among the American public that the federal courts have been corrupted and are manipulated by powerful individuals and by lobbyists for industry and special interests, rendering moot the stipulated limitations placed by the People through the U.S. Constitution on its creature, federal government.

a. James Madison, Father of the Constitution, in his Virginia Resolution of 1798, and Thomas Jefferson, in his concurring Kentucky Resolution, wrote that the States, as the creator parties to the U.S. Constitution, have the right and duty to judge when the U.S. Constitution has been violated by federal government; that the federal government cannot judge of its own infractions

b. In Article III, Section 1 of the U.S. Constitution, the People grant to Congress the authority to create the inferior federal courts, thus the subject matter jurisdiction of the inferior federal courts is entirely within Congress' discretion.

c. In Article III, Section 2 of the U.S. Constitution, the People grant to Congress the authority to withhold subject matter jurisdiction even from the U.S. supreme Court, using "such Exceptions, and...such Regulations as the Congress shall make".

d. In Article VI, Section 2 of the U.S. Constitution, the People stipulate, *This Constitution...shall be the supreme Law of the Land; and the Judges in every State shall be bound thereby...,*which includes *enforcement* as well as obedience.

e. Every federal legislator is now performing his federal duties full-time within his or her own district, which is the jurisdiction of his State Grand Jury and State Court. [This bill will not be attempted until after we have enacted Reform Law #1, the Bring Congress Home Act.]

f. Therefore, pursuant to the power granted by the People to Congress in U.S. Constitution Article III, Section 2, Clause 2, after the effective date hereof, no federal court shall have jurisdiction in any case in which a member of Congress is charged by his or her own State Grand Jury with violating, or conspiring to violate, the U.S. Constitution.

g. In no such case shall removal from state jurisdiction be available to the accused, whether pursuant to 28 USC 1441, or any subsequent federal law.

Section 2. The American People stipulated in Article I, Section 8 of the U.S. Constitution, that *The Congress shall have power...to constitute tribunals inferior to the supreme Court...,* and in Article III, Section 1, that the federal courts are, *such inferior courts as the Congress may from time to time ordain and establish,* and in Article III, Section 2, Clause 2, that the U.S. supreme Court, *shall have appellate jurisdiction...with such Exceptions, and under such Regulations as the Congress shall make.*

In *Turner v. Bank of North America* (1799), Justice Chase wrote, *The notion has frequently been entertained, that the federal courts derive their judicial power immediately from the Constitution; but the political truth is, that the disposal of the judicial power...belongs to Congress. If Congress has given the power to this Court, we possess it, not otherwise: and if Congress has not given the power to us or to any other Court, it still remains at the legislative disposal.*

In *Ex parte Bollman* (1807), Chief Justice John Marshall wrote, *Courts which are created by written law, and whose jurisdiction is defined by written law, cannot transcend that jurisdiction.*

The power of Congress to create inferior federal courts, necessarily implies, as written in *U.S. v. Hudson & Goodwin* (1812), the *power to limit jurisdiction of those Courts to particular objects.*

The U.S. supreme Court held unanimously in *Sheldon v. Sill* (1850) that because the People in the Constitution did not create inferior federal courts but authorized Congress to create them, that Congress by necessity

34

had power to define and limit their jurisdiction and to withhold jurisdiction of any of the enumerated cases and controversies.

The high court even acknowledged Congress' power to re-examine particular classes of questions previously ruled on by the U.S. supreme Court, as stated in *The Francis Wright* (1882): *(A)ctual jurisdiction under the* [judicial] *power is confined within such limits as Congress sees fit to prescribe...What those powers shall be, and to what extent they shall be exercised, are, and always have been, proper subjects of legislative control...Not only may whole classes of cases be kept out of the jurisdiction altogether, but particular classes of questions may be subjected to re-examination and review...*

In *Lauf v. E.G. Shinner & Co* (1938), the U.S. supreme Court declared, *There can be no question of the power of Congress thus to define and limit the jurisdiction of the inferior courts of the United States.*

In *Lockerty v. Phillips* (1943), the U.S. supreme Court held that Congress has the power of, *withholding jurisdiction from them* [federal courts] *in the exact degrees and character which to Congress may seem proper for the public good.*

Section 3. Therefore, Congress hereby excludes from federal court jurisdiction any and all cases involving: a. Taking of human life, from point of conception; b. Sexual practices or the institution of marriage; c. Healthcare; d. Education; e. Official recognition or application of any foreign law or code within these united States or any of them; and f. Claims of United States control, possession, or jurisdiction over any land outside of that granted by We the People and the States, as stipulated in Article I, Section 8, Clause 17 of the U.S. Constitution.

Section 4. What constitutes due process in courts within the United States or any of them shall be determined exclusively from the Bill of Rights and the American common law, in that order of precedence.

Section 5. In Article III, Section 1 of the U.S. Constitution, the People stipulate, *the judicial Power of the United States shall be vested in one supreme Court, and in such inferior Courts as the Congress may from time to time ordain and establish;* therefore within 12 months of the passage of this Act:

a) No 'administrative law' tribunal in these United States shall bind any citizen; b) No administrative adjudicator shall be referred to as 'judge'; c) No administrative tribunal shall be referred to, or refer to itself, as 'court'; d) No administrative process or tribunal shall describe its processes in terms such as 'order', 'subpoena', 'warrant', or 'the record', which are reserved for constitutional judiciary.

Section 6. Pursuant to provisions of Section 3(f) above and the proposed *Return of Sovereign Lands Act,* 24 months after enactment of this legislation and thereafter, it shall be a federal felony for any agency, agent, bureau, department, officer, contractor or other representative of the government of these United States to claim, own, maintain or operate a purported U.S. court or detention facility that is not located within the land or property stipulated in Article I, Section 8, Clause 17 of the U.S. Constitution.

Section 7. No federal judicial rules shall have any bearing or authority over any State Grand Jury.

Section 8. As stipulated in Article I, Section 8, Clause 15 of the U.S. Constitution, the several States retain the power to enforce this legislation by appropriate State legislation and duly authorized Citizen Militia enforcement action within their respective jurisdictions. [End of draft bill.]

Not Like All The 'Restore America' Plans

So. We aren't being hyperbolic or self-aggrandizing, merely factual, when we make the claim that, *AmericaAgain! Trust has created and defined, and is leading a new market and a new way of life called Tactical Civics™, the only full-spectrum, lawful, peaceful solution to the destruction of our republic by organized crime and its bureaucratic hordes, media, and academic allies under the guise of government.*

Our team took 12 years to bring this mission to Americans because digging deep into the crimes of our servants and their masters the billionaires and global corporations, required us to perform *years* of investigative research, legal drafting, 'war gaming' under strictures of Common Law and constitutional precedent, and fine-tuning to make it as comprehensible as possible to American adults of average intelligence.

With each of our proposed reform laws, we didn't just make it up as we went along. We sought out the best minds in America who had already been working the problem and publishing their solution to that problem (crime) before we began constructing that reform law. In the case of this particular reform, our inspiration and information originated at the desk of Professor Philip Hamburger of Columbia University, who has been preaching this truth for decades.

This is called *due diligence.* It is the price of being an American. It's how you become one of *We The People,* when almost everyone around you is too slothful or fearful to lift a finger.

God made mankind for work. *Isn't it about time we did some?*

— CHAPTER 12 —

The People Themselves

Tactical Civics™ is a new way of life that includes the thesis first proposed in 2004 by then-Stanford Law School dean Larry Kramer and in his book *The People Themselves: Popular Constitutionalism and Judicial Review.*

Dean Kramer asserted a truth that is obvious to any third grader reading the first three words of our Constitution: We The People hold the highest public office. We're the boss of government that we created in that supreme Law of the Land. *We are constitutionally (legally) superior to the U.S. supreme Court. Thus, we are obviously far superior to the inferior federal courts.*

Tactical Civics™ is the responsible remnant of Americans, for the first time and from now on *enforcing* our highest law. We'll review Chapter 8, the enforcement mobile app against corrupt federal and state legislators.

When a legislator files a bill it is scanned to determine if it violates the U.S. Constitution and there is a harmonizing State Penal Code section on which to indict the sponsors and co-sponsors of the bill before it becomes law. Determining if the sponsors committed *felony conspiracy* is the analysis and targeting function of our proposed Indictment Engine™ mobile app. That will be a major feat of 'language artificial intelligence'.

On finding probable cause for felony indictment, the Indictment Engine™ will output a felony presentment to each County Grand Jury of each co-conspirator (each co-sponsor of the bill). After those Grand Juries review those statutes and the bill, if they agree with the computer app, they instruct their associated Militia in each district of each co-conspirator to serve that target with a felony indictment.

Why the Militia? Because *the Constitution is our highest law and Militia is the only authorized force to enforce it (see Art I, Sec 8 Clause 15).*

We will cover sheriffs in more detail in Chapter 22, but since the invention in ancient Britain of the *shire reeve* (the origin of *sheriff*) his duty was to be the crown's tax collector and chief enforcer of the crown's rules. And *that is what sheriffs still do.* So at least in the early years of this new way of life, paid 'law enforcement' will not confront powerful politicians. We The People need to make an intimidating show of armed force, as IRS, FBI, BATF, and police or sheriff SWAT teams do in citizens' homes, to prove to criminal legislators that We The People mean business. They either obey the law or we have the court seize their assets and send them to their State Penitentiary to do hard time.

Repentance: Not Words But Action

The enemies of our civilization are many. But a faithful remnant can win this war against D.C. organized crime and its minions in state, county, city, and school district bureaucracies. Not only can we win it more quickly than you might imagine, but We The People of this unique constitutional Republic are the only population on earth at any time in history, who grant to ourselves the highest office in government. The opposite of rebellious or unlawful talk, this is the supreme Law laid down by our founders.

Gaslighting is a Communist Tool

Gaslighting is a criminal tactic in which the perpetrator continually presents lies as truth, and tries to convince the victims that they are going insane.

Since the 9/11 operation, and especially with the Plandemic and Election Steal 2020 operations, there remains no question which side the major media, Big Tech, and Hollywood are on. But it is a simple matter to test our servants who are legislators, judges, and paid law enforcement, to discover which side of this existential war they are fighting for. Do not believe it when they attempt to make you think that basic civics and the Constitution are too difficult for you to grasp. Never believe such liars. *This is not China; at least not yet.*

If we give honest statesmen our support, they will increasingly show themselves and grow in number and influence. But repentance in our civilization must not be limited to our servants. For We The People too, now is the time to take up our duties, and allow the watching world to learn from our faithful example.

— CHAPTER 13 —

Republic, Republic, Republic!

Over a decade ago, 30-year veteran New York City school teacher John Taylor Gatto published a trenchant indictment of government schools entitled *Dumbing Us Down: The Hidden Curriculum of Compulsory Schooling*. But that scholar omitted a crucial point that I will bring to your attention.

Americans are ignorant of civics. We don't know how our system of government works *or even what form of government we have*. I'm not referring to ditzy college kids that Mark Dice interviews. I'm talking about most of our presidents, members of congress, university professors, journalists and others. Like most adults trained in government schools, they believe Abe Lincoln was our greatest president, propaganda on which Washington D.C. has relied for 150 years. In Chapter 5 we linked six books that totally debunk that destructive lie.

But they also cannot comprehend the stipulations set out by We The People in our U.S. Constitution; the most basic fact of civics, that these united States are a *republic*, a form of government guaranteed by We The People to each State, in Article IV, Section 4 of the U.S. Constitution.

You see, *country* can mean many things, but in anthropology, *nation* refers to a common cultural group (see Colin Woodard's book, *American Nations*). In political economy, *nation* refers to a population living under a unitary government. On the other hand, *republic* refers to a confederation of sovereign states each with its own government but unified for only limited and specified purposes. *Read the Constitution; that's us*. It isn't rocket science. In fact, the average sixth grade homeschooler has no problem grasping and remembering it. But senators and presidents apparently do.

These united States of America have been a republic since 1789. America has never been a *nation*, even if many past presidents have used the word because it was handy. If you think this American *republic* is no big deal, watch Europe over the next decade, to appreciate the value of our Christian civilization, constitutional rule of law, and the republic that We The People guarantee to every sovereign State in Article IV, Section 4.

James Madison, Father of the Constitution and the final authority on the matter, explained this clause of the new constitution in Federalist #39: *Each State, in ratifying the Constitution, is considered as a sovereign body, independent of all others, and only to be bound by its own voluntary act. In this relation, then, the new Constitution will, if established, be a federal, and not a national constitution."*

But our ignorance of civics is not limited to the fact that most Americans do not know what form of government we have by law. They also do not know that We The People are the highest level of government, standing over our U.S. Constitution as its creators, interpreters, and enforcers.

For generations, government schools and even private, Christian, and so-called classical schools have trained Americans to demote ourselves with words like *voter* and *grassroots*. Having never read our own Constitution, written at sixth grade comprehension level, most Americans are clueless. Once you recognize our duty and power as America's collective sovereign, you will never again use the word *nation* to refer to our *republic*. You also will stop using propaganda phrases such as 'elected leaders' and 'elected officials' to refer to arrogant criminals. These people are elected to represent and serve us, and to scrupulously obey the Constitution. Instead, they serve themselves and the elite, and violate America's highest law every day, many times per day. And just listen to them; they're proud of it!

If a clueless employer referred to his employees or servants as "my elected leaders", how long would it take the hired help to rule the employer? The 'elected leaders' set their own working conditions, staffing, salary, benefits, luxury travel – and send their IRS thugs after the taxpayers to fund it all.

Mr. Gatto and many others have pointed out the seminal part played by the government schools in destroying our republic. We have swallowed and regurgitated a great deal of destructive foolishness, and the ruins are generations deep. There is work to be done.

By the grace of God, over 50 years, America's growing army of homeschoolers have been training a remnant to take up our duties and powers that our ancestors abdicated. As Europe flies apart under this same curse of criminality, America is pushed to the gates of Hell, with the Millennial generation demanding Communism, courtesy of government schools. It's time to reform our vocabulary and repent our way of life.

Unlike complaining 'save America' groups and websites that do nothing but quote Founding Fathers and ask for donations, Tactical Civics™ chapters have formed in hundreds of counties from Washington State to Florida. It's now easier than ever for We The People to begin rebuilding the fallen walls of our *Republic*.

— CHAPTER 14 —

Our First Right

We can take congress out of Washington DC, making that corrupt city irrelevant again; but to do that, we need Our First Right.

America was hijacked by Washington DC when congress stole our First Right in the original Bill of Rights, which required *2,120* districts as of the 1920 census. But congress passed its *Reapportionment Act of 1929,* arbitrarily fixing the size of the House at just 435 seats, knowing that the original First Amendment was still before the States for ratification. Career politicians' billionaire handlers wanted power, and here's how they got it.

They stole all representation in the U.S. House and Electoral College from residents of America's 31,000+ small towns; about 90% of America's land mass, creating districts with over 750,000 citizens on average. All by using a transcribing error of just *one word.* (See more details in Appendix A.)

The Founding Fathers' Plan

It began on the last day of the Constitutional Convention in 1787. Delegate Nathaniel Gorham made a motion to change one word in Article I of the proposed Constitution – *"the number of Representatives shall not exceed one for every forty thousand..."* to read, "for every *thirty* thousand". George Washington rose to speak for the first and only time to address the convention to pass that change. It was adopted unanimously. On September 25, 1789 congress passed the 12-article Bill of Rights, sending it to the States to ratify. Article 1 guaranteed small districts. When congress officially passed the Bill of Rights, they changed the word *less* in *"the last line less one"* to the word *more.* See the last sentence? It originally said, "nor *less* than..." which is the only word that makes sense, given the preceding sentences:

ARTICLE the FIRST.

After the first enumeration, required by the first Article of the Constitution, there shall be one Representative for every thirty thousand, until the number shall amount to one hundred, after which the proportion shall be so regulated by Congress, that there shall be not less than one hundred Representatives, nor less than one Representative for every forty thousand persons, until the number of Representatives shall amount to two hundred, after which the proportion shall be so regulated by Congress, that there shall not be less than two hundred Representatives, nor less than one Representative for every fifty thousand persons.

41

The copies were sent to all 13 states so their state legislatures could ratify as stipulated in Article V. By 1790, twelve states had ratified: CT, KY, MD, NH, NJ, NY, NC, PA, RI, SC, VA and VT.

Blame it All on Connecticut

But while the Connecticut House voted for the original First Amendment in October, 1789 and its senate voted for ratification in May, 1790, making it the ninth state to vote for ratification out of 12 states at the time (three-fourths of the states, the number required to ratify an amendment per Article V of the Constitution), the House wanted to retract its vote until that one-word error could be corrected (everyone knew the intention of that article was small districts). Since a ratification vote can't be retracted, Connecticut buried its vote record in its archives so it was not recorded.

The only way forward is for the State legislatures to *finish* the ratification process, as we stipulate in Article V. Congress already passed it, so we don't need a constitutional convention and crooked DC can't stop it now. We just need 27 more ratification votes, to give America's 31,000+ small towns our voice again in the People's House at last.

The Internet is shaking humanity as the printing press shook the medieval world. Reclaiming our First Right and restoring the People's House is up to We The People, *the top level of government.* At this writing, a usurper 'resident' acting as president and his thousands of colluding minions in Washington DC are carrying Lincoln's hijacking to a whole new level; many governors are no better. The criminogenic tide is flowing, and only We The People can arrest American Communism, now, on our watch, or our last opportunity may be lost.

Before we can push this unfinished business through state legislatures to get at least 27 of them to vote 'yes', Tactical Civics™ must build our county chapters and membership so we can pack our state palaces when we are ready to push for the votes, all at one time.

We The People must build our numbers and get organized before the Deep Axis kills our rule of law entirely. Please, consider serving God and country in this time of dire need. There's no other plan of action.

— CHAPTER 15 —
The Last D.C. Congress

Imagine Washington DC *with Congress no longer there.*

Envision the American people setting the standard for government reform on earth, by forcing our Congress to become the first distributed legislature of the twenty-first century. Imagine your members of Congress working from a modest office just a few miles from your home, full-time.

Last chapter you learned about Our First Right; our plan to push for final ratification of the original First Amendment, limiting House districts to 50,000 people as the Founding Fathers planned. It will result in over 6,500 members of the U.S. House of Representatives. If you think that's too many, we have *7,383* members in our state legislatures representing the *same* 334 million Americans!

Tactical Civics™ is a responsible new way of life; a self-governing people finally having oversight of what our servants are doing. Citizens should not have to wait weeks just to see their public servant. After passage of the BCHA (Chapter 7), every member of Congress stays in their hometown rather than destroying their families by having a second home (and often a secret second life) in the secretive city-state.

Imagine the Great We-Set™: you will walk into your U.S. congressman's office and see only a staff of two, who treat you as their employer *as indeed you are.* No more trips to the imperial city-state to beg our servants for favors. If you want or need to testify before a committee of congress, you simply show up at your nearby congressman's office, log on to the citizens' workstation, and wait to be called on by the committee. No more wasting time, money, and travel fatigue to go to D.C. to appear before *our servants.*

Elections can never change things. Washington D.C. is the most powerful, corrupt, ruthless city-state in history, operating its own immoral, unethical, economic universe; treachery, fraud, theft and perversion are the norm. Of course this was true in ancient Byzantium, Athens and Rome and it's true in London, Paris, Moscow, Beijing and all the others. But the difference with D.C. is the sheer *scale* of evil power concentrated there.

Today, new freshmen arriving in Washington D.C. are handled by career staffers who run them through orientation. The freshman is first put in awe of the massive scale of D.C. architecture, the countless monuments, and opulent furnishings. Next, he witnesses the ancient, Byzantine, often clandestine traditions of standing committees – each a fiefdom in itself; especially the Rules and Calendar committees. By the end of orientation week, even the most idealistic freshman is overwhelmed.

Then he begins to face the human side of D.C. organized crime; not only are the huge staffs impressive but the sheer range of services available to a legislator with just a call makes a believer out of the new solon. They also learn that many D.C. career staffers earn more than members of Congress do. They were there years before the freshman member arrived and most of them will be there years after the member loses re-election to another freshman with big dreams. Tens of thousands of *unelected* bureaucrats in the Deep State watch presidents come and go. Including the 'Senior Executive Service' of 9,000 industry moles, unknown and untouchable by their sovereign, the American People.

Next, the new freshman discovers who actually writes the laws: law firms with hundreds or thousands of staff, who fill entire buildings on K Street and inside the Beltway, whose largest clients span the globe, having no allegiance to one country. These players in the Big Game enjoy first-name access to federal judges, presidents, cabinet members, and top committee chairs in congress. Once in earth's most powerful, corrupt city-state, a new member of Congress isn't even a blip on the radar. He's a cipher; *a nothing.*

We'd like Trump back in the White House in 2024 because if the Last D.C. congress enacts the Bring Congress Home Act, Trump may be the *only* president who would sign the most powerful reform law in two centuries.

Our First Right is ratified by 27 more states; the first truly representative election in 150 years is held; the huge new congress meets in a large D.C. venue for only two purposes: to pass the BCHA and get it signed into law, and to get their video orientation on how the world's first distributed legislature will work. And that will be the last Washington D.C. gathered action of congress ever required. *Then we can join the 21ˢᵗ century, Congress doing its work under our supervision, back home.*

A generation ago, telecommuting, smart phones, search engines, and countless other innovations were unthinkable; now they're indispensable. Tactical Civics™ can be, too. A logical new way of life for the Information Age; the end of politics and the beginning of popular constitutionalism.

— CHAPTER 16 —

Our Office (above presidents)

Two mega-trends are causing great upheaval around the world in our generation. First, the Internet is threatening corrupt, bureaucratic governments worldwide; no government will come out of this the same size as it entered the Internet Age.

The second mega-trend is the exposure and collapse of Karl Marx's system in America. Over a century, our federal government adopted all ten points in the *Communist Manifesto* as policy. Now, hordes of Latin Americans pour across our southern border, supported by big business, the massive D.C. welfare state, and the Clinton-Obama-Biden machine with its lawless minions almost everywhere employing Saul Alinski's *Rules for Radicals*.

Productive America, *we must get serious.* We cannot continue to live and think as we were programmed, while our republic burns. Americans must stop complaining on social media and *take responsibility.*

Melania Trump was the finest First Lady in history, and Donald Trump proved to be the best president in over a century. But he was *far* from perfect. Anyone who saw him as America's savior was deeply mistaken; presidents can't restore our land. *Only God can,* and He demands our repentance and responsibility! Our forefathers slept and so have we, as predators and parasites took over our culture and government, replacing them with European-style counterfeits. The norms and nobility that animated our founders are fallen and must be rebuilt.

A communist-dominated U.S. House of Representatives began its cancerous work in January 2019, and had a plan backed by George Soros' money, Barack Hussein Obama's 250 field offices of 'Organize For America', tens of thousands of Obama-plant holdovers in the Deep State, D.C. staffers who play for either party as long as they get their cut, and Big Tech giants, each as powerful as a foreign government. What are *we* going to do about this, fellow American?

The Chinese philosopher-general Sun Tzu wrote, *"If you know the enemy and know yourself, you need not fear the result of a hundred battles. If you know yourself but not the enemy, for every victory gained you will also suffer a defeat. If you know neither the enemy nor yourself, you will succumb in every battle."*

Our parents and grandparents didn't know our authority and duty over the Constitution and over our servants that we create by that law. Very few Americans know anything about Grand Jury and constitutional Militia. So Americans don't know their responsibility for this mess, or basic facts such as, American Communism began when Dishonest Abe and Karl Marx were pen pals and mutual admirers. Or the fact that most of Lincoln's illegal, full-time U.S. Army generals were also followers of Marx, the creator of Communism.

Because Americans don't know that American Communism began generations ago, they also don't know that the donkey party is not the whole problem. *Both* parties are distraction theater, designed to keep us waving pom-poms while the Deep State robs us blind and enslaves us forever. Americans are clueless that *politics can never be law enforcement.*

We The People don't face an 'enemy', but massive organized crime in league with a foreign enemy (Chinese Communist Party) and public education from kindergarten to graduate school. Too many Americans think that war is only kinetic conflict: troops, ships, and planes attacking one another. But two Chinese bureaucrats (Qiao Liang and Wang Xiangsui) wrote *Unrestricted Warfare* in 1999, explaining with shocking honesty how China 23 years ago was *already* exploiting America's weaknesses via nontraditional means, especially in our schools and universities and in the culture, with propaganda, technology, sex, drugs, and perversion to break the bonds of American family and society. The COVID scam and Election Steal 2020 were the most sweeping stages of that warfare to date. But the solution is not civil war. *It's law enforcement.*

Tactical Civics™ is not politics, but a responsible new way of life. Restoring our republic is *our* job, not the job of our presidents; it's above their pay grade. We must stop being cheerleaders for presidents and perform *our* responsibilities. We The People occupy the highest office in government.

If we do our job, then what we are witnessing is the ugly *death* of American Communism, *not its birth.* To restore our Republic before it is destroyed, we have to stop cheering for presidents and start doing *our* job, in our *higher* office of government. We must stop writing letters to politicians!

Take the responsibility our Founding Fathers demanded, fellow Christian. As Sun Tzu suggested, you can know yourself and our enemy, and then in the Name of Jesus Christ our King, you can *stand.*

— CHAPTER 17 —

The Fear Porn Industry

Like the horror film genre, the Fear Porn industry is a perverse kind of entertainment that excites the limbic system of the brain, inciting daily cycles of anxiety, fear, and anger. Like all pornography, it is false, cruel, and destructive. But it produces great revenues because Americans are predictable consumers.

Over a generation, many young Americans came to love horror films. In the same way, millions are addicted to conservative talk and 501c3 groups, making Fear Porn potentially *worse* for America's future than communism. Some of these stars admit that they are entertainers; most of them do not, and most listeners cannot discern that conservative talk is just that: *talk*.

During my lifetime, Americans transmogrified from an industrious people with time only for factual news – into self-obsessed consumers, seeking entertainment in place of news. Today, factual news won't garner market share; too many limbic systems are conditioned to want fear, anxiety, and rage, which have become like a drug for millions of conservatives.

Does this describe you? Be honest; do you visit social media to argue, knowing you won't improve a thing? Do you daily listen to talk show hosts, knowing that nothing they say *ever* improves anything?

Conservative radio, TV and Internet 'news' shares an entertainment market with networks, political parties, and non-profits who keep the folks hopping mad. Fear and loathing brings audience to buy the celebrity's branded tea, or his precious metals merchant's stuff, colloidal silver, water filters, emergency food, or the latest 'money bomb' campaign. Joe, Sean, Glenn, Mark, Mike, Alex, Dennis, Laura, Michael – and NRA, GOA, Cato Institute, Heritage Foundation, Hillsdale College, and many other 501c3s comprising 'conservatism' are only *conservative* in *conserving their golden goose*. It's just business. Media moguls, talk stars and 501c3 donation mills are businesses in a Fear Porn market mining a rich demographic vein: productive, disgruntled patriots.

The GOP needs the Democrat party and vise-versa, to remain profitable because politics junkies pay to see a fight. Similarly, Fear Porn conservative talk, media, and non-profits always need a crisis and a bad guy: mass murder, potential war, economic woes, organized crime in government,

BLAntifa riots, natural disasters, rise of the police state – Fear Porn gives you what your limbic system demands every day. They must mentally condition you to inaction and cynicism, so you *never take action* on solutions. They only grow their empire as long as you keep tuning in.

Besides repeating what you've already heard, when have you ever seen any nonprofit lead action for reform? Like government agencies, conservative think-tanks reform *nothing*. They produce papers and sponsor conferences that are reactive, but will never restore what we already lost.

If you listen to the talkers or read WorldNetDaily or Infowars every day, you'll never become part of a solution as a result. You can go buy gold and ammo, hide in the boondocks, feed yourself, and kill the hungry neighbors pounding at your door when the time comes. You can sign up for any of the NewsMax pop-up ads, and receive a *"super-special, eye-opening, life-changing report, FREE!"* – along with a gazillion pieces of junk mail for the rest of your life. But Fear Porn stars will never lead a critical mass of citizens to enforce our Constitution. Have you ever seen a celebrity even *attempt* it?

The same applies to your social media addiction. No amount of posting patriotic quotations or pictures will change anything! Has your favorite conservative website, show, or social media site *ever* promoted a solution, or does it just stir up your fear, loathing, and blood pressure every day?

Over 1,500 American radio stations now play wall-to-wall conservative talkers with their wall-to-wall advertisements. God rest his soul, Rush Limbaugh gave birth to a truly staggering cash cow. It was great for Rush, but passive listening – even if you *scream* at your radio! – changes nothing. It's not a kind of life befitting Americans.

The talkers, nonprofit donation mills and social media are dragging American Christianity down just as the Reagan and Trump presidencies did *and it is more dangerous because Fear Porn addicts can claim it's a solution, though in 35 years it has not been.* Tobias Stockwell posted this excellent explanation of how the Internet is twisting our minds and society. The answer to the Fear Porn industry is: *turn them all off.*

Listening to talkers or hanging around a Facebook 'coffee klatch' for thousands of hours a year instead of taking action will never restore our civilization. Venting at the radio or social media makes you *more* cynical.

Conservative talkers are not conserving anything. But you now can. Turn off Fear Porn, and start walking the talk.

— CHAPTER 18 —

The Founders, Right Again

Like rambunctious Siamese twins from Satan's womb, the fraudulently labeled 'Convention of States' (COS) outfit and 'National Popular Vote' (NPV) scheme call themselves *conservative,* while burning across state legislatures trying to destroy our Constitution under the guise of 'badly needed reform'. Whatever their actual motivations, both schemes march in lock-step with today's unmasked American Communism. Both also align with Progressives and urban metrosexuals against the conservative 95% of American landmass comprising America's 31,000 small towns and the country where Americans still know right from wrong.

The mendacious minions behind the National Popular Vote scheme must be aware that the only way to get their wish is to violate Article II, Section 1 of the Constitution. The Constitution controls, and is clear. If they want a national popular vote for presidents, they must amend the Constitution; the same challenge facing the shameless liars running the COS scheme. Tens of millions of Americans already have their number.

To frame the attempted hijacking of the already terribly adulterated Electoral College, this 1992 article is a good primer on the institution.

Essay in Elections: The Electoral College

(by William C. Kimberling)

In order to appreciate the reasons for the Electoral College, it is essential to understand its historical context and the problem that the Founding Fathers were trying to solve. They faced the difficult question of how to elect a president in a nation that:

- was composed of 13 large and small States jealous of their own rights and powers; suspicious of a central national government

- contained only 4,000,000 people spread up and down a thousand miles of Atlantic seaboard barely connected by transportation or communication (so that national campaigns were impractical even if they had been thought desirable)

- believed, under the influence of such British political thinkers as Henry St. John Bolingbroke, that political parties were mischievous if not downright evil, and

- felt that gentlemen should not campaign for public office (The saying was "The office should seek the man, the man should not seek the office.").

How, then, to choose a president without political parties, without national campaigns, and without upsetting the carefully designed balance between the presidency and the Congress on one hand and between the States and the federal government on the other?

Origins of the Electoral College

The Constitutional Convention considered several possible methods of selecting a president.

One idea was to have the Congress choose the president. This idea was rejected, because some felt that making such a choice would be too divisive an issue and leave too many hard feelings in the Congress. Others felt that such a procedure would invite unseemly political bargaining, corruption, and perhaps even interference from foreign powers. Still others felt that such an arrangement would upset the balance of power between the legislative and executive branches of the federal government.

A second idea was to have the State legislatures select the president. This idea, too, was rejected out of fears that a president so beholden to the State legislatures might permit them to erode federal authority and thus undermine the whole idea of a federation.

A third idea was to have the president elected by a direct popular vote. Direct election was rejected not because the Framers of the Constitution doubted public intelligence but rather because they feared that without sufficient information about candidates from outside their State, people would naturally vote for a 'favorite son' from their own State or region. At worst, no president would emerge with a popular majority sufficient to govern the whole country. At best, the choice of president would always be decided by the most populous States with little regard for smaller ones.

Finally, a so-called Committee of Eleven in the Constitutional Convention proposed an indirect election of the president via a College of Electors. The function of the College of Electors in choosing the president can be likened to that in the Roman Catholic Church of the College of Cardinals selecting popes. The original idea was for the most knowledgeable and informed individuals from each State to select the president based solely on merit and without regard to State of origin or political party.

The structure of the Electoral College can be traced to the Centurial Assembly system of the Roman Republic. Under that system, the adult male citizens of Rome were divided, according to their wealth, into groups of 100 (called Centuries). Each group of 100 was entitled to cast only one vote either in favor or against proposals submitted to them by the Roman Senate. In the Electoral College system, the States serve as the Centurial groups (though they are not, of course, based on wealth), and the number of votes per State is determined by the size of each State's Congressional delegation. Still, the two systems are similar in design and share many of the same advantages and disadvantages.

The similarities between the Electoral College and classical institutions are not accidental. Many of the Founding Fathers were well schooled in ancient history and its lessons.

The First Design

In the first design of the Electoral College (described in Article II, Section 1 of the Constitution):

- Each State was allocated a number of Electors equal to the number of its U.S. Senators (always 2) plus the number of its U.S. Representative (which may change each decade according to the size of each State's population as determined in the decennial census). This arrangement built upon an earlier compromise in the design of the Congress itself and thus satisfied both large and small States.

- The manner of choosing the Electors was left to the State legislatures, thereby pacifying States suspicious of a central national government.

- Members of Congress and employees of the federal government were specifically prohibited from serving as an Elector in order to maintain the balance between the legislative and executive branches.

- Each State's Electors were required to meet in their own States rather than together in one great meeting. This arrangement, it was thought, would prevent bribery, corruption, secret dealing, and foreign influence.

- To prevent Electors from voting only for a 'favorite son' of their own State, each Elector was required to cast *two* votes for president, at least one of which had to be for someone outside their home State. The idea was that the winner would likely be everyone's second choice.

- The electoral votes were to be sealed and transmitted from each of the States to the President of the Senate who would open them before both houses of Congress and read the result.

- The person with the most electoral votes, provided that it was an absolute majority (at least one over half of the total), became president. Whoever obtained the next greatest number of electoral votes became vice president; an office which they seem to have invented for the occasion; it had not been mentioned previously in the Convention.

- In the event that no one obtained an absolute majority in the Electoral College or in the event of a tie, the U.S. House of Representatives, as the chamber closest to the people, would choose the president from among the top five contenders. They would do this (as a further concession to the small States) by allowing each State to cast only one vote, with an absolute majority of the States being required to elect a president. The vice presidency would go to whatever remaining contender had the greatest number of electoral votes. If that too was tied, the U.S. Senate would break the tie by deciding between the two.

In all, this was quite an elaborate design. But it was also a very clever one when you consider that the whole operation was supposed to work *without political parties* and *without national campaigns* while maintaining the balances and satisfying the fears in play at the time.

Indeed, it is probably because the Electoral College was originally designed to operate in an environment so totally different from our own, that many people think it is anachronistic and fail to appreciate the new purposes it now serves. But of that, more later.

The Second Design

The first design lasted through only four presidential elections, for in the meantime, political parties had emerged in the United States. The very people who had been condemning parties publicly had nevertheless been building them privately. And too, the idea of political parties had gained respectability through the persuasive writings of political philosophers like Edmund Burke and James Madison.

One of the accidental results of the development of political parties was that in the presidential election of 1800, the Electors of the Democratic-Republican Party gave Thomas Jefferson and Aaron Burr (both of that party) an equal number of electoral votes. The tie was resolved by the

52

House of Representatives in Jefferson's favor - but only after 36 tries and serious political dealings which were considered unseemly at the time.

Since this sort of bargaining over the presidency was the very thing the Electoral College was supposed to prevent, the Congress and the States hastily adopted the Twelfth Amendment by September, 1804.

To prevent tie votes in the Electoral College which were made probable, if not inevitable, by the rise of political parties (and no doubt to facilitate the election of a president and vice president of the same party), the Twelfth Amendment requires that each Elector cast *one* vote for president and a *separate* vote for vice president rather than casting two votes for president with the runner-up being made vice president.

The Amendment also stipulates that if no one receives an absolute majority of electoral votes for president, then the U.S. House of Representatives will select the president from among the top three contenders with each State casting only one vote and an absolute majority being required to elect.

By the same token, if no one receives an absolute majority for vice president, then the U.S. Senate will select the vice president from among the top two contenders for that office.

All other features of the Electoral College remained the same including the requirements that, in order to prevent Electors from voting only for 'favorite sons', either the presidential or vice presidential candidate has to be from a State other than that of the Electors.

In short, political party loyalties had, by 1800, begun to cut across State loyalties thereby creating new and different problems in the selection of a president. By making seemingly slight changes, the 12th Amendment fundamentally altered the design of the Electoral College and, in one stroke, accommodated political parties as a fact of life in American presidential elections.

It is noteworthy that the idea of electing the president by direct popular vote was not widely promoted as an alternative to redesigning the Electoral College. This may be because the physical and demographic circumstances of the country had not changed that much in a dozen or so years.

Or it may be because the excesses of the recent French revolution and its fairly rapid degeneration into dictatorship had given the populists some pause to reflect on the wisdom of too direct a democracy.

— CHAPTER 19 —

The ConCon Come-On

"Having witnessed the difficulties and dangers experienced by the first Convention... I should <u>tremble</u> for the result of a second." — James Madison

"A constitutional convention is a <u>horrible</u> idea. This is not a good century to write a constitution." — US Supreme Court Justice Antonin Scalia

The staff at Tactical Civics™ is often asked why we do not align ourselves with proposed 'solutions' like an Article V convention or ConCon. A latter-day ConCon movement using the moniker Convention of States (COS) acts as if using that label transmogrifies a constitutional convention into a new creation, impervious to a runaway convention as happened at the first and only ConCon in 1787. This nonsensical position is summarily dismissed by <u>this</u> article by veteran Article V scholar Dan Fotheringham, and it is completely eviscerated by <u>these</u> articles by former JAG attorney and constitutional scholar Joanna Martin, aka 'Publius Huldah'. Finally, <u>this</u> excellent presentation by Robert Brown of John Birch Society ends all debate, in my view.

Scroll down <u>this massive far-left coalition list</u> of Soros-affiliated groups calling for a ConCon. Imagine them amending our Constitution!

Moreover, logic suggests that a ConCon is ludicrous, because more than 11,500 amendments to the Constitution have been proposed since 1789. Washington D.C. violates the Constitution not because it needs *amendment* but because it needs *enforcement*. Criminals will not obey an *amended* Constitution any more than they obey the *existing* one. Tom Glass, a former Texas Attorney General candidate and constitutionalist, makes the case cogently, <u>here</u>.

And finally, there has been an open Article V amendment awaiting action by the States for over 230 years! As an open Article V action, it does not require a ConCon. It was already passed by Congress in 1789 and as stipulated in Article V. As we explained in Chapter 6 and you can read more in Appendix A, Our First Right only awaits ratification by the States, 11 of which have voted to ratify so far.

This would accomplish three powerful reforms. First, it will eviscerate the power of industries and lobbyists to buy political races. Today's huge, gerrymandered U.S. Congressional districts allow only the wealthy and well-connected to compete for a House seat.

Secondly, state legislatures finally finishing their Article V duty on this pending amendment will give a vote in the U.S. House and in the U.S. Electoral College to America's 31,000 small towns *for the first time in over a century.*

Third and most importantly, it will logistically require our Bring Congress Home Act, a reform law removing Congress from D.C. and requiring them to work full-time from their hometowns. *This would mean the end of law firms for industry writing most federal laws and running our lives.*

It is conceivable (I don't know how likely) that Trump could win again in 2024; then by 2026-2027, a president Trump could be cutting the ribbon on the world's most amazing high-end redevelopment project: a new hotel/retail/office rehab of the former U.S. Capitol.

Imagine dining, shopping, staying the night, or even having a lease office in the former imperial palace of today's DC mafia, who will never again sit as though they are our masters, under that celestial granite dome.

No ConCon can do that.

— CHAPTER 20 —

Allegiance to What?

I do not recite the Pledge of Allegiance.

This gets me in a trouble with some of my fellow Americans. If you want to be despised by otherwise good, patriotic Americans, just tell them that you don't recite the pledge.

Here's the irony: Americans' childhood programming was like that of any Soviet or Chinese citizen, rendering us ignorant of our history and what the D.C. government has done to us over five generations.

As we explain in the segment from 8:14 to 8:47 in *AmericaAgain!- The Movie*, the Bellamy Pledge was developed by a fascist/socialist to program America's children. If you are interested in the birth of the Bellamy Pledge, you can find more history here.

In his article entitled *What's Conservative About the Pledge of Allegiance?*, Gene Healy of the CATO Institute analyzes Bellamy's pledge and asks why any constitutionalist should chant a pledge to Washington D.C.?

Well, because most Americans are programmed and ignorant of facts of history. For instance, you now know that Dishonest Abe Lincoln and Karl Marx were mutual admirers, and that Lincoln was the original hijacker of our Constitution, as Chapter 5 explained with links to six books.

Americans for six generations have been cheated in school. With the exception of homeschoolers, every generation alive today is a victim of fascist conditioning that began over 150 years ago. The Marxist Obama wrought destruction on our society but did not launch American communism; *Abe Lincoln did*. By Woodrow Wilson's administration a century ago, seven of the ten points of the Communist Manifesto were D.C. policy; today, it's all ten. As we demonstrated in Chapter 13: by law, America is a constitutional *republic* of sovereign States, not a unitary *nation;* a vital distinction. Centralized power is dangerous! So, I do not pledge allegiance to D.C. organized crime agencies and career politicians.

Tactical Civics™ is our mission to rebuild America's walls as in the Book of Nehemiah; a new way of life for self-governing Americans. Popular constitutionalism can truly be called the Great We-Set™.

A major goal: detox our minds of 150 years of communist programming in government schools, colleges, universities, and bureaucratic agencies reinforced daily by mainstream media.

The first three words of the Constitution make clear that the sovereign power and duty of We the People over our servant government is *perpetual*. As Mark Twain said, *"No country can be well governed unless its citizens as a body keep religiously before their minds that they are the guardians of the law and that the law officers are only the machinery for its execution, nothing more."*

It's time to repent our sloth, gullibility, and misplaced allegiance; time to learn basic civics, and to take responsibility. This book is designed to give you true history and civics, to empower you as no generation of Americans has been empowered in two centuries.

Of course, true liberty is impossible without Christ. As Jesus said of Himself and His gospel, *"You shall know the truth, and the Truth will make you free"*. It's true in civil affairs, too.

So no; I do not recite the Bellamy Pledge. I pledge allegiance to Christ and the Constitution.

I hope you will, too.

— CHAPTER 21 —

Support Our Troops?

My first wish is to see this plague of mankind, war, banished from the earth. **General George Washington**

I hate war as only a soldier who has lived it can, only as one who has seen its brutality, its futility, its stupidity. **General Dwight D. Eisenhower**

Even now, the families of the wounded men and of the mentally broken and those who never were able to readjust themselves are still suffering and still paying...There are only two reasons why you should ever be asked to give your youngsters. One is defense of our homes. The other is the defense of our Bill of Rights and particularly the right to worship God as we see fit. Every other reason advanced for the murder of young men is a racket, pure and simple. **General Smedley D. Butler**

The world has achieved brilliance without wisdom, power without conscience. Ours is a world of nuclear giants and ethical infants. We know more about war than we know about peace, more about killing than we know about living. **General Omar Bradley**

America is in greater social and political upheaval than ever before; we face what can accurately be called a constitutional crisis. What we need is true, constitutional law enforcement because the Founding Fathers designed a system of law and order specifically designed to avoid or deal with exactly what we face today: tyrant servants, rioting lunatics, and an alien flood across our borders. That system of self-defense can be put back in place in an amazingly short period of time in your state.

But first, we must deal with a very unpopular subject. As every politician and Country Western singer knows, the quickest way to cash is to 'support our troops', unquestioningly. To restore our land and rule of law, we must return to the law itself, and enforce it – even if it means roasting a lawless, much-loved sacred cow, the war industry.

Most of the U.S. military is illegal, according to the Constitution. This monograph will give you basics and point to more resources. Every assertion herein is true. Any veteran reading this: it will make you furious — and then challenge you *not* to hang your head in shame but be a leader right here at home, rather than a hired killer abroad.

59

Christ said that no man can serve two masters; every former or current military employee or family needs to choose their allegiance: their service branch, or the Constitution? Every American should support our troops, but 'our troops' means two mutually exclusive things:

1) the U.S. Constitution defines 'our troops' as the Militias

2) the military industry and employees claim 'our troops' means *them*

Verify this in the U.S. Constitution, Article I, Section 8, Clauses 12-16. Those are the only references besides the Second Amendment that relate to national defense (go to Appendix I to confirm it).

Constitutional Definition of 'Our Troops'

Okay, you can read right there that 'our troops' are defined in the U.S. Constitution as only a Navy (clause 13), and Citizen Militias *"to execute the Laws of the Union, suppress Insurrections, and repel Invasions"* (clause 15).

Representative Elbridge Gerry, on August 17, 1789 in debate on what later became the Second Amendment, wrote:

"What, sir, is the use of a militia? It is to prevent the establishment of a standing army, the bane of liberty. Whenever Governments mean to invade the rights and liberties of the people, they always attempt to destroy the militia, in order to raise an army upon their ruins."

Clause 12 stipulates that Congress can only fund Militia ground operations for two years at a time, whereas Clause 13 suggests that the Navy can be full-time to defend our shores.

So forget the Second Amendment and the century-old Dick Act; citizens owning and bearing *military grade* arms — semi-auto, selective-fire, and fully automatic is not only a right stipulated in the Second Amendment, it is a *duty* of every citizen in Militia, as stipulated in Article I, Section 8, Clause 15 of the Constitution.

The *Posse Comitatus* Act and the 1903 Dick Act only reiterate what the Constitution had already guaranteed, and what God had granted from the beginning. As for the Coast Guard, that branch logically extends from the Navy and provides invaluable lifesaving service to Americans and others in U.S. waters every day. Air Force and space-based defense might even be said to be a modern-day equivalent of the US Navy defense perimeter concept of the 18th century. The Constitution has to be amended to make them legal, but in principle they're a high-tech extrapolation of the founders' intentions for the Navy: defending our coasts.

But this is not true of the U.S. Army or Marines; the idea of a standing army on American soil or plundering foreign lands for industry would have been anathema to every Founding Father. The Citizen Militia of the several States was the only armed force that they ever intended on American soil. The founders passionately believed that free citizens in Militia would keep America free, but paid government troops would destroy our republic.

But I am *not* against military employees. Let me repeat, *I have absolutely nothing against military employees.*

As I will explain below, I believe that most members of the United States armed forces are among the most honorable, dedicated Americans alive. But an even greater number of courageous, honorable Americans have never been in the military industry. We consider most military employees a valuable asset to the republic, though a few of them are sociopaths looking for a legal way to kill, even as some gang members satisfy that lust.

As horrible as their deployment(s) may have been on their spirit and mind, the military veteran can become a vital resource in America's near-term future. He can restore the righteousness of the duty he believed he was performing for his country. Read on.

Our Troops: arming for national defense NOW

Obama claimed to have taught constitutional law, so he has read Article I, Section 8, Clause 15 many times. He knew that Americans buying millions of firearms and tens of billions of rounds of ammunition while he was in the White House, were responding to his idiotic threats exactly as Clause 15 and the Second Amendment indicate that Americans should. Like a giant organism, We the People respond as antibodies against a looming threat to our lives, liberties, and property. During the 'Obamanation', Americans bought millions more firearms and billions more rounds of ammunition. The problem is, we're still doing no more than that, so we're not meeting the Founding Fathers' plan for national defense: the Militias of the Several States.

Civics & History Resources

First, if you still don't know how the military industry has evolved into possibly our greatest domestic threat, learn some facts about the industry's history since 1890 in Stephen Kinzer's book <u>Overthrow: America's century of regime change from Hawaii to Iraq</u>. No matter how much you may love employees of that industry and think it is 'defending liberty', by remaining ignorant of 20th century history, you support exactly what the Founding Fathers hated and warned against.

Kinzer demonstrates that not a *single* foreign action/invasion by the U.S. military has ever been conducted for the national defense of these sovereign States of America. *Not one!* Andrew Bacevich formerly taught at West Point and was a decorated officer in Vietnam. His book *The New American Militarism* explains that the military built since Lincoln's time is *antithetical* to everything the Founding Fathers fought for. The smallest book on this subject but possibly the best, is a classic written by the most highly-decorated U.S. Marine in history, General Smedley Butler. In his classic booklet *War is a Racket,* the repentant old war-horse writes…

"I helped make Mexico…safe for American oil interests in 1914. I helped make Haiti and Cuba a decent place for the National City Bank boys to collect revenues in. I helped in the raping of half a dozen Central American republics for the benefit of Wall Street….I helped purify Nicaragua for the international banking house of Brown Brothers in 1909-12. I brought electricity to the Dominican Republic for American sugar interests in 1916. In China, I helped to see to it that Standard Oil went its way unmolested." (pg. 10)

Secondly, presidents cannot initiate wars. As James Madison, Father of the Constitution, wrote…

"The declaring of war is expressly made a legislative function. The judging of the obligations to make war, is admitted to be included as a legislative function. Whenever, then, a question occurs whether war shall be declared, or whether public stipulations require it, the question necessarily belongs to the department to which those functions belong—and no other department can be in the execution of its proper functions, if it should undertake to decide such a question."

Some Troops Plunder…Others Keep Us Free

In my lifetime I've seen the domestic enemy that president Eisenhower, a former 5-star general, warned about. He dubbed it the 'Military-Industrial Complex' and it is *huge* business for industries of every kind.

When I was a child, those U.S. troops (unknowingly) defended the Rockefellers' rubber plantations and offshore oilfields in Vietnam; but for the past century the U.S. troops also provided free mercenary forces for the petrochemical industry in Central and South America and the Middle East. It's a symbiotic relationship: while providing free mercenary services for U.S. industry overseas, the war industry is a massive business in itself. Its supply train is long, wide, and complex, affecting almost every sector of industry. Great jobs, great pensions, and great public acclaim.

For much more on this subject, read any book by Peter Dale Scott, especially _American War Machine_ and _The American Deep State_. It will make your blood boil to learn how the Deep State fools millions of patriotic Americans into working _against_ the U.S. Constitution and for their industry profits. The criminal operations of the CIA and NSA are also covered in great detail in many of Scott's books, but that subject is beyond the scope of this chapter.

Contrary to war industry propaganda, U.S. military employees deployed overseas and every foreign military base operated by that industry is _illegal_ and has _nothing_ to do with keeping us free.

Not only that, but the war industry, beyond destroying the lives of countless American veterans and their families, have made large parts of Southern Iraq, Afghanistan, Kuwait, and Saudi Arabia uninhabitable for the rest of history, by firing over 1,300 tons of depleted uranium munitions in those areas. If you want to learn the horrific extent of the cancers, deformities and other maladies just from the depleted uranium treachery, watch this full-length documentary _Beyond Treason_, by the late Captain Joyce Riley, founder of The Power Hour.

You will never again think of presidents Reagan, Bush I, Clinton, Bush II, or Obama the same way again (Trump was much better, and Biden was never a president; only a lawless puppet of organized crime occupation).

Resources for Those Suffering From PTSD

For a detailed analysis of how we are taught to kill other human beings, read the book _On Killing_ by Lt. Col. Dave Grossman, explaining why we are naturally unwilling to kill, except in self-defense or the defense of home or family. The Founding Fathers designed our military around the Citizen Militia, a purely defensive force, because this is the only ethical national defense. Americans are now programmed from early childhood by the 'entertainment' and computer gaming industries to love killing. The war industry uses this programming to 'deploy' you to kill in homes and neighborhoods on the other side of the world, with no declaration of war. This is not only illegal; your moral soul fights it all the way.

One last book, by psychotherapist Edward Tick, is _War and the Soul: Healing our Nation's Veterans From Post-traumatic Stress Disorder._

That's America's dirtiest big secret and it has been making life a living hell for America's vets. They're only human; having killed others has made them want to kill themselves. For God's sake, *they must seek help*. Drugs are all they get from the VA, to 'get people processed'. The spiritual need is greater than anything – and their training can become a profound blessing for their fellow Americans and a meaningful new career for the vet.

I've shaken a veteran's foundations with truth: they were defrauded by their employer. They *believed* their indoctrination. As General Butler said, *war is a racket*. To live the rest of life with restored sanity they must face the truth, learn how they were abused – and then forgive themselves.

Let me repeat that: *the first thing a vet must do is forgive himself*. God knows our heart; we all sin, some worse than others. But what they did in ignorance, having been defrauded by a ruthless industry, God will never hold against them. They should go to God in repentance for any lives they took, and know that God is in the business of forgiveness.

Duty of a True Oathkeeper: Be a National Resource

Oath Keepers tries to convince military employees not to turn against their sovereign, the American people. I think we must do much more than keep public servants with firearms from abusing citizens. The Army and most of the operations of the U.S. Marines are technically unconstitutional, as I demonstrated. But vets were paid by taxpayers to 'defend the Constitution from enemies foreign and domestic', and that is still in their DNA.

Eight of the past ten presidents and their congresses have cut deeply at the Constitution's roots. Bush II, Obama, and *Resident* Biden were finally the bridge too far. Their open disdain for the sovereign People and the Constitution placed We The People on high alert. Yet we are unprepared to defend the Republic. Trump did what Reagan did; added fuel to the war industry fires and waved the flag, oblivious to the Constitution's stipulated limits on federal military. Every politician and country singer knows that if you wave the flag and 'support the troops', you'll be popular.

Tens of millions of Americans have fine firearms, even almost military-grade; but most could not serve effective Militia duty to save their souls. We need Militia training and by law, our state is supposed to provide it. But *not a single constitutional Militia exists today*. Veterans with recent or specialist training, will be among the most valuable citizens in this Republic. If they're still a federal employee, they should *retire*. Then they can serve the republic as never before.

Restoring the Citizen Militias

We should have Militia officers in every community, and county Militia ordinances meeting the intent of Article I, Section 8, Clause 16 of the U.S. Constitution, because the states are derelict. This is not a debatable political issue; it is the highest American law, and We The People must get our county governments to do what state governments refuse to do. Today's so-called militia groups have no accountability beyond their inner circle, *which is true of every street gang or vigilante group.*

Some of the officers must be tactical firearms trainers; others might train members in logistics, communications, emergency response, first aid, survival techniques, anti-terrorism drills, riot control and suppression, emergency infrastructure, heavy equipment operations, and the like. Every community has unique challenges due to geography, topography, climate and culture. There are vast differences between urban, suburban, small town and rural environments, culture, and infrastructure.

Within a few months, those who are called and interested, like Volunteer Fire Department duty, will have the first constitutional Militia in their community in over 150 years.

Our sovereign States abdicated their duties because We the People first abdicated ours. To restore the 'Homeland Security' of our Founding Fathers (Militias), the first step is Tactical Civics™ chapters helping newly-forming County Militia units to push through our proposed County Militia Ordinance.

Veteran, stop hanging your head in shame. I've been tough on you not because I don't appreciate your service but because you've been violating the Rule of Law you swore to defend. Please consider helping your fellow citizens by using the leadership skills you learned at their expense to now rebuild the Founding Fathers' constitutional homeland security force. The greatest military veteran stories are yet to be told. Yours needs to be one of them. Americans by the millions are waiting to be trained to do our duty as citizens. Will you stand in the gap of history?

Today's Nonsensical Second Amendment Debate

After every mass shooting, gun-grabbers and armed citizens go at it again. This is nothing new; the body of our free republic is healing itself. It is defending itself as antibodies do against infection. But we're asking the wrong questions and fighting the wrong battle.

To help you understand why the Second Amendment is not even the right battle to fight, Chapter 22 will explain how the gun lobby works against restoring Citizen Militia required by law. In 25 years of arguments about the Second Amendment, we've not heard anything about America's constitutional military defense, the Militia. Our upcoming book, *Time to Start Over, America,* provides the most complete, concise education on the subject available today.

American veterans are vital to the next phase in our history. Thanks to the evil plans of the so-called 'Great Reset' cabal, almost every country on earth faces turmoil and upheaval. But no other people can lawfully, peacefully do what Americans can, through Tactical Civics™. The duty of well-trained veterans is to prepare *every* American to be always ready to defend our homes and Republic against all enemies foreign *and domestic.*

There are over 70 million armed citizens in America; according to our own stipulation in the U.S. Constitution, *all of us* are the U.S. military and have a duty for Militia. By working wisely and diligently at this critical time in history, we can *all* keep America free, by the grace of God.

— CHAPTER 22 —

Shooting Second Amendment Blanks

With every real and false-flag shooting in this republic, statists and liberals re-kindle their heated attacks on 'our rights under the 2nd Amendment'. Constantly focusing on that Amendment instead of the *duty* and *authority* we have under Article 1 of the Constitution is a self-destructive habit. Led by gun organizations supposedly on our own side, we keep handing easy victories to gun-grabbers by simply not knowing the powers and duties of We The People that we codified in the Constitution.

Tactical Civics™ is a new way of life that can finally put full-spectrum popular sovereignty in the hands of every American who will accept the responsibility. If only half of 1% of the American people will take our duty and authority seriously, we turn the tables forever on Washington D.C.'s Deep State and collusive media.

Firearms are necessary – but not sufficient

We The People are arming ourselves as never before. That's fine; but free republics and their rule of law are maintained by *wisdom*, not primarily by force of arms. Imagine: We The People, the sovereigns over the Constitution and the government we created and limited by that law, have never attempted to enforce the Constitution; *not a single time*. Why start shooting lawless public servants when we haven't yet taken the first law enforcement step?

Notice that in real life and even on television, only criminal defense lawyers appeal to the Constitution; the prosecution never does. That is because We The People never created a mechanism to *enforce* our highest law. As we stipulate in Amendment X, we *retain the power* to do it at any time. Tactical Civics™ is the only solution in the republic today designed for that purpose.

No mere armed citizens can perform this law enforcement mission in total alignment with the Founding Fathers and our Constitution.

National Firearms Act of 1934 is Unconstitutional

We explained that *We The People are the U.S. military according to the Constitution*. It is grossly illegal for Congress, with the National Firearms

Act of 1934, to have forced manufacturers and dealers to use the 'military and law enforcement use only' designation for all the best firearms and equipment. There is no *constitutional* limit to the type, caliber, fire-control system, or optics of the arms that citizens can and should own. The 1934 act forces tactical arms and equipment manufacturers to tip the scales against the constitutional citizen Militia stipulated in Article I Section 8.

Today, millions of citizens argue with gun-grabbers who remain on the offensive, infringing on magazine capacity, barrel length, pistol grip stocks, bump stocks, noise suppressors, flash hiders, and fire control systems. We fell to this ludicrous position because we cower in the face of Congress' 79-year-long violation of the Constitution. The military industry and local police departments side with their career interests, against the People's authority, duty and liberty.

Congress making any law infringing on the right of citizens to buy, build, repair, trade, sell, carry and use *military-grade* weaponry for Militia use is precisely the situation the Second Amendment was meant to avoid. But because We The People first abdicated our *authority, power* and *duty* that we stipulate in Article I, Section 8, Clause 15 and we refuse to make our state governments obey their duty that we stipulate in Clause 16, it is *not* a Second Amendment *rights* issue but an Article I People's law enforcement *powers* and *duties* issue.

The Gun Rights Lobby is Peddling Fear Porn

Had it wanted to, the NRA could easily have restored constitutional Militia anytime over its 150-year existence; but it refuses to do so. As Adam Winkler explains in his book *Gun Fight*, the NRA was a *gun control* organization before it became a gun rights lobby group. The ancient, self-serving behemoth institution with its huge headquarters and careerist staff first creates 'crises' in DC and then pretends to end them. Actually, NRA is only playing footsies on The Hill.

As we explained in Lesson 17, every non-profit and conservative talker is part of a mammoth industry that is very active on the Right. Fear Porn raises billions in tax-exempt donations and advertising revenues each year.

If you think they are actually trying to *solve* the problems they complain about, you don't understand the revenue model: feed a regular stream of fabricated crises to keep the member/donor/listener afraid and coming back for more.

The brain's limbic system is the target for pornography, horror movies, violent sports, and murder mysteries featuring execrable villains. As they daily exercise their followers' limbic system of the brain with doses of fear and anger, they create addicts; and addicts come back daily. Advertising, product sales, and donation revenues rise.

This is why the NRA will never solve any of the crises; if the problems are ever solved, the victims stop giving. Rush Limbaugh spun this along for over 35 years, but the NRA has done so for over 150 years!

I was an NRA member for decades; the only thing it has *never* been is an effort to restore the Militias as stipulated by We The People in the Constitution. Gun Owners of America is no better; at best, it pays lip service to Militia.

It does not even frame the enemy in the right terms. Notice this GOA bumper sticker sending exactly the NRA 'gun rights' message...

A *right?* In the U.S. Constitution Article I, Section 8, Clause 15, We The People stipulate that *'to execute the Laws of the Union, suppress Insurrections, and repel Invasions'* is the *duty* and the *power* of the Militia. No police force, sheriffs, or standing army are stipulated in the law; only Citizen Militia as law enforcement.

Especially enforcing the Constitution itself against organized crime in our legislatures; but also riot control against thugs in Antifa, neo-Nazi and Black Lives Matter hordes. And especially these days, border security against current invading hordes of Muslims and Latin American drug mules, gang-bangers, illegal workers, and welfare queens.

The Basic Civics

Forget Second Amendment 'rights' until you first exercise our Article I power and duty. In the first three words of the Constitution, We The

People stipulate that we are the highest power in government, creating it. In Article I Section 8, we gave them only 17 powers that standardize our public services such as mail service, coining gold and silver money, copyrights, naturalization laws, etc.

In the Tenth Amendment, We The People stipulate that *we retain every imaginable power for ourselves and only grant our servants the powers we enumerate.*

Our arrogant servants puffed themselves up as we sat by and watched for five generations. They arrogated hundreds of illegal powers to themselves over the past 150 years. Now the best we can do instead of law enforcement is to beg our criminal employees for *rights?*

Partial List of Our Servants' Felonies

Our servants in the U.S. Congress now take it on themselves almost weekly to attack the retained sovereign powers of We The People and these sovereign States. Every member of both houses took a solemn oath, then violates it on a regular basis.

Every member is constructively, even if only by ignorance or professional negligence, violating the Constitution with respect to infants' right to life, our stipulations for lawful money, honest banking, the very limited land that federal government can claim or use, and our stipulation of a well-trained Militia of the Several States.

Before Trump, the Deep Axis tried a fake 'war on terror' and Islamic jihad or Iranian saber-rattling kindled and reinforced by the CIA; then the saber-rattling little North Korean, who could be taken out tomorrow by U.S. Special Forces but instead was goaded by the globalist war industry because it's good for them.

The arrogant organized crime operation known as The Deep State now makes the U.S. Congress the second most destructive enemy of these sovereign States and People (the *most* potent is the massive population of stupid people).

It is long overdue that We The People begin to 'execute the Laws of the Union' against this Democrat/Republican machine that:

- Invites enemies across our borders (cheap labor for industry)
- Refuses to throttle the lawless courts under its aegis
- Continues to run earth's largest counterfeiting operation (FED cartel)
- Continues to operate an extortion/payroll-skimming scheme (IRS)
- Continues the largest gaslighting operation in history (COVID scam)

- Swept under the rug the first openly stolen election *(stole our government)*
- Continues to load its sovereigns down with rules, regulations, fees, and programs that it does not have to live under
- Continues to engage in felony insider trading every day, making millions by buying and shorting stocks of industries that it regulates or supports
- Pays itself whatever it decides, from *our* payroll accounts, including *fat benefits and pensions to the grave, even after we kick them out of office* – while we struggle to make ends meet!

I could go on for pages; but you get the idea. We The People are now at that point in the movie where we have the opportunity to trap the mafia kingpins and finally bring them to justice. Tactical Civics™ has developed the best solution in American history.

Going on Offense in Our Counties

Instead of demanding that Congress and our State legislatures stop violating stipulations in law, gun rights organizations have trained generations of Americans to argue about a last-ditch Second Amendment 'right' when we are not performing the only *duty* that We The People demand of ourselves in the entire Constitution!

If we want to obey the Constitution *over which we ourselves are the highest authority*...first we need to pass our model County Militia Ordinance in every county possible, because *every state legislature is violating the stipulation for constitutional Militia* (Art I, Sec 8, Clause 16, U.S. Constitution). We stipulate that *every* state appoint its Militia officers and set regular training of Militia, but few States are doing so. We have a long way to go before our state legislatures are obeying the Constitution. So we revitalize our Grand Jury in every county via our County Grand Jury Ordinance, and with our County Militia Ordinance we put teeth back in the Constitution. Once we have seen to it that our counties recognize well-regulated, properly-officered Militias, then We The People ourselves will *'execute the Laws of the Union, suppress Insurrections and repel Invasions'* (Clause 15).

Making Militia Cool, Fun, and Affordable

As we explain in our book *Time to Start Over, America,* we need to restore our constitutional Militias rather than allowing liberals and statists after every shooting to make new arguments about red flag laws, barrel length, magazine capacity, open carry rules, full-auto or select-fire, flash-hiders, noise suppressors, bump stocks and more.

Instead of complaining about out-of-control cops and biting our fingernails over 25 Muslim training camps scattered across rural America, millions of Americans should be mustering, training, and gathering as neighbors and friends once did in America. When we have *thousands* of constitutional Militia units, Second Amendment talk will become a relic. There are over 32,000 municipalities and towns in our Republic so there should be over 32,000 Militia training camps across America. Militia training should be as common as baseball games; as popular, cool, fun, and enjoyable as golf, hunting, or fishing.

Wake up; It's Morning in America!

The most effective step Americans can take is to go on tactical *offense* today. So-called 'militia groups' are operating outside the Constitution's stipulations that We The People set for ourselves. They will never be legitimate until they get over their mere desire to train in the field without re-training their attitude as responsible to oversee government.

Exactly the same problem plagues the so-called 'common law grand juries' attempting to appoint themselves. Before we had a Constitution, the two fundamental institutions of American law enforcement were the Militia of the State or community, and the Grand Jury of the county. Those two fundamental institutions must work in tight coordination as we explained in Chapter 8; that's the mission of Tactical Civics™.

There has never been a better time to be alive in America. Americans have never been more ready to take our lives back, but we need to do far more than any president can do; We The People must turn the tables ourselves. We were warned by General Smedley Butler in the 1930s, by General and President Dwight Eisenhower in 1961, by criminologist Donald Cressey in 1969, and by Professor Thomas DiLorenzo in 2012, that our most dangerous enemy is D.C. – the independent, lawless, ruthless city-state that fell under control of evil men and corporations long ago.

Now, We The People must begin to 'execute the Laws of the Union', not with a last-ditch right stipulated in the Second Amendment, but using a full-spectrum tactical plan, most of which does not involve force.

By God's grace, we begin turning the tide of history just when the evil ones thought they had won. And we will do it not only by using arms, but by using *brains*.

— CHAPTER 23 —

Sheriffs: Fake History

Teaching fake history as truth is even more dangerous than 'reporting' fake news. For instance, besides teaching that the sheriff is the highest constitution enforcement officer in each county, KrisAnne Hall doesn't even get basic history correct. She says,

The Declaration of Independence is the Sixth liberty charter in the long history of British law. It catalogues the grievances of the colonists and lay out [sic] the principles upon which they separate from Great Britain. It is rooted in the principle of sovereignty – that no one is naturally the ruler of another. This principle is at the heart of individual liberty. Walk through this foundational document and learn the precise foundation that was laid for our future. See that the singular principle of liberty permeated all of our founders' motivations. Arm yourself with the truth that you need to counter the dispersion's [sic] about our Republic's origins.

With all due respect, KrisAnne continues wrongly citing the provenance of our Anglo-American rule of law, as we've informed her for many years. All she has to do is corroborate what we have told her many times.

The TRUE Origins of our Rule of Law

Our Anglo-American rule of law, 'liberty charters' as KrisAnne calls them, originated in the *Compact of Ethelred* in 1014 A.D., when the English people forced a king to meet their demands. For the first time, kings could not do as they pleased. The rest of our Constitution's genealogy is:

#2 *Charter of Liberties* (1100 A.D.)

#3 *Magna Carta* (1215 A.D.)

#4 *Provisions of Oxford* (1258 A.D.)

#5 *Declaration of Arbroath* (1320 A.D.)

#6 *Mayflower Compact* (1620)

#7 *Petition of Right* (1628)

#8 *Grand Remonstrance* (1641)

#9 *English Bill of Rights* (1689)

#10 *Declaration of Independence* (1776)

Those were all established by Englishmen, over there and over here. Then, the two purely *American* entries in the ancient lineage of our Anglo-American rule of law are:

#11 Articles of Confederation (1781)

#12 U.S. Constitution (ratified 1789)

Like our People's ancient law enforcement institutions, Grand Jury and Militia, this rule of law was born and matured in England, but now exists *only* here in America. So our rule of law is called *Anglo-American,* but the people of England allowed it all to crumble.

KrisAnne Hall is still teaching her fans/customers, and former sheriff Richard Mack (founder of CSPOA, Constitutional Sheriffs and Peace Officers Association) is still teaching his fans/customers that the sheriff is the highest constitutional officer in America; *that's a dangerous falsehood.*

You can learn the true history of sheriffs in our books and articles in the Tactical Civics™ Training Center; but in brief, the sheriff *cannot* be the highest constitution enforcer because...

A) We don't authorize, or even *mention,* sheriffs in the Constitution;

B) The *shire reeve* was the king's tax collector/enforcer against the People;

C) Today's sheriffs *still perform that same duty in every county.*

As we explained in Chapter 1, the People cannot actually *own* property in America; sheriffs and tax collection lawyers make that impossible. So, like all communists, even after we pay off the mortgage we can only *rent* our home, business, or farm from those taxing authorities who are living high on the hog. *On our backs.*

If you believe that you own the farm or home that you paid off years ago, just don't pay the next property tax bill on it. The sheriff will sell it at a foreclosure sale on the courthouse steps, and put your family on the street. It was never your property because *private property doesn't exist anymore in America.* Organized crime wearing the label school district, city, or county have embezzled all private property in America. So-called owners have no voice in the transaction. *That's life in America under God's judgment.*

One duty of the sheriff is to assure that you pay bureaucrats their pound of flesh for the privilege of living in your own home. Another major activity of sheriffs is running their mouths about being 'constitutionalist' during re-election campaigns. That's either shocking ignorance, or fraud.

In Times of Universal Deceit

...telling the truth will be a revolutionary act". That was one of Orwell's zingers, and it perfectly fits our lawless era. Plain truth sounds _very_ harsh today.

We are no scofflaws at Tactical Civics™; our mission educates, supports, and organizes the willing remnant of the People to again exercise our authority and *duty* of law enforcement in every county. Even in the most Marxist or atheist county, *law is still law.*

This is basic history and civics that every homeschooler can learn, but government schools cannot teach, or they'd have to stop taxing Americans through the nose to pay for opulent new school buildings, bureaucrat fleets and fat salaries, football stadiums, indoor pools, and so on.

America is corrupt because Americans have been lazy and ignorant. Now, by the grace of God, some of us are reforming ourselves. We are teaching hard truth to *very* lazy people, so of course it's not popular. But truth followed by repentance in action are the only way to restore our land, now under God's judgment.

When comparing 'save America' organizations, the first consideration should be: *does the organization offer a comprehensive, long term plan of action with projects on the ground to execute on the plan...or is it all just more talk?*

The second consideration: *what is the background of the organization's founder; could they have a former career bias?* For instance, KrisAnne Hall's prior career was a state assistant prosecutor and Richard Mack's prior career was county sheriff. My prior career was architectural engineer with side jobs as cattleman, homebuilder, missionary pilot, Tax Honesty author, and founder of K-12 classical Christian schools. I never took a dime from tax coffers and I never will.

We don't wish to besmirch a Christian (Hall) or even a Mormon (Mack) but our mission is often compared to theirs. That's *preposterous.* They are teaching the *opposite* of history as *fact.*

Presentation style aside, truth is terribly important on earth just now.

— CHAPTER 24 —

'Rights' is Wrong

If the upset parents of wild, criminal children were to pout and insist to the children, *"I have rights!"*, would that make sense?

Our Three Ugly Babies

We The People — collectively, not individually — are the 'parent' of government. We gave birth to our federal government in an era of relative honor and morality, but in the past 160 years it became a lawless, wicked, massive monster. Still, the legal relationship of sovereign-to-servant is stipulated in our highest law. No one can deny the birth process: *We The People...do ordain...*and then following that Preamble in the U.S. Constitution come Articles I, II, and III.

Those were our three servants, newborn and innocent in 1789.

The Anti-Federalists Were Right

Alas, James Madison seems to have been saying, *"Now, be sure to check on one another, children!"*, because his checks-and-balances sound *absurd* today. I suppose that the idea was rational back then to the Federalists, but the so-called 'Anti-Federalists' saw red flags.

I can understand Madison's confidence: bracketed by that Preamble and our open-ended reservation of powers in Amendment X, there is, *'Militia, to execute the Laws of the Union'*. What could go wrong? Most honorable, diligent folk of that time could not foresee the collapse of norms and nobility that began in the generation of Lincoln, Marx, and Darwin and grew to open D.C. global crimes throughout the 20th century.

The Anti-Federalists *did* foresee it; but they were the political minority, so they were voted down and we got this Constitution with its 'elastic clauses'. But I will say in defense of both this Constitution and of the Federalists: they assumed that the People would always do our collective sovereign duty like a responsible parent. But even Ben Franklin had his reservations, answering Lady Powell, *"A Republic, Madam, if you can keep it."*

It's unfortunate but understandable that the Founding Fathers used the term *rights* so often. They knew what it was to be a subject of a monarch from whom you had to beg *rights*. But we are only subjects of our own indolence. Having been born in a century grown so corrupt, the parents should *never* have expected their three children to check and balance one another; our ancestors should have known better! *But they didn't.*

Well, *we* certainly know better *now,* don't we? In this surreal, hijacked condition (I am writing in 2022 Marxist-occupied America) everything good is called evil by Communists and atheists, who will do or say *anything* to win. While we won't stoop so low, we do need to watch our language when it comes to civics.

Remember, in our system the simple definition of civics is, *Who is Boss?.*

Metaphorically, Communists and atheists have stolen our words, twisted and hardened them, gutted us with them, decapitated us, and are urinating down our collective windpipe! The forces of evil are determined that American Communism not die; but by God, *we are determined to kill it.*

The overthrow of our laws, creating 'sanctuary' cities and states openly violating our laws is only one of many crimes of late-stage American Communism. America's only hope now is *sincere repentance before God.*

'Rights' is Wrong

This is not a 'kinetic' war; armed conflict. It is a plunder-and-occupation scheme waged with words and ideas. The 'enemy', predators and parasites of society, have been winning for generations. They lie, steal, cheat, and are masters at gaslighting. *Yet Americans allow them to train up their children!*

We tell the truth and play by the rules. But the predators and parasites don't intend to slack off, so neither can we. It's not about 'rights'!

We The People have *authority* over the Constitution; so use *that* word.

We have a *duty* to enforce it, as we stipulate in that law; so use *that* word.

But please, fellow Christian, never speak of *rights* again.

— CHAPTER 25 —

The Greater Magistrate

The framers of our Constitution knew the Scriptures. The memories were still fresh in their minds, of being subjects of the British throne. They were also intimately familiar with the command in Romans 13:

Let every soul be subject to the higher powers. For there is no power but of God; the powers that exist are ordained by God. Whosoever therefore resists the power, resists God's ordinance; and they that resist shall receive to themselves damnation. For rulers are not a terror to good works, but to the evildoer. Would you wish to not have fear of the power? Do that which is good, and you shall have praise from the same, for he is the minister of God to you for good. But if you do that which is evil, be afraid; for he bears not the sword in vain. He is the minister of God; an avenger to execute wrath on him that does evil. (Rom 13:1-4)

The magnificent law they wrote, the highest human law in this Republic, in opening with the words, *We The People...do ordain and establish this Constitution...*, set out the most powerful, unique human law in the history of this planet. Having won their war for our independence from the tyrant monarch across the Atlantic, those men took their wish lists and went for broke, crafting a written Constitution for our blessed, unique Republic.

Pastor, America Has No Caesar

As we explained in Chapter 4, these States are a unique republic because in the opening three words of our highest law, We The People give ourselves the hardest, most liberating authority that men have ever granted themselves: the duty to *govern our governors*. We give ourselves the authority to assure that the servants we create through the Constitution, will obey it or we "execute the Laws of the Union". Among all the governments ever created on earth, only in this Republic of sovereign States are the People themselves the actual Big Boss. *By law.*

Forever.

But only if we know the Constitution and enforce it, as Romans 13 says that *God ordained us to do.* Collectively, we are supposed to be "the higher powers". If you don't believe that God ordained that our original founders should arrive here in Jesus' name, and that He inspired our systems of law, economics, ethics, government and family structure for at least the first 250 years of this experiment, then you don't know American history. Those *are* our spiritual roots.

As to civil government and law, as I demonstrated above, We The People are the Big Boss. The higher powers. We The People — collectively, not individually as anarchists — are, in the words of the 16th century German confessions, the *Greater Magistrate* above our federal, state, county, and local governments, the *lesser* magistrates. They are our *servants* that we elect and pay to perform *only* the functions we enumerate in our constitutions and in our county and city charter documents.

NOT 'Sovereign Individuals'

We are not suggesting that every *individual* American is sovereign in our system of government; only *collectively*. That is why we have government in the first place: to avoid the every-man-for-himself attitude of the anarchist and libertarian. Those who peddle the 'sovereign individual' fantasy have no foundation under their feet: no examples, no history, no law, no tradition or custom – and certainly *no Constitution.*

But the Romans 13 command, *be subject to the higher powers* applies to each of us individually, as it does to every public servant from school district to congress, the White House, and the U.S. supreme Court.

To sit in the Big Boss position of the Greater Magistrate, you do it as a member of either your County Grand Jury or Militia. Only in those two primordial law enforcement institutions of Western civilization do you occupy the office of the Big Boss in your county.

And only during good behavior.

And *only when that Grand Jury or Militia are not making it up as they go along.*

Our mission to America is called Tactical Civics™ because this new way of life restores basic civics and teaches Americans tactics that make up Popular Constitutionalism. We show you what the Constitution requires of you as an American, especially when serving in Militia and Grand Jury. We show you the lies we've been programmed in, and the powerful truth and solemn duties in the Constitution. Soon, you have enough good news and solid foundation to tell others in your circle, giving them hope.

Until a critical mass of Americans take responsibility and learn, train, and muster for duty, the Greater Magistrate that God ordained for our Republic will stay hiding in a corner while lesser magistrates and criminals of every description take turns running the tables on one another.

Big Boss is Clueless

The conventional wisdom programmed into every American by government schools, Marxist colleges, the treacherous Deep State, and the 20 million career government employees is that that voting is the extent of the People's power to seize or reform criminals in public office.

Others, like the clever 'Q' psyop, just tried to keep us in our cages by assuring us that the unconstitutional 'department of justice' or other lesser magistrates, would begin indicting bad guys soon. They said for years… *trust the plan.* As pathetic as that may have been, it's the conventional wisdom peddled by every political party, law school, Political Science course, and 'reform' book, course, national speaker, think tank, or website.

But it's not what we read in the plain language of the Constitution, is it?

No indeed; in that law, We The People do not authorize any FBI, DOJ, police, or sheriffs. We don't even *mention* any of those. And the only place we mention an army (Article I, Section 8, Clauses 12-16), We The People limit it to two years' existence, then these 'armies' raised by Congress must go back to the duties as State Militias.

Isn't that amazing? Believing the nonsense fed to us in government schools and colleges staffed by Marxists, atheists, and unionists, We The People have allowed our servants and lesser magistrates to create their own lawless fiefdoms, in open violation of the Constitution.

The bedrock of our Constitution: We The People, in Grand Juries and in Militias duly established, task *our own selves* as the *Greater Magistrate.* We're supposed to *ordain,* as we stipulate in America's oldest, highest law. But we don't, because we're busy playing golf or keyboard warrior, or paying for a fancier house than we need, or…well, you get the idea. So here we are, the collective Big Boss, just doing as commanded by every petty, blue-light bureaucrat in D.C. or in our state palace, county palace, city palace, or school district palace.

The bent servants are so sure of themselves that they even get us to pay for every agency, bureau, program, regulation, fancy building, vehicle fleet, junket, or fat pension package they design for themselves. No matter how unconstitutional — in other words, *criminal* — all these things may be, the property owners and productive citizens just keep paying.

As for 'savior' Trump: at his insistence and the imperious commands of dozens of emperors in state palaces, tens of millions of Americans became masked zombies and took dangerous, unproven 'vaccinations' just to keep their jobs, buy groceries, eat at a restaurant, or go to any public venue. Can't be different than the flock. Must comply!

This was (and still is) the most chilling, astounding mass reconditioning experiment in history. Blatantly unconstitutional and demonstrably fraudulent, yet the Masters of the Universe, today's gatekeepers of the public square, will cancel and destroy the career of any truth-teller even if they've published peer-reviewed medical reports.

The latest of three massive racketeering and attempted coup operations has been the most effective. Democrats and Communist Chinese are much smarter than conservatives are. And all governors love power trips; it's why they became governors. Meanwhile, the Higher Magistrate remains clueless of our authority and *duty* to arrest this ongoing hijacking of an entire civilization and economy. The 9/11 debacle was experiment #1; this was experiment #2, and *far* more chilling in terms of mass reconditioning of a formerly self-governing People, into fearful, compliant zombies.

It's bizarre. How foolish can the collective Greater Magistrate be? I'm not sure yet; my fellow Americans continually shock me. Trump surprised me, too; either he was always on the enemy's side with Bill Gates and the vaccine industry, or just gullible. Yet, his staff knew perfectly well the several inexpensive, effective antidotes for the China virus. Why did Trump still push the monster Fauci on us? Why did he push Bill Gates' and Big Pharma's vaccine on hundreds of millions of Americans? More chillingly: *why did his fans accept it?* (Read Paul's description in Romans 1; God's judgment is a tough place to live.)

But repentance is always an option. We pray for a great wave of real repentance in American hearts. In our American system of government, repentance must include learning your Greater Magistrate duties, and performing them. So let's review some civics.

Nullification and Interposition

After the ratification of our Constitution, James Madison and Thomas Jefferson posed two contesting principles on how to respond to our federal servants when they violate the supreme Law that We The People laid down, and by which we created those servants' offices. Jefferson favored *nullification* by the States of any lawless federal act or pronouncement. Fans of nullification still abound today; but two facts stand in the way of Jefferson's preferred solution.

First, each of the 50 States is running a unique racket in its state palace. Some have grown much worse than others, but all are running rackets for people and industries with money. So it's beyond naïve to think at this hour of the day that *any* of the 50 state palaces will begin operating as servants, with We The People their boss. So the first problem with nullification is that the crooks in state governments *just won't do it.*

Secondly, if each of the 50 States make up their own response every time our *federal* servants are outlaws, we'll have worse coast-to-coast confusion than what we already do. Nullification won't fix the mess; *it will add to it.*

James Madison favored another principle, called *interposition…*when federal servants go rogue, the *State* interposes between the federal bad guys and the People who are their victims. As a practical matter, exactly *who* in the State would do the interposing depended on the nature of the threat from federal rogues. The interposition force might have been an attorney and his staff from the state palace. But have you ever seen a state attorney general preen in front of the camera? It's as theatrical as when governors or sheriffs do it. Or it might have been, as Alexander Hamilton posited in the 28th Federalist, the *State Militia* who would interpose. But other than toothless resolutions and other political tricks, it has never worked.

Madison's analysis of the much-despised Alien and Sedition Acts, provided justification for such interposition. As University of New Mexico law professor Christian Fritz writes:

The people of the states "as co-parties to and creators of the constitution" could exercise their ultimate authority by amending the Constitution or finding other ways to express their constitutional understanding. Madison later conceded that the resolutions and his Report lacked specifics about "what mode the States could interpose in their collective character as parties to the Constitution." However, given "the object and reasoning" of those documents, specifics were "not necessary." "It was sufficient to show that the authority to interpose existed, and was a resort beyond that of the Supreme Court of the United States." If the sovereign people invoked their ultimate right to intervene, how they did so was their "own choice."

Madison knew that We The People had open options because he led the committee that drafted and finalized the Bill of Rights. But back to our law enforcement options; in the original 'Article the Twelfth', what we know today as the Tenth Amendment, We The People stipulate,

"The powers not delegated to the United States by the Constitution, nor prohibited by it to the States, are reserved to the States respectively, or to the People."

Or in modern language:

We The People, as the Big Boss, retain every power imaginable, except those that we delegated to the servants in our Constitution. What powers those may be, and in what form, and how executed, is entirely up to us.

Some pastors today claim that the Magdeburg Confession's 'Doctrine of the Lesser Magistrate' is how Madison's interposition idea works out today. What?? When your *high*-level lawless servant attempts to take the People's rights, the People's only recourse is to get a *lower*-level servant to stand between the People and the bad guy?

Two serious problems with the 'Doctrine of the Lesser Magistrate'. First, it references a German religious confession of 1555 instead of the U.S. Constitution which is our highest law. Secondly, too many pastors who even dare preach about our murderous, lawless, ruthless civil government, change the subject from *our servants perpetrating criminal acts,* to the servants just taking 'our rights'.

Does a mature parent beg the rebellious, bratty 6-year-old for rights? Of course not; the parent lays down the law in the home. Societies only hold together as long as everyone plays by the rules. We The People need to *enforce* our Constitution, just as we stipulate in that law. It's our *duty* to future generations and to God; *rights* have nothing to do with it.

Pulpit CEOs Are to Blame

Charles Finney once said,

"If Satan rules in our halls of legislation, the pulpit is responsible for it. If our politics become so corrupt that the very foundations of our government are ready to fall away, the pulpit is responsible for it."

I say to you today, Joe Farah, Chuck Baldwin, John McArthur, Hugh Hewitt, Bill Bennett, John Hagee, Max Lucado, Dinesh D'Souza, John Whitehead, Rick Warren, Os Guinness, Charles Stanley, Chuck Swindoll, Dave Ramsey, James Dobson *and dozens more* who have made your names into national brands: I have begged you but you do nothing to support our mission to wake and teach Americans to do their duty. As an American, none of you Christian so-called leaders can use the excuse "It's not my ministry," nor can you plead ignorance. *Satan rules in our halls of government local, county, state and federal, and you are responsible for it.*

Referring to a January 20, 2020 armed march in Richmond, VA by over 15,000 Americans including a great many self-proclaimed 'militia' against an attempted gun grab by then-governor Ralph Northam, one pastor framed the problem like this,

The fundamental divide in America right now can be characterized as a difference over the nature of rights. What are rights? How are we to understand them? When we understand that, and not until then, we can understand gun rights. ... The legislature cannot have the authority, and does not have the authority, to alienate the rights of the people from the people. Any attempt to do so is, by definition, a lawless attempt.

See? There's that silly talk about *rights* again. Americans still hold pastors in high regard. When Paul says in Romans 1:31 that God gives rebels over to be rendered stupid ('without understanding' is among 22 other sins that Paul lists), what part do incompetent shepherds play in that stupidity? In the unwillingness to lift a finger to enforce the law?

NRA Seminary

Pastors are posing the wrong questions and framing the wrong issues because apparently they don't know basic American civics. By simply espousing a nonsense principle, *as the NRA has done for almost 150 years,* the American pulpit has had 'the sheep' chasing their tails for five lifetimes. The NRA, countless think tanks and conservative groups, and America's pastors, by teaching their followers to get the U.S. Constitution exactly backwards, allow massive criminal activity by our servants to continue for yet another generation. Along with the flow of donations.

Take the fiery Chuck Baldwin, who decamped from a good gig in Florida to a safer good gig in Montana. For decades, I followed and listened in rapt attention to Chuck. Then I noticed that he was preaching great sermons while avoiding *duty,* just like the National Rifle Association, one of the largest, longest-running hoaxes in American history, second only to Congress' FED cartel and IRS heists, or the myth that Abraham Lincoln was a great president.

Before we move on to illustrate academia's similar malpractice, one last illustration of a pastor retrenching; trying to apply 16th century German law to our constitutional Republic. He writes,

One of the things that happened in the Reformation is that in various countries, the Protestants came into conflict with the magistrates who were wanting to suppress the reform efforts. Places where this conflict could be seen in high relief were France, the Netherlands, and Scotland. And when the magistrates took to the sword and stake, one of things that resulted was a theology of Protestant resistance...a three-step theology of resistance. The first was prophetic denunciation of the civic evil. When the magistrate is defying God, then courageous men in the pulpit should be authoritatively naming what is happening, and denouncing it…

A fat lot of good 'courageous men in the pulpit' have done (if that's not an oxymoron). Yet, this pastor continues digging himself in:

The second stage is for the believers to flee the persecution. Jesus said to do this — when you are persecuted in one city, flee to the next…

By which I can only assume he will soon lead an exodus to Canada? Yet he digs:

The third and final stage is to take up arms defensively…it is not permissible to undertake a revolution whereby the rebels seek to overthrow the existing authority. But taking up arms defensively is an option. And stating that you will refuse to comply if required by the tyrants to is also an option…

That is the logical and ethical equivalent of parents taking up defenses against their bratty children, telling them that they (the parents) refuse to comply with the brats' demands. Finally, this 'Reformed' pastor reaches his teacher's desk, invoking Calvin to twist American civics into 16th century German shape:

In his magisterial Institutes, John Calvin gave us another layer of protection against lawless anarchy. He taught that when the supreme ruler is resisted, it should be undertaken by the lesser magistrate, and that the people…should resist tyranny from the central government by means of submission to local authorities who are fulfilling their oath of office. Every lesser magistrate has the obligation (not the right, the obligation) to disobey unlawful orders from above. And, when they do this, the people have an obligation to rally behind them.

The governor wants to seize as many weapons as he can, and this is where we see Calvin's doctrine of the lesser magistrate on display… At this time of writing, over 90% of Virginia's counties have declared themselves to be Second Amendment sanctuaries. They have said to the state government that they will not comply with the usurpation of this unjust law.

Oh, Thou Pretty Resolution!

Actually, by passing toothless, non-binding political 'resolutions' (a very different thing from a binding city or county law, called an ordinance), 90% of Virginia's county governments simply took the quickest route to dispersing the crowds in late 2019 and early 2020, before the Communist Democrat machine found in its China Virus hoax a much more effective way to keep citizens from meeting in public or private, or even going to work or school – and the perfect way to manufacture *millions* of fake mail-in ballots. These crimes will be exposed eventually, but don't hold your breath. Still, do we Christians have to be *this* gullible?

Blind Men in Frocks

The point to notice here is this universal practice by American preachers, of twisting Romans 13 into a total refutation of American civics. They preach and write as though we do *not* actually have a written Constitution; as though We The People do *not* clearly stipulate in that highest law that collectively, we are the top level of government and 'the higher authorities'.

The preacher we quote above simply refuses to grasp that 'submission to authorities' is not what the Greater Magistrate is supposed to do when the lesser magistrates turn to lives of crime:

And so this means that the rally in Virginia's capital — and which included a number of Virginia sheriffs — was not simply a mob. It was more than a crowd. It was not simply a protest. These were citizens were assembling in their state capital, declaring their intention of submitting to the existing authorities…They were citizens in submission to the law and to their authorities…

He even unwittingly plugs Tactical Civics™:

Some might complain…[about] *a gun rights rally like this… [but] this is how it is to be done. We should all do it more…everyone take note. This is how it is to be done. As it happens, in order to respond as an informed citizenry, the citizens have to be instructed, taught, catechized. They have to know what their rights are, how they are to be protected, and what the response should be whenever they are threatened. But this requires civics classes…*

Back to Grade School

As we have reiterated from the beginning of this article series, American civics (the law enforcement that We The People stipulate in the U.S. Constitution) is not about citizens' *rights,* but about our *authority* and our *duties* as the Greater Magistrate. I reiterate: We The People are the only human authority (collectively!) *over* the U.S. Constitution.

I should not have to point out to preachers that the unique foundation of American civics, right in the opening three words of our highest law, is third grade civics. Yet they refuse to grasp it, though I've instructed and catechized them for years (in the aforementioned pastor's case, over 20 years). He ends his discombobulated civics lesson with delicious irony:

It requires Christian leaders to write about this stuff. And it requires, when they write about this stuff, that they get it right. When that starts to happen, we can then be — as the meme has it — the America that Hong Kong thinks we are.

This brother founded his own church, denomination, and college! Don't upbraid me for my tough treatment of blockhead pastors; I stumble behind our King, Jesus of Nazareth. Of all the people Jesus spoke and preached to, the only ones He was truly tough on were those lofty, sniffy religion-men. When a pastor who has been teaching dangerous, backwards civics learns the truth, he has the duty to make it clear to his followers! The American People have lawful authority over the corrupt servants and must exercise it before it's too late. *That's* reformation, Mr. 'Reformed faith'!

Preening, Puzzled Professoriate

This is not to say that religious careerists are the only demographic group working for the enemy while pretending to be on our side in the public square. It is now generally accepted that American education from kindergarten to graduate school has been deep-captured by godless Marxism, now having haughtily removed its mask. Parents who send their children into those places will reap the whirlwind for sending their children to Pharaoh for training.

I will not waste space even dignifying the openly godless, destructive practices of K-12 and post-secondary teachers today; there are many books on the subject. And because this chapter is already too long, I'll only illustrate one example of dozens I could cite, of professors *supposedly* on the conservative side of American civics.

I mentioned Christian Fritz above; he teaches at the University of New Mexico School of Law. His book *American Sovereigns: The People and America's Constitutional Tradition Before the Civil War,* is a classic case of hundreds of pages of academic blather that misses basic civics. In a 2012 article about Interposition and Nullification, Fritz writes,

Political arguments frequently use history for justification. Invariably, such efforts are less about taking the past on its own terms than the desire to make symbolic historical references that resonate with modern audiences in order to achieve particular political objectives, whether liberal or conservative.

A fine kettle of fish; a professor pointing out one of the daily tactics of every member of his guild! But Fritz appears to be truly confused about who is boss in our system of government:

Who were "the people" that underlay the national constitution, and how could that sovereign act, and be recognized in action? ... Madison's views about the constitutional implications of governments resting on a collective sovereign were easily overlooked then just as they are today.

Indeed; overlooked by law school professors writing about American constitutional history. But like the pastor above, Mr. Fritz doggedly keeps digging his students a trench.

I'm no admirer of Alexander Hamilton. Yet in his 28th Federalist we see the basic principle: whether the federal or state servants ran afoul of the Constitution, We The People would simply employ the non-offending servant (state or federal) to bring the other one back in line:

The obstacles to usurpation and the facilities of resistance increase with the increased extent of the state, <u>provided the citizens understand their rights and are disposed to defend them</u>. The natural strength of the people in a large community, in proportion to the artificial strength of the government, is greater than in a small, and of course more competent to a struggle with the attempts of the government to establish a tyranny. But in a confederacy the people, without exaggeration, may be said to be entirely the masters of their own fate. Power being almost always the rival of power, the general government will at all times stand ready to check the usurpations of the state governments, and these will have the same disposition towards the general government. <u>The people, by throwing themselves into either scale, will infallibly make it preponderate. If their rights are invaded by either, they can make use of the other as the instrument of redress</u>. [Underlined emphasis mine.]

Okay, now see Mr. Fritz walk up to the water's edge repeatedly, but always refusing to drink:

The right to monitor the constitutional operation of government was a central issue of American constitutionalism after the adoption of the Constitution in 1787. The struggle over that right revealed a fundamental disagreement among Americans over the puzzle at the heart of the new federal system: What did rule by a collective sovereign mean under a national constitution when the people who held this sovereignty were also the sovereign of their individual state governments? ... In America, the people were the sovereign. A half-century after Americans established their governments on this principle, the concept remained as elusive as it was when it first energized the Revolution ... For purposes of the national government, all agreed that the people were the sovereign, but how could they exercise their sovereignty? ...

As the Constitution's sovereign creator, the people were not subordinate to their creation, the national government. The people had a final authority. The Constitution was merely "a description of those powers which the people have delegated to their Magistrates, to be exercised for definite purposes."

For Madison... the sovereign who gave life to the Constitution did not limit its own powers as the sovereign in adopting the Constitution. ...Simply because there were physical difficulties in manifesting an authentic action by that collective sovereign did not preclude the power of that sovereign to act on constitutional questions.

As he does in his 400+ page book *American Sovereigns,* Mr. Fritz surveys different events in early American history when We The People attempted to amend, change, or ignore the Constitution. He constantly reiterates that We The People are the sovereign in this Republic, yet he never concludes with action. Like far too many pastors in our day, the professor talks a great deal but *never acts.*

Summary

At this point, I'd forgive you for considering me a pompous ass. But truth is vital at this stage in America's self-destruction. If you know the truth on a tactically and strategically vital point of life, you had better put it out there, regardless how many people call you a judgmental know-it-all. The pulpit and university have lost their former credibility because the blind have been leading the blind into a trench for generations. So while I do not pretend to have these men's credentials, to quote Erasmus of Rotterdam, *in the land of the blind, the one-eyed man is king.*

I close by reiterating the most fundamental principle of American civics, putting Romans 13 in proper context for every American:

We The People, collectively, are the Greater Magistrate over all other levels of government.

In his career writing and speaking about constitutional law and history, Mr. Fritz has never cited a case in over 230 years where We The People *enforced* the law by which we created the lesser magistrates because we, the Greater Magistrate, have *never once* attempted it.

To teach, support, equip, and organize the responsible remnant of We The People to enforce it finally, and for the rest of American history, is the mission of Tactical Civics™.

— CHAPTER 26 —
Constitutional Money Returns!

A Tactical Civics™ member asked me, *"I just learned of the existence of 'goldbacks' being issued by several states. Whatever happened to Article I, Section 10?"*

Nothing happened to our supreme Law of the Land; it's still the law. But common sense dictates that if the People don't give a damn that our servants violate a law, our servants will violate it all day long.

"Laws Are For the Little People"

There are few more glamorous, powerful gigs in this world than being a member of congress. Especially now. They *openly* defy laws high and low. They steal elections. They operate mask-and-jab gaslighting campaigns (Trump was the poster boy of that scam, and still is), and have fun slinging the 'general public' from pillar to post while they remain *untouchable!*

Crime can be heady stuff, when the money is abundant enough. Consider the textbook case. It's not in North Korea, Venezuela, or an African banana republic, but a previously unknown Muslim communist from Chicago. He suddenly wins the presidency – two terms! – ignites race war, tells the world that this is a Muslim country, salts the Deep State with 300% more Marxists...then retires with hundreds of millions of dollars, a huge mansion on Martha's Vineyard, and is now finishing construction of an even more expensive mansion in Hawaii. Americans once made jokes about European, Mexican, or African politicians who did crimes like that.

The Mother Lode D.C. Crime

But as pathetic as the Obamas are (perfect follow-on to the Clintons and Bushes), congress has been perpetrating *far* bigger financial crime for 160 years. *And Americans just don't care.* Think of any neighborhood where crime is winked at and even laughed at, and everyone accepts it. You *think* you wouldn't want to live in such a neighborhood. But in real life, most Americans seriously couldn't care less.

In our highest law, We The People created and defined a common federal servant for ourselves and our sovereign States. With respect to lawful money, our federal servant has been in perennial violation of Article I, Section 8, Clause 5... *"Congress shall have power...to coin Money, regulate the Value thereof...*". Since Lincoln waged war against his own sovereign and spawned a perpetual illegal national army – that is, for 160 years now – congress has only *coined* a token amount of gold and silver (lawful) U.S. money. Over 97% of the *currency* now in use in our Republic is only two things:

1) Counterfeit U.S. Dollars...worthless paper manufactured by U.S. Bureau of Printing & Engraving by order of the FED banking cartel, and

2) 'Loans' (trillions of dollars' worth) created from thin air and keystrokes.

Total, open, arrogant, untouchable *organized crime*. Many books have been written about both of these crimes, in great detail. I'd estimate that at least a significant minority of Americans know all about this ongoing organized crime. But few people give a damn that congress is organized crime; they'll use counterfeit paper as long as it works to buy more stuff.

We The People own enough gold to completely stop using that fake paper *within one year*. The D.C. cabal is hiding that gold; keep reading this article to the end. Then if you're a Tactical Civics™ member, listen to our November 11, 2018 podcast **HERE**.

First Steps of Repentance

Since the federal servant is so totally derelict, the States have begun to take matters into their own hands. They're making honest, lawful U.S. money again, because Washington D.C. will not do it until We The People remove congress from that criminal hellhole.

Goldbacks are the world's first voluntary currency made in a spendable (sufficiently small) denomination of physical gold. The Utah Legal Tender Act started it all in 2011, giving official recognition (at least in that state) to goldbacks as legal tender.

Vacuum-deposition technology is quite exacting, allowing .9999 fine gold to be precisely metered to far less than $1/1000^{th}$ of a Troy Ounce. That is the amount of .9999 fine gold that is layered on a nominal $1 Goldback.

Nevada was the second state to begin 'coining' goldbacks. Next came New Hampshire, and a dozen others are considering the move. States with huge economies like Texas already have a state gold depository and do not tax precious metals sales or purchases.

So, back to the original question. *Yes, of course it is lawful* for a State to use Goldbacks, a precise quantity of .9999 fine gold pressed onto a sheet of fine paper.

Our federal servants are addicted to their counterfeiting operation with the FED cartel. Congress refuses to do what We The People empowered them to do, so that we could have true money. Thus We The People can, should, and *must* allow – even *demand* – that our State servants fill the need for lawful U.S. money. See U.S. Constitution, Article I, Section 10, Clause 2:

"No State shall... coin Money; emit Bills of Credit; make any Thing but gold and silver Coin a Tender in Payment of Debts...".

No one can allege a violation against Utah, Nevada, New Hampshire, or any other State that becomes responsible and offers relief from congress' money crime. Read the clause above, again: the Goldback is a precisely metered layer of .9999 fine gold on high quality paper. If anyone alleges that this isn't *coining lawful money,* show them the clause above. Goldbacks are much closer to coined gold than what DC is selling via its FED counterfeiting operation. A small step in the right direction...repentance in action, praise be to God.

We thank and honor the legislatures and governors of Utah, Nevada, and New Hampshire for taking first bold steps out of the life of crime that all of us have been forced to live, by the criminals in the satanic city-state on the Potomac.

Now, The Exciting Part

When you read our AmericaAgain! Declaration (Appendix F), you will see 19 reform laws that we propose. The one that you might think is the most insanely ambitious is our *Lawful U.S. Money and Banking Act.* But let me explain why it is totally rational.

First, a large number of Tactical Civics™ chapters have to be planted by repentant Americans. We finish ratifying Our First Right (small districts; small-town America has a vote at last). Next, we bring congress home! Then we get those 6,500 new statesmen in our House of Representatives to force the servants in D.C. to show us the location and exact amount left, of our 288,000 metric tons of gold that the U.S. military seized from Japan and Germany in WWII. Read the book *Gold Warriors* if you doubt the existence of that massive hoard.

How much is 288,000 metric tons of gold worth, if you converted it into Goldbacks? I just checked the market; spot gold is at $1984 per Troy Ounce. Next, 288,000 metric tons equals 9,259,415,136 Troy Ounces. Multiply that by today's gold price ($1984)...our corrupt government is holding *$18.371 Trillion* in gold!

93

The U.S. money supply is calculated in three parts: M0, M1, and M2, with M0 being the most liquid money in our republic: coin, bills, and other assets readily convertible into cash. Presently, America's money supply M0 stands at $6.041 trillion. So do the math. Our criminal D.C. government has enough gold hoarded away to replace every counterfeit bill in America by monetizing just *one-third* of its hoard!

So What Are We Waiting For?

The gold is there; we just need to get the wheels of law enforcement turning, so we have to get enough Americans to repent and join us.

There are several issues. First, Goldbacks are 'frail'; they can't be folded, or they slough off small amounts of gold from the creased areas. They are pretty, and much harder to counterfeit than coins or bars, but still not ideal for everyday use.

What *would* be ideal is gold and silver certificates, like we used to have: a U.S. government paper bill, backed 100% by, and convertible in any bank to, physical gold or silver.

Another issue is that D.C. criminals surely have been ripping us off since WWII. Say the criminals have slowly stolen a ton of gold here, ten tons of gold there, over the past 75 years. Well, we owned *three times* as much gold as the average money supply. Let's say that half of it has been stolen by the criminals in DC and that's why nobody has been willing to confess to the American People how much of it still exists, or where it is. One way or another, *that's clearly embezzlement* and a capital crime at that level.

We need to have our federal government disclose our 288,000 metric tons of gold that the corrupt D.C. servants have been hoarding and probably stealing for decades. When we determine how much we still have, here's one way to recover our losses: the gold/silver ratio these days is 79:1, which is *five times higher* than the 15:1 gold-silver price ratio through most of history. We can make congress sell off some of our gold each year during the transition period, and we can buy *five times as much silver as normal.* Ever since the first U.S. Treasury Act, silver has been the metal stipulated as a U.S. Dollar.

We have the servants keep our store of silver in certified, monitored national vaults to back paper silver certificates issued by the U.S. Treasury, <u>not</u> by a private crime syndicate. Those will be regular, easy-to-use paper bills, fully backed by physical silver in a monitored, certified vault.

If we didn't want to bother with increasing our precious metal reserve by 500% by buying silver to monetize, We The People can also just have congress issue gold certificates and assure that they keep that amount of assayed, tested, physical gold in our national vaults.

A return to lawful U.S. money is attainable *right now*. But it requires a large enough, educated and dedicated American remnant living out Tactical Civics™ and pushing through our reform law to restore lawful money and honest banking. *So people have to care.* Tactical Civics™ is hard at work teaching civics and the tactics of popular constitutionalism: doing the job of We The People, America's highest office in government.

Once we have a sufficient army of educated, faithful saints, by God's grace we *can* arrest history's largest, longest-running financial crime. So stop moping in hopelessness! Turn off the daily fear porn! Join us and plug in to your State group and county chapter. *As long as you keep doing nothing but complain, you are an accessory to the corruption that you complain about.*

But repentance is always an option.

— CHAPTER 27 —

Some Days, the World Just Changes

June 15, 2021 was the 806th anniversary of the day that King John of England sealed Magna Carta, one of the most important documents in the history of western civilization.

An earlier law is more fundamental: the *Compact of Ethelred* (1014 A.D.), whereby the People demanded concessions of King Ethelred in order to return to his throne. Still, that day in the valley Runnymede, when John put his royal seal on Magna Carta, was a day when the world changed.

America has often been called an experiment, and surely it is that. From their writings and speeches we know that the Founding Fathers, including the framers of the U.S. Constitution, believed in an ineffable, all-powerful God and in the basic sin nature of mankind. The evidence of that belief is found in the limits and *disabilities* of servant government expressed and implied in the U.S. Constitution.

The framers had a visceral distrust of governments, that was expressed in Ben Franklin's axiom as he left the Philadelphia convention. When Lady Powell asked, *"Doctor Franklin, what kind of government have you given us?",* Franklin's cogent reply was, *"A republic, madam…if you can keep it."* On the day (Sept 25, 1789) that the Constitution was finally sent to the States to be ratified, the world changed again.

Losing Our Phlogiston

At the time of our War of Independence, the science community believed about combustion that everything had an indeterminate amount of an almost weightless substance called *Phlogiston.* Some materials like metals were supposed to be rich in Phlogiston; others, like soil, were considered to have very little of it. Phlogiston theory held that during combustion, phlogiston was released from a material, resulting in the reduced weight of the remaining product. *The fire comes, the phlogiston disappears…poof!* was the sum total of combustion science in George Washington's time.

Then, a Frenchman named Antoine Lavoisier wrote a treatise in 1777 that eventually earned him the title, *Father of modern chemistry.* Demonstrating that Phlogiston theory was bunk, Lavoisier humbly proposed,

"I claim to substitute for it [the theory of 'Phlogiston'] *not a rigorously demonstrated theory, but only a more probable hypothesis which presents fewer contradictions…*[it] *explains with marvelous ease almost all of the phenomena of physics and chemistry."*

Lavoisier's simple experiments burned material with and without carbon, measuring the difference in the weights of the remaining product. His hypothesis was demonstrated in the tests; material burned in the presence of carbon produced *carbon dioxide,* proving that the process of combustion did not *lose* material (so-called phlogiston), only *rearranged* it into airborne products of combustion.

Lavoisier's work led to chemist John Dalton and others eventually discovering the atomic nature of matter, and beginning to understand how elements combine. But someone had to take that first radical step that 'changed the world' in chemistry and materials science, and that someone was Antoine Lavoisier.

Plato Had it Right

Plato was a philosopher and mathematician in Classical Greece; the first and most important mind to develop our philosophy in Western civilization and its first institution of higher learning. It was in Athens; he called it the Academy. One of my favorite Plato aphorisms is, quote, *"There are two things at which a person should never be angry: what they can help, and what they cannot."*

I'm amazed at the level of anger we see from conservatives today, because we can *help* it; we can *change* things. That's what Tactical Civics™ is about. It's *exciting* even though very few people know about it. Do you know why?

It's a Remnant Thing

First, because these united States are a *very big* republic. And second, ever since Plato and Cicero complained about it centuries before Jesus came, most human beings are clueless and very *happy* to stay that way. That's not an elite statement; just a fact of life that has nothing to do with wealth or social standing. Some of the wealthiest people are also the stupidest. Remember, *ignorance* is lack of information; *stupidity* is *avoiding* information or not *acting* on the information that you have because it may change your comfortable circumstances.

So if you feel angry at the stupidity of your fellow Americans, listen to Plato and give it up! Paul says in Romans 1 that God will give faithless people over to stupidity ('lacking understanding') and you can't fight God.

You can be joyful in Christ, because however crazy things look presently, God always has His remnant, and *repentance will always bring restoration*. It just takes time, diligence, and faith.

Some Days, The World Just Changes

I am a whale about aphorisms; little ditties that convey a vital truth about life. With respect to this new way of life, I think of Tactical Civics™ as an extended family, or a church, or a school. We're the body of Christ, attempting to glorify Him by doing the chores. And I always say that the mission will take off when God has ordained it should take off, and almost certainly not by anything *we* do. While God certainly doesn't want us sitting on our hands, the mission will take off by God's grace, despite our floundering around. So my aphorism is, *"Some days, the world just changes"*.

For instance, there was a period lasting almost three generations when the steamboat was all that stood between life and death for countless American villages and towns. In the winter, the last steamboat deliveries before the river or bay became un-navigable, iced in; that steamboat brought all that you would see of the outside world until late spring.

The first steamboat whistle of late spring brought men, women and children, pig-herds and pastors, millers and matrons, running to the docks to greet their iron and thread; their fabric and rifles; their tea, coffee, and sugar; their oil lamps and lumber and civilized books and magazines. No one in those generations could imagine life without the steamboats.

But! Then the railroad came, pushing the steamboats off the pages of history as surely as spring pushes winter out of our lives; as though the snows and cold had never been, and new life is everywhere. The railroads carried civilization to a whole new level.

Those steam- (and then diesel-) driven behemoths became like rolling villages on rails, transporting people, animals, and commodities over mountains and across the great plains. They shrunk America as the steamboats in their fixed, watery courses could *never* have done. The railroads were king, as summer seems to engulf all of life with its seemingly endless heat and humidity. Surely nothing could beat the mighty railroads.

But! Then came the automobile, with its increasing web-work of paved roads across the republic from sea to sea, and gasoline stations and tire stores and the ubiquitous American invention, the motor hotel, or 'motel'. No longer constrained by railway schedules, the traveler could go where he pleased when he pleased, stay as long as he pleased, and then move along with total liberty of travel. No official stations full of crowds; no ticket-punching officials poking their head in your room. For ease and speed of travel, nothing could supplant the automobile. There was just one fly in the ointment: to travel beyond our shores, Americans still faced the crowds in loading areas, with their ticket-punchers and then a long, slow steamship or later diesel-burning cruise ship voyage.

But! Then came the commercial airliner; the final season, as it were, in human travel and shipping commodities. Now you can be in Europe in a matter of hours, although we still have to face the indignities of ticket-handlers, and far worse at the hands of the TSA Gestapo.

My point is, no one would think of using a steamboat for their daily needs or travel anymore because…*some days, the world just changes.* Yet back in the days of the steamboat, no one could *imagine* something better, faster, simpler and safer. Someone had to *invent* it and do the hard, risky work of executing on that vision. It happened in transportation, manufacturing, power generation, medicine, agriculture.

Every area except government.

This seems bizarre; government is the most crucial area of life! It impacts our lives, liberty and property more than any other area of human endeavor. Yet for two and a half centuries, one arrogant, lawless city-state, has ruled our lives as an emperor rules his subjects...since well before the steamboat era until today, in our era of space travel.

But! Then came Tactical Civics™.

— CHAPTER 28 —

A New Way of Life Begins

Unlike most 'save America' books, the one that you have now completed furnishes you the basic materials for a new way of life. The 72 books and resources listed in Appendix J make a Liberty Library for any American, can easily be read in 3-5 years, and will make you a truly useful teacher to your family's younger generations.

Your duties as an American include taking responsibility for our servants in every level of government. It is critical to understand that the founders meant what they wrote in the opening words of the U.S. Constitution: *We The People...do ordain.*

Our civilization is unraveling at an alarming rate, and we have no one to blame but ourselves. We can't blame our parents and grandparents who never taught us this basic civics because *their* parents and teachers never taught *them*...because *their* parents and teachers didn't know it, either. Trace it back, and you find it began when Dishonest Abe and the 37th Congress finally hijacked America as the elites had been trying ever since Alexander Hamilton was their errand boy. As reiterated many times in this book: the hijacking of our lawful money, Militias, and Constitution did not begin with Obama but in the generation of Lincoln, Marx and Darwin.

Americans find the time for so many hobbies, but have no time to study our condition, recognize *organized crime, not politics,* and roll up their sleeves. Criminals in public office and private industry have been running our lives for five generations, while We The People have met Einstein's definition of insanity: *Repeatedly doing the same thing, and always expecting a different result.*

God has shed His grace on us, showing us popular constitutionalism for the few who will take responsibility. Many of us have begun doing this in counties from coast to coast. Just a few people in each county at first. As is true of all new things, our mission won't mature overnight. But you can now become part of the Great We-Set™: the lawful, peaceful, full-spectrum solution to the 'Great Reset' plan of earth's evil ones.

It's not easy, but it's exciting and fulfilling. And it will eventually change the world by God's grace. *Again.*

— APPENDIX A —

Our First Right

This is the story of a crime. Of how a tiny mistake 140 years earlier set us up for it, how We the People have always had the power to reverse it, and how we can take congress forever out of Washington DC, making that corrupt city irrelevant again.

America was hijacked by Washington DC – the most ruthless, powerful, criminal city-state in the history of the world – when congress stole our First Right in the original Bill of Rights. This hidden mega-crime stole all representation in the U.S. House and Electoral College from residents of America's 31,000+ small towns, about 90% of America's land mass.

The millionaire lapdogs of billionaires and industry distract us with week-to-week nonsense as they fund pork, multibillion-dollar wars and multimillion dollar campaigns for huge districts with as many as 900,000 citizens – all because of a small error of just *one word*.

The Founding Fathers' Plan

It began on the last day of the five month long Constitutional Convention in 1787. Delegate Nathaniel Gorham made a motion to change one word in Article I of the proposed Constitution – "*the number of Representatives shall not exceed one for every forty thousand...*" to read, "*for every thirty thousand*".

George Washington rose to speak for the first and only time to address the convention. On page 644 of *Records of the Federal Convention*, James Madison describes the scene:

"*When the President rose…he said that although his situation had hitherto restrained him from offering his sentiments…he could not forbear expressing his wish that the alteration proposed might take place… The smallness of the proportion of Representatives had been considered by many members of the Convention an insufficient security for the rights and interests of the People. He acknowledged that it had always appeared to himself among the [disagreeable] parts of the plan…as late as the present moment was for admitting amendments, he thought this of so much consequence that it would give much satisfaction to see it adopted.*" The change was adopted unanimously.

State legislatures deliberated about ratifying the Constitution. Madison's committee proposed 39 amendments; on September 25, 1789 congress

103

passed 12 articles, sending them to the States to ratify. Article 1 guaranteed small districts...

Article the First. After the First Enumeration required by the First Article of the Constitution, there shall be One Representative for <u>every Thirty Thousand</u>, until the Number shall amount to One Hundred; after which the Proportion shall be so regulated by Congress that there shall not be less than One Hundred Representatives, nor less than One Representative for <u>every Forty Thousand</u> Persons, until the number of Representatives shall amount to Two Hundred, after which the Proportion shall be so regulated by Congress that there shall not be less than Two Hundred Representatives, nor more than One Representative for <u>every Fifty Thousand</u> Persons.

Some people contend that *'not more than'* in the last sentence means they sought to *restrict* the number of representatives. But that word *'more'* in the last sentence was a transcribing error, as you see from Washington's speech, the convention vote, the underlined clauses above, and the photocopy below.

A Slip of Mister Otis' Pen

On the day before congress officially passed the Bill of Rights, they agreed to correct a transcribing error to change the word *less* in *"the last line less one"* and to insert the word *more*. So the last sentence should end, "nor less than..." as you see in this newspaper broadside of the time:

Though confusing, the final phrase fits with the prior sentences. But the scribes making copies for the States received bad instructions from Samuel Otis, who reported that they should replace the word 'less' in the last *place* in the article, rather than in *'the last line less one'*. So the copies sent to the states contained an error that made the last passage read nonsensically; exactly *opposite* of what the Founding Fathers intended.

The handwritten copies were sent to all 13 states so their state legislatures could ratify as stipulated in Article V. By 1790, twelve states had ratified: CT, KY, MD, NH, NJ, NY, NC, PA, RI, SC, VA and VT.

Our First Right, Hidden in the Basement

In 2011, a disbarred New Jersey attorney named Eugene LaVergne discovered that Connecticut's vote sat unrecorded, so only eleven votes were counted...all because of Mr. Otis' pen. LaVergne discovered that the Connecticut House voted for the original First Amendment in October, 1789 and its senate voted for ratification in May, 1790. That made Connecticut the ninth state to vote for ratification out of 12 states at the time; exactly three-fourths of the states, the number required to ratify an amendment per Article V of the Constitution. The number is now 38.

When its senate voted to ratify, the Connecticut House wanted to retract its earlier vote until Otis' error could be corrected. The transcription error was trivial; everyone knew the intention of that article was *small districts.* Since a ratification vote can't be retracted, Connecticut just buried its ratification vote record in its state archives in the basement, and it was never recorded.

Although LaVergne sued in 2012, in Article V, we do not give the courts jurisdiction in the matter. The only way forward is for the State legislatures to finish the ratification process. The congress already passed it, so we don't need a constitutional convention; just 27 more ratification votes. DC can't keep 27 more State legislatures from restoring our First Right at last. But you may wonder, *why did we wait so long?*

Congress' Crime of '29

The founders designed the People's House to keep politicians from amassing power. The number of districts of the House of Representatives was supposed to increase after every census to *keep districts small.* But the shock-and-awe of Lincoln's War and 'Reconstruction' were a devastating 16-year distraction. Elite puppeteers bought politicians, increasing their power and riches as their districts grew. Then, their only job was to distract America with an unending series of political scandals...

The congress reapportioned districts in 1872 with a random formula creating 292 districts, yet our First Right required _765_ districts at that point. In 1890, the House changed its calculation to ensure that no state lost a seat due to shifts in population, yet Our First Right required _1,844_ districts as of the 1910 census, when congress shunted it at a random 435 districts.

Our First Right required _2,120_ districts as of the 1920 census, but using convoluted math, congress passed its Reapportionment Act of 1929, that did not even *mention* districts! When they used the excuse that the House chamber couldn't accommodate over 435, congressman Ralph Lozier said:

I am unalterably opposed to limiting the membership of the House to the arbitrary number of 435... There is absolutely no reason, philosophy, or common sense in arbitrarily fixing the membership of the House at 435...

Openly violating the Constitution, congress arbitrarily fixed the size of the House, knowing that the original First Amendment was still before the States, open for ratification. Career politicians wanted power and their billionaire handlers wanted it even more; now you know how they got it.

It's Our Responsibility

Isn't it amazing? This hijacking began with a one-word clerical error, followed by a shock-and-awe war and counterfeiting operation by Lincoln, a president that most American schools teach was one of our greatest. For copious evidence that Lincoln and the 37th congress hijacked our lawful (silver) U.S. Dollar and defrauded us into a civil war, read any of three books on the subject by Thomas DiLorenzo, or any of the six books that I linked to in Chapter 5.

Several of those books also explain that Lincoln and Karl Marx were mutual admirers, and most of Lincoln's Union generals were fans of Marx. By the time Tom 'Woodrow' Wilson was in the White House, eight of Marx's 10 points in his Communist Manifesto were already federal policy. Yes, *our federal servant has been Communist for generations.*

At this writing, a usurper 'resident' acting as president and his thousands of colluding minions in D.C. are carrying Lincoln's hijacking to a bizarre new level. We The People either end American Communism on our watch, or our historic window of opportunity may be gone. The Internet is shaking humanity as the printing press shook the medieval world. Reclaiming our First Right and restoring the People's House is up to We The People, the top level of government.

First Things First

Before we can push this unfinished business through state legislatures to get at least 27 of them to vote 'yes', Tactical Civics™ is building our county chapters and membership, so we can pack our state palaces when we are ready to call for the vote in *all the legislatures in one phalanx.*

106

There is Precedent

The original Second Amendment was ratified by one man, after more than two centuries sitting idle in the states. In 1983, a University of Texas student named Gregory Watson began working to get 29 more State legislatures to ratify the amendment, which stipulates that if Congress gives itself a pay raise it does not take effect until an election intervenes. After ten years nagging the state legislatures, in 1992 that one young man got it ratified! It became the 27th Amendment. If one citizen did it, surely we can get 27 more state legislatures to ratify Our First Right!

State Legislators

Remember, this is merely a state legislature ratification *vote*, not legislation. The vote can be taken in a single day. No legislation, reconciliation bill, or governor's signature required. Below, see the Fact Sheet and a draft Joint Resolution that they can use to call for the vote. But as explained in Chapter 10, *never trust a legislator. Granite Dome Syndrome is real!*

You pay for it, so look carefully. Imagine that this instant opulence became *your* playground for the rest of your life. It's like a middle-class person being given a free mansion with staff and amenities. The architecture alone makes them consider themselves special, and suck-up staff reinforce this self-assessment. Politicians learn to think: *"The people pay all my bills…the fools even come hat-in-hand to my door every day! They pose for pictures with me! They send their children by the busload to get a glimpse of me! They call me 'Honorable'! This is better than being a drug lord; I'm a rock star and my constituents are idiots!"*

As their sovereigns, we must put our foot down as our ancestors failed to do. Can you do that? Because that's what it will take to turn America around. We must stop expecting criminals to reform themselves. Why is the Internet not being used for self-government, as citizens become daily more aware of the corruption in government?

The Bring Congress Home Act

As we said in Chapters 7 and 15, we reiterate here…since 6,500 members will definitely not fit in the House chamber, it's time to bring them home. Modeled roughly on the MOBILE Act of 2013, our legislation called the Bring Congress Home Act stipulates:

- No member of congress can have an office in D.C.

- Every member gets one modest lease office, *in their town*

- Congressmen get 50% of their present salary

- Congressmen get a staff of two (senators, six)

- All members are limited to two terms

- We end all benefits immediately

- They work via telepresence, off-the-shelf tech today

In each congressman's office space there will be one extra telepresence workstation for citizen use when we testify before a congressional committee or subcommittee. We don't have to take time off, fly to them in DC, and pay for travel just to have them look down their noses at us.

A New Chapter in American History

Once we set the precedent by bringing Congress home to modest lease spaces and small staffs, Americans in every state capital will get other great ideas. Gubernatorial candidate and businessman John Cox of California launched a state-level project, neighborhoodlegislature.com, to break up the *state* legislature to make them serve full-time from their hometowns.

It will take time to reclaim life in America from the Deep State and its puppeteers in the banking, war, oil, insurance, tech, media and other industries. But Our First Right *can* help stop the Deep State and industries sparking wars and plundering the world in our name.

What About The Expense?

An employer who lets employees set their own salaries, benefits, fancy offices, working conditions, staffing levels, and opulent perks is a recipe for business failure.

Americans complain about government excess, but still send the kids on D.C. bus tours to gawk at 535 politicians who *each* spend an average *$11 million annually* on their operations; who *each* have as many as *eight* offices and staffs; whose Capitol Hill palace is more opulent than those of kings, popes, and emperors: white-glove exclusive dining rooms, gold-plated china, limousines, spas, private jets and more. All paid for by us, their sovereigns; $5.85 billion annually for congress' operations.

We The People abdicated our role, allowing our arrogant, corrupt servants to control every aspect of our lives, steal us blind, and tighten the chains more with each generation. We allowed them to rack up $23 trillion in debt and $190 trillion in unfunded liabilities.

Will smaller districts cost us more? No; a decentralized congress made of normal Americans *will cut tens of billions and possibly hundreds of billions* in federal expenditures and save us over $800 million annually in congress' operations (see below). Melancton Smith said in the 1788 New York ratification debate:

"The man who would seriously object to this expense to secure his liberties, does not deserve to enjoy them. By increasing the number of representatives, we open a door for…the substantial yeomanry of our country, who, being possessed of the habits of economy, will be cautious of…expenditures…a greater saving will be made of public money than [needed] to support them."

Imagine, for every *one-tenth of one percent* congress cuts federal spending, they offset the entire cost of operations for 6,400 congressmen and 100 senators!

The Best Time in American History

The massive politically-generated anger and resentment in America today between factions *is by design*. Nothing serves D.C. better than the American People fighting one another. This distracts us from the multi-billion-dollar crimes they're perpetrating in clear violation of the U.S. Constitution, right under our noses.

Had enough? Take responsibility, and join us. If you live in KY, MD, NH, NJ, NY, NC, PA, RI, SC, VA or VT, your legislature already ratified the original First Right, but you can start or join your Tactical Civics™ county chapter to work on all our other action projects and spread the great news of this new way of life. In over 200 years, We The People have not had such a golden opportunity to improve our own lives. Join us!

Congressional Operating Budget

Each year, 535 members spend $5.85 billion; per member that equals:	$10,934,579
If 6,400 House & 100 Senate members split same $5.85B, each gets:	$900,000

House Operations Budget Item Description	Annual
Legislator $98,000 salary plus 40% burden	$137,200
Senior staffer (ofc manager) $65,000 salary plus 40% burden	$91,000
Junior staffer, research & clerical $45,000 salary plus 40% burden	$63,000
Office rent ($3000/mo)	$36,000
Utilities ($800/mo)	$9,600
Phone & Internet service ($1500/mo)	$18,000
Publications (no mailing; website only, plus PDF) allow $3,000/mo	$36,000
Research expenses and publications ($5,000/mo)	$60,000
Copying services (for legislative and other publications; $5,000/mo)	$60,000
Legislative drafting services ($5,000/mo)	$60,000
Computer systems support ($500/mo)	$6,000
Website maintenance ($400/mo)	$4,800
Insurance (fire/theft/casualty; $500/mo)	$6,000
Very limited travel	$25,000
Office supplies, furniture rental ($3,000/mo)	$36,000
(4) computer systems (one for the People testifying before committees)	$14,000
Alarm & security services ($500/mo)	$6,000
Gasoline allowance (to attend events only in the district; $500/mo)	$6,000
Auditor selected by the People of the district ($1500/mo)	$18,000
Total Budget (less contingencies)	$692,600
Contingencies (10%) audited and posted quarterly on website	$69,260
Total Budget Required per U.S. House member	**$761,860**

(See next page for Senate and combined operating cost)

Senate Operations Budget Item Description

Description	Amount
Legislator $198,000 salary plus 40% burden	$277,200
(2) Senior staffers $75,000 salary plus 40% burden	$210,000
(4) Junior staffers, research & clerical $50,000 salary plus 40% burden	$280,000
Office rent ($5000/mo)	$60,000
Utilities ($900/mo)	$10,800
Phone & Internet service ($2500/mo)	$30,000
Publications (no mailing; website only, plus PDF) allow $7,500/mo	$90,000
Research expenses and publications ($8,000/mo)	$96,000
Copying services (for legislative and other publications; $10,000/mo)	$120,000
Legislative drafting services ($5,000/mo)	$60,000
Computer systems support ($1,000/mo)	$12,000
Website maintenance ($400/mo)	$4,800
Insurance (fire/theft/casualty; $500/mo)	$6,000
Travel	$75,000
Office supplies, furniture rental ($5,000/mo)	$60,000
(8) computer systems (one for the People testifying before committees)	$28,000
Alarm & security services ($750/mo)	$9,000
Gasoline allowance	$9,600
Auditor selected by the People of the district ($1500/mo)	$18,000
Total Budget (less contingencies)	$1,456,400
Contingencies (10%) audited and posted quarterly on website	$145,640
Total Budget Required per member	**$1,602,040**
Total expense for 6400 congressmen at $761,860 each:	$4,875,904,000
Total expense for 100 senators at $1,602,040 each:	$160,204,000
Total Congress Operating Expenses after we Bring Congress Home	**$5,036,108,000**
Current Operating Expenses (535 members total)	**$5,850,000,000**
The Bring Congress Home Act can save us $814 million!	

28th Amendment Fact Sheet

Text of the 1789 Amendment

Article the First. – After the First Enumeration, required by the First Article of the Constitution, there shall be One Representative for every Thirty Thousand, until the Number shall amount to One Hundred; after which the Proportion shall be so regulated by Congress that there shall not be less than One Hundred Representatives, nor less than One Representative for every Forty Thousand Persons, until the number of Representatives shall amount to Two Hundred, after which the Proportion shall be so regulated by Congress that there shall not be less than Two Hundred Representatives, nor more than one Representative for every Fifty Thousand Persons.

Q: If we ratify this 28th Amendment with a U.S. population of 320 million, we'll have 6,400 members of the U.S. House! Where would we put them all?

A: *Which government puts greater burdens on the American people – State or federal? The same 320 million Americans have 7,382 state legislators but only 535 federal ones.*

After ratifying the amendment, during the massive redistricting process in every state, AmericaAgain! will be pushing passage of the Bring Congress Home Act (BCHA) – a far more comprehensive version of HR287 filed in 2013. Congress must move out of the 19th century.

Q: But won't the added cost be astronomical?

A: *Congress' operating budget would be approximately equal to the present $5.85 billion. Rather than the present 3-6 offices and staffs, U.S. congressmen under the BCHA would have a single office and paid staff of two. The BCHA will also end opulent perks and pensions and limit all members of Congress to two terms, either house.*

Q: Doesn't the 20th Amendment say, "The Congress shall assemble at least once in every year, and such meeting shall begin at noon on the 3rd day of January"?

A: *Yes; but people attend meetings every day via teleconference and videoconference; during the fake COVID operation, Congress met virtually too. We The People need* *to end D.C. organized crime, and we begin with the original first article in the Bill of Rights finally becoming the 28th Amendment.*

Q: It has been 223 years since the last ratification vote was held on this original First Amendment; hasn't the statute of limitations run out on this process?

A: *No. Unless there is a ratification deadline in the body of the article, a constitutional amendment has no expiration date for ratification. The original Second Amendment was not finally ratified by the required 38th state legislature until 204 years after Congress sent it to the states for ratification in 1789.*

Q: If this amendment was so important, it would have been ratified when Congress first passed it.

A: *It was ratified when Congress first passed it! See the draft Joint Resolution; the Connecticut House of Representatives in October 1789 voted to ratify; the CT Senate in May 1790 also voted to ratify. The House sought in 1790 to alter its vote due to a transcribing error, but the Senate rejected the idea, so CT didn't send its vote to the archivist in DC. It was ratified, but not recorded as ratified.*

The process is not finished because at this point there are many more states than there were in 1790. Yes, the CT legislature blew it. Yes, New Jersey attorney Eugene LaVergne filed a federal lawsuit on that point. But a 2012 federal appeals court threw it out for not having jurisdiction. That was proper for the court to do. In Article V, We The People do not authorize courts to involve themselves in the amendment process. LaVergne was wrong to think that 230 years later, with 36 states added since the last ratifying vote on the original 'Article the First', and none of those state legislatures having considered the article of amendment, that some federal court could just decide this for all Americans. For proper representation; we must have at least 27 more states' legislatures decide this, on behalf of the People of those states.

Q: With 6400 seats in the U.S. House, we will be faced with a massive redistricting project. Given our workload on budgetary and operational matters in our state, why should the State legislature spend time on this frivolous political issue?

A: *George Washington did not speak publicly at the 1787 Constitutional Convention until the next-to-final day of that historic four-month gathering. When he finally rose to speak, Washington's first words were to urge his fellow delegates to support apportionment of representation at one congressman per 30,000 people rather than 40,000. (See it, right in Article I, Section 2, Clause 4 of the Constitution!)*

As a practical matter, this is simple: no committees, reconciliation bill, or governor's signature for a ratification vote. We provide your draft Joint Resolution. This is not

114

rocket science. As to redistricting your state for proper apportionment of U.S. representatives, there are GIS mapping companies and redistricting attorneys who can work with your legislature's designated staff and/or redistricting committee to help draw final boundaries and GIS/TIGER maps for your state's new U.S. congressional districts.

Q. Some people argue that the amendment has a fatal flaw in the last sentence, "*there shall not be less than Two Hundred Representatives, nor <u>more</u> than one Representative for every Fifty Thousand Persons.*" That should say, not <u>less</u> than one for every 50,000 persons; so if we ratify, we could have as few as 200 members in the U.S. House.

A. *Read the amendment; as the 12 legislatures knew when they ratified the amendment, it is clear that the progression is 1: 30,000 then 1: 40,000 and finally 1: 50,000 people. Those who raise this objection either have ulterior motives or are ignorant of the history of Article I, Section 2, Clause 4.*

The 71ˢᵗ Congress, in restricting the House to only 435 districts, hijacked the Constitution. As explained on page 5 of the book FEAR The People, the Founding Fathers made this their first article of amendment because, as George Washington made clear during the Convention, adequate representation was paramount. It is time to turn the tables on Washington D.C., bring Congress home, and restore rule of law.

This first vital step in that process cannot be stopped by Washington D.C.; the amendment was passed by Congress, sent on to the state legislatures, and arguably already ratified once. Now, state legislature, it is <u>your</u> duty to perform!

Model Joint Resolution recording the Vote on the Original First Amendment (now 28th)

Original Constitutional Amendment #1 (to be 28th Amendment)

Offered by Rep. _____

WHEREAS, The First Congress of the United States of America, at its first session begun and held March 4, 1789, sitting in New York, New York, in both houses, by a constitutional majority of two-thirds thereof, adopted the following proposition to amend the Constitution of the United States of America in the following words, to wit:

"RESOLVED, by the Senate and House of Representatives of the United States of America in Congress assembled, two thirds of both houses concurring, that the following (Article) be proposed to the Legislatures of the several States, ... which (Article), when ratified by three fourths of the said Legislatures, to be valid to all intents and purposes, as part of the said Constitution, viz.: (An Article) in addition to, and Amendment of the Constitution of the United States of America, proposed by Congress, and ratified by the Legislatures of the several States, pursuant to the fifth Article of the original Constitution.

"Article the First. – After the First Enumeration, required by the First Article of the Constitution, there shall be One Representative for every Thirty Thousand, until the Number shall amount to One Hundred; after which the Proportion shall be so regulated by Congress that there shall not be less than One Hundred Representatives, nor less than One Representative for every Forty Thousand Persons, until the number of Representatives shall amount to Two Hundred, after which the Proportion shall be so regulated by Congress that there shall not be less than Two Hundred Representatives, nor more than one Representative for every Fifty Thousand Persons." And

WHEREAS, on the last day of the 1787 Constitutional Convention, delegate Nathanael Gorham proposed a change in Article I, Section 2, Clause 4 of the new U.S. Constitution, to limit the size of a U.S. congressional district to 30,000 people rather than 40,000 people – and this was the only subject about which President George Washington felt strongly enough to publicly address the Convention, urging the revision to smaller districts because 40,000 was too large; and

WHEREAS, of the first 12 amendments passed by Congress on September 25, 1789 the subject amendment was placed in first position for the reason given by Melancton Smith at the New York ratifying convention: *"We certainly ought to fix in the Constitution those things which are essential to liberty. If anything falls under this description, it is the number of the legislature"*; and

WHEREAS in one of the Anti-Federalist letters, the prophetic 'Cato' admonished: *"It is a very important objection to this government, that the representation consists of so few; too few to resist the influence of corruption, and the temptation to treachery, against which all governments ought to take precautions..."* and

WHEREAS, Article V of the Constitution of the United States allows the ratification of the proposed Amendment to the United States Constitution by the Legislature of the State of _____ , and does not dictate a time limit on ratification of an amendment submitted by Congress, and the First Congress specifically having not provided a time constraint for ratification of the above-quoted Amendment; and

WHEREAS, The Supreme Court of the United States in 1939 ruled in the landmark case of <u>Coleman v. Miller</u> that Congress is the final arbiter on the question of whether too much time has elapsed between Congress' submission of a particular amendment and the most recent state legislature's ratification of same if Congress did not specify a deadline; and

WHEREAS, the Legislature of the State of _____ finds that the proposed Amendment is today even more meaningful and necessary to the United States Constitution than in the eighteenth century when submitted for adoption, given the level of corruption and lobbyist tampering resulting in multi-million-dollar U.S. congressional elections and inability of the United States Representative to meaningfully interact with the citizens he or she is supposed to represent; and

WHEREAS, the original First Amendment was designed to avoid precisely what we suffer today: multimillion-dollar campaigns for U.S. congressmen whose districts include up to 750,000 citizens and more – a population that they can never personally know, much less represent; and

WHEREAS, the proposed amendment to the United States Constitution has already been ratified by the legislatures of the following 11 states on the dates indicated, to wit: New Jersey on November 20, 1789; Maryland on December 19, 1789; North Carolina on December 22, 1789; South Carolina on January 19, 1790; New Hampshire on January 25, 1790; New

York on March 27, 1790; Rhode Island on June 15, 1790; Pennsylvania on September 21, 1791; Vermont on November 3, 1791; Virginia on December 15, 1791; and Kentucky on June 24, 1792; and

WHEREAS, the original First Amendment did actually receive sufficient votes for ratification once Kentucky's vote was recorded, due to the fact that the Connecticut House of Representatives in October 1789 voted to ratify Article the First, and the Connecticut Senate in May 1790 also voted to ratify it, and although the House sought by May 1790 to alter its vote due to a transcribing error, the Senate rejected the idea, thus technically, Kentucky's 1792 vote was the twelfth vote in 15 states at the time, the original First Amendment thus having been ratified by more than three-fourths of the states, making this present-day campaign truly a *re*-ratification of the People's original Right in the Bill of Rights; and

WHEREAS in 1993, the thirty-eighth State Legislature ratified the original Second Amendment, which had been ratified by the first State over 204 years earlier, at which time the Archivist of the United States declared it ratified as the Twenty-Seventh Amendment to the United States Constitution; and

WHEREAS this joint resolution only calls for the ratification vote of the original First Amendment to the U.S. Constitution under the stipulations of Article V thereof, and is not state legislation requiring committee deliberations, a reconciliation process or signature by the Governor; and

WHEREAS all due deliberation on this matter has been held on the floor of both Houses of this Legislature, it was found in the best interests of the people of _____ that the ratification vote be held without delay, and such vote having been held in favor of ratification;

THEREFORE, be it RESOLVED, BY THE HOUSE OF REPRESENTATIVES OF THE _____ LEGISLATURE OF THE STATE OF _____, THE SENATE CONCURRING HEREIN, that the foregoing proposed Amendment to the Constitution of the United States is ratified by the Legislature of the State of _____; and be it further RESOLVED, that the Secretary of State of _____ shall transmit certified copies of this resolution to the Archivist of the United States, to the Vice-President of the United States, and to the Speaker of the United States House of Representatives with a request that it be printed in full in the Congressional Record.

Model County Grand Jury Ordinance

An ORDINANCE Providing for Citizens to Volunteer for Grand Jury and Assuring that the County Court shall Call for a Grand Jury When the People so Demand, in the County/Municipality

of_____,

in the State of_____

Short Title: County Ordinance on Grand Jury   [Revision 04]

Preamble

We, the [name of county board or commission] *of* [fill in] [COUNTY, PARISH OR BOROUGH], [fill in STATE], *in pursuance of our oaths to uphold the Constitutions of our State and of the United States, and of our duty to our community under Divine Law, hereby secure the fundamental right and authority of our Citizens to volunteer for Grand Jury service within this* [County, Parish or Borough].

Article I. Justification

§1 WHEREAS, in the preamble to the Constitution for the United States, the American People declare that, "We The People...do ordain and establish this Constitution", thus clearly establishing that The People collectively occupy the highest sovereignty over all American government; and

§2 WHEREAS, the United States supreme Court in Chisolm v. Georgia, U.S. 2 Dall 419, 454 (1793), affirmed that, "The People are Sovereign...at the Revolution, the sovereignty devolved on the people; and they are truly the sovereigns of the country...equal as fellow citizens, and as joint tenants in the sovereignty"; and

§3 WHEREAS, in Amendment X of the U.S. Constitution, we state, pari materia with the Preamble, that We The People, as well as the State governments that We elect to represent us, retain all powers not specifically enumerated by us in the U.S. Constitution; and

§4 WHEREAS, the Grand Jury, along with the Militia, are the two ancient and pre-constitutional institutions intended and stipulated by the U.S. Constitution to maintain our rule of law and to 'execute' that and all other laws in our Republic; and

§5 WHEREAS, if our State enacts any statute that violates or is repugnant to the U.S. Constitution, that State law is null and void ab initio; and

§6 WHEREAS, no State legislature can sideline or outlaw the Grand Jury institution or impair its functionality, as it remains an independent institution of the People, pre-dating the U.S. Constitution but demanded thereby; and

§7 WHEREAS, Rule 6(a)(1) of the Federal Rules of Criminal Procedure stipulates, "When the public interest so requires, the court must order that one or more grand juries be summoned."; and

§8 WHEREAS, in times of corruption and lack of public confidence, the public must be the sole determinant of its own interest rather than public employees deciding what is the public interest; and

§9 WHEREAS, different county and state governments observe a variety of protocols allowing or disallowing the citizens to place their names on a volunteer roster for Grand Jury service;

Article II. Ordered

§1 NOW, THEREFORE, BE IT RESOLVED, that the [Board, Commission,] of _____ [County, Parish or Borough] hereby orders that within this jurisdiction, any citizen and resident who has not been convicted of a felony and who applies to be placed on a standby roster for Grand Jury duty, shall be placed on that roster by the county clerk; and

§2 For any given occasion requiring seating of a Grand Jury, all names on the volunteer standby roster shall be added to any other list used as a source of names for random jury selection, and from this aggregated list Grand Jurors shall be selected truly at random, in no particular order nor assigned to any particular case or Grand Jury target; and

§3 Each random selection session of Grand Jurors by county clerk staff shall be witnessed in person by a three-member committee of this governing body to assure that the process is uncorrupted by any staffer or potential Grand Jury target or the target's minions, contractors, or associates; and

§4 If any judge in our jurisdiction shall refuse to call for a Grand Jury venire when demanded by petition signed by a number of County residents equal to or greater than half of one percent of the number of ballots cast in the prior county election, this representative body shall seek from the State Court of Appeals or Supreme Court a writ of mandamus compelling drawing of a venire, or the appointment of an alternate judge to call for such Grand Jury to grant relief to the community; and

§5 The County shall make a page or pages available on its web site or prominently post there links, for County Grand Jury education, information, volunteer application with the County Clerk, and for Citizens to submit legitimate complaints of possible crimes, and calls for a Grand Jury if a panel is not sitting at that time.

Article III. Miscellaneous Provisions

§1 SEVERABILITY. If any section, part or provision of this Ordinance is declared unconstitutional or invalid by a court of competent jurisdiction, then it is expressly provided and it is the intention of the [name of county board or commission] in passing this Ordinance that its parts shall be severable and all other parts of this Ordinance shall not be affected thereby and they shall remain in full force and effect.

§2 EFFECTIVE DATE. This Ordinance shall take effect immediately upon its passage.

ORDAINED *by the* [name of county board or commission] *of* [fill in] [COUNTY, PARISH OR BOROUGH], [fill in STATE], *this* _____*Day of* [month] *in the Year of our Lord 20*____

_____

[Board/Commission Member]

_____

[Board/Commission Member]

_____

[Board/Commission Member]

_____

[Board/Commission Member]

_____

[Board/Commission Member]

Model County Militia Ordinance

An **ORDINANCE SECURING THE U.S. CONSTITUTION** and **ESTABLISHING AND WELL-REGULATING MILITIA** in the County/Municipality of_____, in the State of_____

[Short Title, "Constitution Enforcement and Militia Ordinance"]

Preamble

We, the [name of county board or commission] *of* [fill in] [COUNTY, PARISH OR BOROUGH], [fill in STATE], *in pursuance of our oaths to uphold the Constitutions of our State and of the united States, and of our duty to our community under Divine Law, hereby establish our County as a Constitutional County, with the purpose of securing the fundamental and natural rights, powers, and authority of our Citizens, including but not limited to the right of self-defense, and defense of family and property, and hereby declare and exercise our right, authority and duty to restore and perpetually maintain the Constitutional Militia within this* [County, Parish or Borough], *for all purposes of Militia as stipulated by the People themselves in the United States Constitution.*

Article I. Justification

§1 WHEREAS, in the preamble to the Constitution for the united States, the American People declare that, "We The People...do ordain and establish this Constitution", thus clearly establishing that The People collectively occupy the highest sovereignty over all American government; and

§2 WHEREAS, the United States supreme Court in Chisolm v. Georgia, U.S. 2 Dall 419, 454 (1793), affirmed that, "The People are Sovereign...at the Revolution, the sovereignty devolved on the people; and they are truly the sovereigns of the country...equal as fellow citizens, and as joint tenants in the sovereignty"; and

§3 WHEREAS, when the Declaration of Independence, recognized in American jurisprudence as Organic Law of this republic, recounting crimes of King George III, stated that, "He has dissolved Representative Houses repeatedly...whereby **the Legislative powers, incapable of Annihilation, have returned to the People at large for their exercise***", the American People collectively established that powers delegated by the People return to them, when the servant body*

to which they have been delegated abdicates, neglects, or refuses their proper exercise; and

§4 WHEREAS, the Virginia Resolution of 1798 states, "in case of a deliberate, palpable, and dangerous exercise of other powers, not granted by the [Constitution], the States who are parties thereto, have the right, and are in duty bound, to interpose for arresting the progress of the evil, and for maintaining within their respective limits, the authorities, rights and liberties appertaining to them"; and

§5 WHEREAS, the United States supreme Court in Printz v. United States, 521 U.S. 898 (1997), affirmed that, "The Constitution thus contemplates that a State's government will represent and remain accountable to its own Citizens" and quoting James Madison, "[T]he local or municipal authorities form distinct and independent portions of the supremacy, no more subject, within their respective spheres, to the general authority than the general authority is subject to them, within its own sphere" and further affirmed that, "This separation of the two spheres is one of the Constitution's structural protections of liberty"; and

§6 WHEREAS, in the same case, the United States supreme Court concluded, "The federal government may neither issue directives requiring the States to address particular problems, nor command the States' officers, or those of their political subdivisions, to administer or enforce a federal regulatory program…such commands are fundamentally incompatible with our constitutional system of dual sovereignty" – which applies as surely to the county/state relationship as to the state/federal; and

§7 WHEREAS, the Second Amendment of the United States Constitution reads "A well regulated Militia, being necessary to the security of a free State, the right of the people to keep and bear Arms, shall not be infringed"; and

§8 WHEREAS, the United States supreme Court in United States v. Miller, 307 U.S. 174 (1939), affirmed that firearms which are part of ordinary military equipment, or with uses that could contribute to the common defense, are protected by the Second Amendment; and

§9 WHEREAS, the United States supreme Court in District of Columbia v. Heller, 554 U.S. 570 (2008), affirmed the individual's right to possess firearms, unconnected with service in a militia, for traditionally lawful purposes such as self-defense within the home; and

§10 WHEREAS, the United States supreme Court in McDonald v. Chicago, 561 U.S. 742 (2010), affirmed that the right of an individual to "keep and bear arms," as protected under the Second Amendment, is incorporated by the Due Process Clause of the Fourteenth Amendment against the States; and

§11 WHEREAS, Article [fill in], *Section* [fill in] *of the Constitution of* [STATE] *affirms,* [fill in actual language such as, "A person has the right to keep and bear arms for the defense of self, family, home and state, and for lawful hunting and recreational use"]; *and*

§12 WHEREAS, certain legislation which has been or may be enacted by the legislature of this State, and which has been or may be enacted by the United States Congress, may infringe on the right, duty and authority of law-abiding Citizens to keep and bear arms to fulfill their duty stipulated in Article I, Section 8, Clause 15 of the United States Constitution and Article [fill in], *Section* [fill in] *of the Constitution of* [fill in STATE]; *and*

§13 WHEREAS, any 'red flag' 'ERPO' or similar process violates the Second, Fourth, Fifth, Sixth and Fourteenth Amendments of the U.S. Constitution; and

§14 WHEREAS, the [Board, Commission] *of* _____ [County, Parish, Borough] *believes that the legitimate and justifying role of government is to secure the rights to life, liberty and property of the People as articulated in our Declaration of Independence; and*

§15 Whereas, the Congress of the United States and the Governor and Legislature of [State] *have for too long utterly neglected their Constitutional duties in support of Militia; and*

§16 WHEREAS, within its jurisdictional boundaries, the [County, Parish or Borough] [Board, Commission] *is the most efficient and lawful body to which this power and duty, incapable of Annihilation, shall have returned for its exercise,*

§17 IN ORDER to secure its Citizens' authority and duty to possess the means of self-defense and other unalienable rights, and to execute its essential and indispensable duty to organize and regulate Militia for the same and related purposes, and to honor its oath to uphold the Constitutions of this State and of the united States,

Article II. Ordered

§1 NOW, THEREFORE, BE IT RESOLVED, that the [Board, Commission,] *of* _____ [County, Parish or Borough] *hereby expresses its intent to perform within our jurisdiction the abdicated duties required of the State as stipulated by We The People in Article I, Section 8, Clause 16 and in the Second Amendment, and our intent to oppose by all lawful means any enactment that may unconstitutionally infringe the rights of its Citizens to keep and bear arms; and that*

§2 The [Board, Commission] *of* _____ [County, Parish or Borough] *hereby ORDERS that NO public funds under its control, nor time of employees, nor physical property and equipment of the* [County, Parish

127

or Borough] *may be used to restrict or infringe Constitutional Rights, including the Second Amendment rights of our Citizens, or to aid or cooperate with federal, state, or other agencies in any such restriction or infringement of said rights; any County employee cooperating in such infringement being subject to dismissal; and that*

§3 The [Board, Commission] *of* _____ [County, Parish or Borough] *hereby ORDERS that its human and material resources SHALL be applied as necessary to oppose, resist, obstruct, and interpose against any infringement on the authority and duty of its Citizens, including the authority and duty to keep and bear arms in Militia and the right to keep and bear arms for personal and home defense, using such legal means as are recognized and expedient to deter, prevent and obstruct any other crime, including but not limited to court action, with failure of any County employee to do so within the scope of her/his employment being grounds for dismissal; and that*

§4 Searches and Seizures of Firearms and other Militia Accoutrements Under 'Red Flag' Laws.

To secure the guaranteed due process and other rights of County residents, NO search for or seizure of a citizen's firearms, ammunition, Militia accoutrements and/or related personal property, under any 'red flag', 'ERPO' or similar purported law, enactment, or regulation shall be allowed to proceed in the County. Any complaint, application, or process intended to result in such an order or action, shall be immediately transmitted to the Grand Jury for investigation of all parties and witnesses named or participating therein. If no Grand Jury is sitting, one shall immediately be impaneled for the purpose, and the information transmitted thereto; and that

§5 The [Board, Commission,] *of* _____ [County, Parish or Borough] *hereby establishes that it shall be an offense to make a complaint under any "red flag", "ERPO" or similar law or purported law alleging a danger that cannot be proven beyond reasonable doubt to exist, with each such offense punishable by a fine of no less than $1,000 or one year in jail, or both. If any trespass or seizure has taken place as a result of such unprovable complaint, in addition to the specified fine or imprisonment, the individual or entity that filed the complaint leading to the 'red flag' action ('Complainant') shall within 30 days of notice pay to the Court its stipulated reimbursement to Target for all costs arising from the Action ('Damages'), including but not limited to a) Target's demonstrated loss of earnings; b) All of Target's property seized and not restored in like condition to that in which it was seized in the Action; c) any other damage to any of Target's property; and d) Attorneys' fees, court costs and all other costs demonstrably arising from the Action. If Complainant fails to pay the Damages within 60 days from date of notice by the Court, Damages are hereby statutorily tripled and the County Grand Jury and*

128

Militia shall seize, in ex parte action, all such property of Complainant as required to satisfy the Court's stipulated Damages payable to Target; and that

§6 The [Board, Commission] *of* _____
[County, Parish, Borough] *hereby establishes its Constitutional Militia, to include all County Citizens without criminal records or history of adjudicated mental incompetence, who are willing and able to aid in defending this community and upholding the Law; and that*

§7 The [Board, Commission] *of* _____ [County, Parish or Borough] *shall provide in the most timely way possible and in no case later than sixty (60) days from the date hereof, for the necessary staffing and public funding to restore the Militia in this County, during any and all such periods as the State Legislature shall continue in abdication and/or violation of duty as stipulated in Article I, Section 8, Clause 16 of the Constitution for the United States; and that*

§8 The [Board, Commission] *of* _____ [County, Parish or Borough] *shall administer and regulate its County Militia as follows:*

1. Nomination and Appointment of Officers.

This Body shall appoint officers nominated by their respective units and according to a uniform command structure mutually agreed on by all units in the County. Said power of appointment of officers shall revert to the State Governor during all such times as the State Legislature has ceased its abdication or avoidance of its constitutional duty for the same.

No nominee may have been convicted of a felony in any State, or may have been adjudicated mentally incompetent, or be regularly taking any drugs proven to be mentally incapacitating, and all officers must take an oath to uphold, defend, and enforce the Constitutions of this State and of the united States and all laws made in pursuance thereof, before entering upon their official duties.

2. [County, Parish or Borough] Militia Liaison and Coordination.

All units of County Militia must choose and report one officer from among all of them to serve as County Militia Liaison Officer, and one to serve in the incapacity of the first. Duties of the County Militia Liaison Officer shall be to coordinate operations among the several units, to coordinate operations with Militias of other jurisdictions and with paid law enforcement agencies, and to coordinate with the State at all times during which the State is performing its duties for constitutional Militia as stipulated by the People in the Constitution.

The County Militia Liaison Officer shall report to this Board/Commission on all Militia activities within the County and involving County Militia units, when requested by this Board/Commission.

3. Minimum Standards of Mental and Physical Fitness.

Uniform minimum standards of mental and physical fitness shall be adopted and updated as necessary by all militia units in the County; shall include freedom from any adjudication of mental incompetence, freedom from drugs proven to be mentally incapacitating, and the taking of an oath to uphold defend and enforce the Constitutions of this State and of the united States and all laws made in pursuance thereof, prior to the individual entering upon official duties, and shall be reported to this Board/Commission.

4. Arms, Ammunition and Accoutrements.

Citizens shall provide their own firearms, ammunition and tactical accoutrements, meeting uniform standards adopted by all County Militia units, and keep them in good repair. However, as funds allow, the County may provide ammunition and other equipment.

5. County Militia Training.

A uniform, minimum mandatory training program and schedule for new recruits and for existing members shall be adopted and updated as necessary by all County Militia units, and shall be reported to this Board/Commission.

6. Coordination and Cooperation With Paid Public Peace Officers.

All County Militia units shall cooperate and coordinate with existing paid municipal, County, and State public peace officers, upon the official request of these agencies, made through the County Militia Liaison Officer.

However, County Militia shall be responsible to the Citizens of the County and to the Constitutions of this State and of the united States, and shall NOT cooperate in, or permit, the enforcement of any enactment or supposed law which is null by reason of its conflict with the natural rights of Citizens or with the Constitutions of this State or of the united States. In <u>Marbury v. Madison (1803)</u> *the U.S. Supreme Court affirmed that "(a) Law repugnant to the Constitution is void."*

7. Minimum Standards of Personal Grooming and Respectful Public Behavior.

Uniform minimum standards of personal grooming and respectful public behavior for Militia members shall be adopted and updated as necessary by all militia units in the County, to protect the effectiveness of members and promote public confidence in our Militia. Excessive or inappropriate use of coarse language and display of symbols associated with death, lawlessness, rebellion, or wanton violence shall not be permitted.

8. Law Enforcement Duty Coordinated With and Directed by Grand Jury.

130

Especially in cases in which one or more members of paid public law enforcement or other public officials are being investigated by the Grand Jury, law enforcement duty including but not limited to collection of evidence and service of search and arrest warrants, shall be a core function of this Militia, as coordinated with, and directed by, the Grand Jury of this [County, Parish or Borough].

9. Grand Jury Anonymity.

Uniform protocols shall be adopted by all County Militia units to protect and preserve anonymity of subjects of investigation and of members of the Grand Jury, particularly in investigations of public officials or paid law enforcement personnel or agencies.

10. Removals for Cause.

Violation by any Militia member or officer of his or her Oath to defend and enforce the Constitutions of this State and of the united States and all laws made in pursuance thereof, shall be punishable by removal from membership or office.

11. SEVERABILITY *If any section, part or provision of this Ordinance is declared unconstitutional or invalid by a court of competent jurisdiction, then it is expressly provided and it is the intention of the [name of county board or commission] in passing this Ordinance that its parts shall be severable and all other parts of this Ordinance shall not be affected thereby and they shall remain in full force and effect.*

12. EFFECTIVE DATE. *This Ordinance shall take effect immediately upon its passage.*

ORDAINED *by the* [name of county board or commission] *of* [fill in] [COUNTY, PARISH OR BOROUGH], [fill in STATE], *this* _____ *Day of* [month] *in the Year of our Lord 20*_____

_____

[Board/Commission Member]

_____

[Board/Commission Member]

_____

[Board/Commission Member]

_____

[Board/Commission Member]

_____

[Board/Commission Member]

AmericaAgain! Declaration

When a government has ceased to protect the lives, liberty and property of We The People from whom its legitimate powers are derived, and for the advancement of whose happiness it was instituted, and so far from being a guarantee for the enjoyment of those inestimable and inalienable rights, becomes an instrument in the hands of evil rulers for their oppression;

When the federal republican Constitution, which they have sworn to support, no longer has a substantial existence – the whole nature of our servant government having been changed without our consent, from a restricted republic of sovereign States to a consolidated central despotism in which productive Americans are forced to work for imperious bureaucrats and government functionaries, favored industries, tyrannical and abusive Big Tech corporations more powerful than governments, and a growing parasitic population that has rendered our Republic fully Communist;

When, long after the spirit of the Constitution has departed, moderation is thrown to the wind by those in power, the semblance of freedom removed, and the forms of the Constitution discontinued as in the arrogant violation of the Second Amendment's proscription against any infringement of the right of the People to keep and bear arms (which Article I, Section 8, Clause 15 assumes is the duty of all able-bodied Americans);

When for five generations, We The People have suffered the general government's instigation, perpetration, funding, and defense of organized crime;

When, far from our petitions being regarded, citizens who show public concern for these infringements and usurpations are marked as 'terrorists' or arrested by tyrannical new city, state, and federal agencies hatched under the guises first of 'war on terror' then of a hoax 'pandemic';

When, with each new legislature, administration, and federal Supreme Court, the public servants of We The People more openly and arrogantly burden us and encroach on our privacy; on our liberty to travel freely; on our ability to enjoy our own property freely or to raise our children as we see fit; on our ability to actually own our property free and clear; to operate our farms, shops, or businesses as we see fit without posing any harm to others; on our ability to even open our small businesses, eat in restaurants or even gather in our own homes and churches! – all under the threat of a proven Chinese-engineered hoax 'pandemic'; and now have colluded in both corrupt political parties to openly, cynically steal a national election in which one candidate received easily 80 million true votes, yet was 'defeated' by a nearly senile puppet candidate whose gaslighting operation enlisted a massive, Communist-style phalanx of state-owned media (Google, Twitter, YouTube, Facebook, ABC, MSNBC, CBS, CNN, NPR, Fox News and others);

In consequence of such acts of malfeasance and abdication on the part of the servant government, anarchy threatens to dissolve civil society into its original elements, the first law of nature and the right of self-preservation, the powers reserved by We The People as stipulated in the U.S. Constitution, Amendment X, enjoins not only our right but a sacred obligation to our posterity, to enforce the specific limits of federal power as enumerated in that supreme Law of the Land, by all the lawful and necessary means provided in that Constitution, including but not limited to the Courts of our sovereign States and such federal legislative reforms as We The People may effect, to secure our welfare and happiness.

Nations, as well as individuals, are amenable for their acts to the public opinion of mankind. A statement of a part of our grievances is therefore submitted to an impartial world along with the peaceful, lawful, and legitimate enforcement steps that We The People of these United States now intend to take, to which the nations of the earth are witness.

We The People of the fifty sovereign States of America, creators of the U.S. Constitution, acknowledge the duty of every American to preserve, protect, and defend that Supreme Law. We hereby announce to a watching world our intention to restore the original form, purpose, and enumerated limits of our government, superintending from this day forward our State courts and federal servants so that we may once more secure the Blessings of Liberty to ourselves and to our posterity.

These United States have a solemn duty to serve their citizen masters by enforcing our supreme Law of the Land when one or more branches of federal government violate it. When the States neglect this duty, our Declaration of Independence establishes that this duty and the power to execute it return to the people at large for their exercise. The three

134

branches of federal government are creatures — things created by us in the U.S. Constitution, the highest law in this Republic.

In the Constitution, We the People clearly enumerate the powers of federal government. We retain any powers not specifically enumerated therein, to ourselves and our sovereign States. Any exercise of power by government beyond those listed powers is an egregious violation of the Supreme Law.

President Jefferson said that *"in questions of powers...let no more be heard of confidence in man, but bind him down from mischief by the chains of the Constitution"*. Such "binding down" can be peaceably accomplished by binding the federal purse and by We the People and sovereign States enforcing that Law of Limitation for the first time in American history.

The present $3.9 trillion annual federal revenue – and the far larger mountain of financial derivatives that Congress allows the financial industry to create from thin air and our labor – have spawned a brood of corruptions as unlimited oceans of money always do. This ocean of illicit D.C. cash has spawned unconstitutional federal powers, cabinet departments, agents, agencies, programs, projects, offices, regulations, and financial industry 'assets' that for sheer number are impossible to list here but that threaten our liberties, property, livelihood, posterity, and public morals, making a joke of our Supreme Law.

In Federalist #28, Alexander Hamilton said that by merely exercising our power as creators of the federal government, we can prevail: *"the larger the American population would become, the more effectively we can resist federal government tyranny... Power being almost always the rival of power, the general government will at all times stand ready to check the usurpations of State governments, and these will have the same disposition towards the general government. The People, by throwing themselves into either scale, will infallibly make it preponderate. If their rights are invaded by either, they can make use of the other as the instrument of redress.."*. The mission of AmericaAgain! is to make good on the guarantees offered in the Federalist Papers to our fore-fathers.

All three branches of our federal creature have ceased to check-and-balance one another, instead colluding over the past 150 years abusing the "necessary and proper", "general welfare", and "interstate commerce" clauses to fashion a lawless, limitless system of power, pork, and perquisites warned against by James Madison, the primary author of the Constitution: *"...it is evident that there is not a single power whatever, which may not have some reference to the common defense or the general welfare; nor a power of any magnitude which, in its exercise, does not involve or admit an application of money. The*

135

government, therefore, which possesses power in either one or other of these extents, is a government without the limitations formed by a particular enumeration of powers.

"Consequently, the meaning and effect of this particular enumeration is destroyed by the exposition given to these general phrases… Congress is authorized to provide money for the common defense and general welfare. In both, is subjoined to this authority an enumeration of the cases to which their power shall extend…a question arises whether (any) particular measure be within the enumerated authorities vested in Congress. If it be, the money requisite for it may be applied to it; if it be not, no such application can be made.

"It is incumbent in this, as in every other exercise of power by the federal government, to prove from the Constitution, that it grants the particular power exercised.

"With respect to the words 'general welfare', I have always regarded them as qualified by the detail of powers connected with them. To take them in a literal and unlimited sense would be a metamorphosis of the Constitution into a character which there is a host of proofs was not contemplated by its creators."

Congress and presidents for many generations have violated the highest law in America in precisely this blank-check manner, at a cost of tens of trillions of dollars – and at the further cost of our liberty, privacy, and rights to property and peaceful self-government. When a government of, by, and for The People stands in perennial, collusive violation of the Constitution, We The People have constitutional authority to take enforcement action. The duty of constitutional law enforcement falls on We the People, not by resisting government's lawlessness with lawlessness of our own, but by having the courts of our States bring law enforcement power to bear as our right and duty under that Law.

With respect to compliance with his "Oath or Affirmation, to support this Constitution", no public official can be allowed to be the judge of his own case, as Presidents Jefferson and Madison observed.

The nefarious practice of executive orders is nowhere authorized in Article II of the Constitution. Numerous such executive fiats are demonstrable violations of the limited powers stipulated in Article II, yet We The People have had no voice in said imperial edicts issued by presidents. The same principle holds true for treaties signed by tyrannical presidents under the noses of the American people to our detriment, without popular review before being trundled through a complicit U.S. Senate.

Every public official's oath is made to We the People; the Constitution commands that the official be bound by that oath; thus We the People

136

have the right to enforce that oath and the power to do so as well, for no right can exist without an effective remedy, including remedy via State courts.

With the Chinese virus hoax, Congress' corrupt, imperious practices to oust a sitting president then infested State, county, and municipal governments; as U.S. Supreme Court Justice Louis Brandeis suggested in his 1928 dissenting opinion in Olmsted v. U.S.: *"In a government of laws…Our government is the potent, the omnipresent teacher. For good or for ill, it teaches the whole people by its example. Crime is contagious. If the government becomes a lawbreaker, it breeds contempt for law…"*.

Congress has perennially refused to balance its federal budgets.

The flow of illegal aliens across our borders reached epidemic proportions long ago, yet Congress refused to allow President Trump to seal the border, instead arming a ticking time bomb against our culture and civil order; saddling Taxpayers with the cost of socialist programs for politicians' future political pawns. America was a melting pot Republic with a common language, currency, culture and work ethic; now it is polyglot warring factions seeking African-America, Mexican-America, Israeli-America, and Muslim America.

The U.S. Congress was intended to be populated by citizen-statesmen for limited terms so that no lifelong political oligarchy would rule over the citizens as is now the case, with members of Congress being wealthy, insular individuals with little affinity with, or empathy for, the average citizen. Members of Congress shamelessly enjoy fat pensions, insurance policies, private spas, limousines, private jets hidden in federal budgets, and much more – paid for by citizens who never enjoy such free luxuries.

The original intent of the Constitution's framers was to balance the Legislative branch with two bodies, the House of Representatives representing the interests of the People, and the Senate representing the interests of the States. Prior to 1913, the individual State legislatures appointed representatives to serve in the US Senate who were expected to act and vote in the interest of the State or were subject to immediate recall and replacement.

During the administration of Woodrow Wilson, Congress introduced the Seventeenth Amendment, which was ratified under questionable circumstances. The new amendment stripped away a critical power of the States to control D.C. by balancing the desires of the mob with cooler heads in their deliberative legislatures. Making both houses of Congress elected directly by the People opened the Senate to even greater corruption by moneyed interests and their lobbyists.

Many socialist accretions that have drained America's private sector wealth and inflated dependent populations, could never have passed if the sovereign States had retained direct control of the U.S. Senate as designed by the framers. Repealing the 17th Amendment will restore this critical check-and-balance mechanism as our founding fathers intended when they designed the U.S. Constitution.

Because the 13th Amendment disallows slavery or involuntary servitude, national conscription for military or other national service is illegal.

In the interests of a massive industry rather than national security, the U.S. Congress has refused to cut off funding for undeclared, unprovoked foreign attacks and invasions ordered or maintained by presidents who cannot prove they serve a national defense purpose. There will always be men in the world whose goal is plunder, to amass insane wealth; such chieftains buy and trade politicians as game pieces, world without end. They amass plunder using the U.S. military as free mercenaries.

The U.S. Constitution only authorizes Congress to use military power in declared war with a Navy, or with a Citizen Militia mustered for national purposes for a maximum of two years, or to use the Citizen Militia of the Several States, with officers and training provided by the States, "to execute the Laws of the Union, suppress Insurrections, and repel Invasions". No other federal armed forces are authorized by the Constitution.

Thus, it is illegal for full-time U.S. military ground forces to even exist, much less to plunder foreign resources or threaten foreign people who present no threat to us, under the guise of 'democracy', 'peacekeeping', 'war on terror', or 'protecting American interests abroad'.

The only difference that the United States military industry brings to conquered lands is replacing Arab family crests or banana republic dictators' logos with U.S.-based corporate logos. While this lawless plunder continues, We the People will continue to be regarded as enemies by citizens of the world.

The majority of Americans was once Christian; most still profess Christianity at least in name. The melting-pot culture that made America the envy of the world was not theocracy, but was demonstrably the ethic of Christ, not of Mormonism, Judaism, or Islam. We The People refuse to have America become as Europe – another battleground for a 1,400-year old Islamic jihad.

The legislation labeled 'Legal Tender Act' beginning in 1862 and collusive rulings by the U.S. Supreme Court in 1871 and 1884 violated the U.S. Constitution's stipulations in Article I, Sections 8 and 10. By law, only Congress has the power only to coin gold and silver, and every State shall use only gold and silver coin as legal tender. All paper scrip – and the tens of trillions of dollars annually in derivative financial instruments – are illegal and immoral, yet enabled under the protection of Congress, whose members have overseen and acquiesced in a 150-year-old conspiracy to defraud, embezzle from, and place into servitude the citizens they pretend to serve and represent.

It is *illegal* for Congress to declare that paper shall be considered lawful money. It is *illegal* for Congress to grant a concession to a private cartel using the Federal Reserve brand to manufacture counterfeit (paper) money and to require the People and sovereign States to pay face value plus interest for the worthless scrip. Before Great Depression II falls on our heads, we declare *this will not stand*.

Congress has willfully allowed the Internal Revenue Service to perennially violate the federal tax laws, regulations, and its own operating manual, transforming Taxpayers by terrorist coercion into pack-mules to carry the financial burdens of Congress' demonstrable crimes. We refuse to allow Congress to burden future generations with an equally corrupt revenue-neutral 'fair tax', so-called, that would continue to amass over four times the revenues required to fund enumerated federal powers.

It is *illegal* for Congress to allow its servants, federal judges, to hold the entire population in 50 sovereign states hostage to the 1% sexual pervert lobby. In the Constitution, nowhere do We The People empower Congress or a federal court to hold the population hostage to an immoral minority by the imperial whim of five people in robes who on June 26, 2015 in their preposterous opinion, suggested that sexual perversion would now become 'marriage' in America. *This will not stand.*

Trillion-dollar tech corporations have occupied, captured, and dominate Town Square in every American community. Every major news outlet and social medium is working in lock-step towards Communist, environmental-anarchist goals inimical to our civilization and economy, while stratospherically enriching a tiny band of monopolist billionaires at Google, Facebook, Twitter, YouTube, Microsoft, Apple, Amazon and others who declare their hatred for conservative and Christian America. Year after year, Congress held pointless hearings and promised relief that never comes. Over 150 million Americans' lives remain occupied, dominated, and driven by godless globalists. *This will not stand.*

On a Sunday night in March 2010, the Democrat members of Congress conspired to transform the IRS into an American Gestapo – finally unmasking its terror organization to enforce its unconstitutional 'health care' scheme in which Barack Hussein Obama was also complicit. Now with the GOP members of Congress fully on board with arrogant tyranny, history proves that if Congress is allowed to fully arrogate this lawless new power, it will never relinquish them. *This will not stand.*

It is illegal for Congress to allow illegal aliens to enter this country and be catered to by federal government — the exact opposite of enforcing immigration laws that every productive American expects to have enforced. Individual works of mercy and foreign missions are biblical outreach; unrestrained communism and open borders are not. The Obama administration and Congress held several hundred million productive Americans hostage on behalf of a militant, tactically shrewd lobby of a few thousand activists. Those who pay property taxes are forced to pay the education, food, clothing, medical, incarceration, and law enforcement bills of an illegal horde, invited in and catered to by a lawless, arrogant, dismissive Congress. *This will not stand.*

Now, the militant Islamist army is following the path opened by the abortionists, by militant sexual perverts, and by the illegal alien lobby. It is illegal for Congress to allow any federal judge to enforce, support, enable, or even allow any alien law-code — whether Islamic sharia or any other — to be recognized or enforced in place of the established civil and criminal laws of these sovereign States. *This will not stand.*

After our long failure to perform our citizen duties, bearing the cost of our abdication on every hand, We the People of these fifty united States intend to lawfully, peacefully begin enforcing the Constitution in each of the 3,141 counties of our 50 States against its violation by our U.S. congressmen and senators, effecting such law enforcement through local AmericaAgain! members singly and statewide in a process called TACTICAL CIVICS™ and using a mechanism called the AmericaAgain! Indictment Engine™. This Declaration is the perpetual deed of AmericaAgain! Trust, a private, irrevocable, perpetual trust and member organization created by David M. Zuniga.

When this Declaration uses the term 'We The People', it refers only to those Americans who agree to work for, support, and enforce the principles and action projects stipulated herein – the same as is true of the term 'We The People' as it appears in the U.S. Constitution.

We the People hereby announce our intention to draft, refine, and push through the passage of the following reform legislation. As a plea-bargaining package offered to any member of Congress indicted by using the AmericaAgain! Indictment Engine™, or as an immunity package for those who have not yet been targeted, We The People will demand that members of the U.S. House of Representatives and the U.S. Senate agree in writing to enact the following:

1) The **Bring Congress Home Act**, or 'BCHA', stipulating: Whereas a general principle of constitutional law in these United States holds that no legislature can bind a subsequent one; and whereas the Apportionment Act of 1929 set a totally arbitrary 435-district limit to the U.S. House of Representatives in clear violation of the intention of Article I, Section 2, Clause 4 and also in clear contravention of the original first Article in the Bill of Rights as passed by the first Congress and sent to the States; and whereas a sufficient number of States have ratified that amendment and it has been recorded as the 28th Amendment to the U.S. Constitution; and whereas the expanded size of the U.S. House demanded by the U.S. Constitution, in light of the benefits and cost savings of modern technology and the security risk of Congress operating from one location, therefore:

Section 1. No member of Congress shall have a private office or staff located in Washington D.C..

Section 2. All members of Congress shall serve a maximum of two terms.

Section 3. No district of the U.S. House of Representatives shall contain more than 50,000 people, as stipulated in the original First Amendment passed by Congress in 1789 and recently ratified by the State legislatures as the 28th Amendment.

Section 4. To remain properly accountable and accessible to the sovereigns People that (s)he represents, every member of the U.S. House of Representatives shall be provided with a single office located within his/her district, paid staff not exceeding two persons, reasonable office expenses, and the hardware, software, and encryption technology and services required to conduct the business of the U.S. House of Representatives, working from his/her own district.

141

Section 5. To remain properly accountable and accessible to the sovereign States that the U.S. Senate was originally de-signed to represent, every member of the U.S. Senate shall be provided with a single office located within close proximity to the State capitol, also with paid staff not exceeding six per-sons, reasonable office expenses, and the hardware, software, and encryption technology and services required to conduct the business of the U.S. Senate, working from his/her own State capitol pursuant to such time as the 17th Amendment shall be repealed.

Section 6. Public funds used by any member of Congress shall be limited to the member's salary — which shall in the case of a congressman, effective immediately, be 50% of present salary; office staff, space rent and expenses; self-operated vehicle lease payment, fuel and insurance; coach-class airfare for public business; and mail costs to communicate with his/her sovereigns. An annual audit of expenditures for each member of Congress and his/her staff and office operations shall be posted online on that member's public web page accessible to the public, no later than 60 days after the close of each congressional session.

Section 7. Beyond those listed in Section 6 above, any and all other publicly-funded expenditures inuring to the benefit of a member of Congress shall hereafter be considered illegal use of public funds, including but not limited to: pensions and insurance premiums (retroactive), foreign travel under the guise of legislative business, limousines or other special conveyances, spas, hairdressers, and club memberships.

2) The **Constitutional Courts Act**, stipulating:

Section 1. A consensus exists among the American public that the federal courts have been corrupted and are manipulated by powerful individuals and by lobbyists for industry and special interests, rendering moot the stipulated limitations placed by the People through the U.S. Constitution on its creature, federal government.

> *a. James Madison, Father of the Constitution, in his Virginia Resolution of 1798, and Thomas Jefferson, in his concurring Virginia Resolution, wrote that the States, as the creator parties to the U.S. Constitution, have the right and duty to judge when the U.S. Constitution has been violated by federal government; that the federal government cannot judge of its own infractions*

> *b. In Article III, Section 1 of the U.S. Constitution, the People grant to Congress the authority to create the inferior federal courts, thus the subject matter jurisdiction of the inferior federal courts is entirely within Congress' discretion.*

> *c. In Article III, Section 2 of the U.S. Constitution, the People grant to Congress the authority to withhold subject matter jurisdiction even from the U.S. supreme Court, using "such Exceptions, and…such Regulations as the Congress shall make".*

d. In *Article VI, Section 2 of the U.S. Constitution, the People stipulate, "This Constitution...shall be the supreme Law of the Land; and the Judges in every State shall be bound thereby...", which binding includes enforcement as well as obedience.*

e. Every federal legislator is now performing his federal duties full-time within his or her own district, which is the jurisdiction of his State Grand Jury and State Court.

f. Therefore, pursuant to the power granted by the People to Congress in U.S. Constitution Article III, Section 2, Clause 2, after the effective date hereof, no federal court shall have jurisdiction in any case in which a member of Congress is charged by his or her own State Grand Jury with violating, or conspiring to violate, the U.S. Constitution.

g. In no such case shall removal from state jurisdiction be available to the accused, whether pursuant to 28 USC 1441, or any subsequent federal law.

Section 2.   The American People stipulated in Article I, Section 8 of the U.S. Constitution, that "The Congress shall have power...to constitute tribunals inferior to the supreme Court...", and in Article III, Section 1, that the federal courts are, "such inferior courts as the Congress may from time to time ordain and establish", and in Article III, Section 2, Clause 2, that the U.S. supreme Court, "shall have appellate jurisdiction...with such Exceptions, and under such Regulations as the Congress shall make".

In 1799 in Turner v. Bank of North America (1799), Justice Chase wrote, "The notion has frequently been entertained, that the federal courts derive their judicial power immediately from the Constitution; but the political truth is, that the disposal of the judicial power...belongs to Congress. If Congress has given the power to this Court, we possess it, not otherwise: and if Congress has not given the power to us or to any other Court, it still remains at the legislative disposal."

In Ex parte Bollman (1807), Chief Justice John Marshall wrote, "Courts which are created by written law, and whose jurisdiction is defined by written law, cannot transcend that jurisdiction".

The power of Congress to create inferior federal courts, necessarily implies, as written in U.S. v. Hudson & Goodwin (1812), "the power to limit jurisdiction of those Courts to particular objects".

The U.S. supreme Court held unanimously in Sheldon v. Sill (1850) that because the People in the Constitution did not create inferior federal courts but authorized Congress to create them, that Congress by necessity had power to define and limit their jurisdiction and to withhold jurisdiction of any of the enumerated cases and controversies.

143

The high court even acknowledged Congress' power to re-examine particular classes of questions previously ruled on by the U.S. supreme Court, as stated in The Francis Wright (1882): "(A)ctual jurisdiction under the [judicial] power is confined within such limits as Congress sees fit to prescribe…What those powers shall be, and to what extent they shall be exercised, are, and always have been, proper subjects of legislative control…Not only may whole classes of cases be kept out of the jurisdiction altogether, but particular classes of questions may be subjected to re-examination and review…".

In Lauf v. E.G. Shinner & Co (1938), the U.S. supreme Court declared, "There can be no question of the power of Congress thus to define and limit the jurisdiction of the inferior courts of the United States".

In Lockerty v. Phillips (1943), the U.S. supreme Court held that Congress has the power of, "withholding jurisdiction from them [federal courts] in the exact degrees and character which to Congress may seem proper for the public good".

Section 3. Therefore, Congress hereby excludes from federal court jurisdiction any and all cases involving:

> *a. Taking of human life, from point of conception;*
>
> *b. Sexual practices or the institution of marriage;*
>
> *c. Healthcare;*
>
> *d. Education;*
>
> *e. Official recognition or application of any foreign law or code within these united States or any of them; and*
>
> *f. Claims of United States control, possession, or juris-diction over any land outside of that granted by We the People (the sovereign People and States) as stipulated in Article I, Section 8, Clause 17, U.S. Constitution.*

Section 4. What constitutes due process in all courts within the united States or any of them shall be defined and determined exclusively from within the Bill of Rights and the American common law, in that order of precedence.

Section 5. In Article III, Section 1 of the U.S. Constitution, the People stipulate, "the judicial Power of the United States shall be vested in one supreme Court, and in such inferior Courts as the Congress may from time to time ordain and establish"; therefore within 12 months of the passage of this Act:

> *a. No 'administrative law' tribunal in these United States shall bind the citizen in any way;*
>
> *b. No administrative adjudicator shall be referred to as 'judge';*
>
> *c. No administrative tribunal shall be referred to, or refer to itself, as 'court'; and*

144

d.   No administrative process or tribunal shall describe its processes in terms such as 'order', 'subpoena', 'warrant', or 'the record', which are reserved for constitutional judiciary.

Section 6.   Pursuant to provisions of Section 2(f) above and the proposed Return of Sovereign Lands Act, 24 months after enactment of this legislation and thereafter, it shall be a federal felony for any agency, agent, bureau, department, officer, contractor or other representative of the government of these United States of America to claim, own, maintain or operate a purported U.S. court or detention facility that is not located within the land or property stipulated in Article I, Section 8, Clause 17 of the U.S. Constitution.

Section 7.   Because Federal Rules of Criminal Procedure Numbers 6 and 7 appear to create an unconstitutional barrier to the established prerogative power of the People when serving in their State Grand Jury, no federal judicial rules shall have any bearing or authority over any State Grand Jury. As U.S. Supreme Court Justice Antonin Scalia wrote in U.S. v. Williams (1992):

"(T)he Grand Jury is an institution separate from the courts, over whose functioning the courts do not preside...Rooted in long centuries of Anglo American history, the Grand Jury is mentioned in the Bill of Rights, but not in the body of the Constitution. It has not been textually assigned, therefore, to any of the branches described in the first three Articles. It is a constitutional fixture in its own right...

In fact, the whole theory of its function is that it belongs to no branch of the institutional government, serving as a kind of buffer or referee between the government and the People...The Grand Jury requires no authorization from its constituting court to initiate an investigation, nor does the prosecutor require leave of court to seek a Grand Jury indictment...[T]he Grand Jury generally operates without the interference of a presiding judge. It swears in its own witnesses, and deliberates in total secrecy."

Section 8.   As stipulated in Article I, Section 8, Clause 15 of the U.S. Constitution, the several States retain the power to enforce this legislation by appropriate State legislation and duly authorized Citizen Militia enforcement action within their respective jurisdictions.

3) The **Non-Enumerated Powers Sunset Act,** stipulating:

Section 1.   Congress hereby acknowledges as unconstitutional, any and all past enactment of legislation, 'positive law' Code sections and regulations, consent to treaties, or provision of federal funds applied to executive orders that confer on federal government any power not specifically enumerated in the U.S. Constitution or reasonably inferred from the powers enumerated, notwithstanding past creative interpretations applied by all three federal branches, to the terms 'interstate commerce', 'general welfare', and 'necessary and

145

proper', and notwithstanding any and all 'positive law' Code sections drafted, finalized, promulgated, and/or enforced by federal employees who have no direct oversight by, or accountability to, the American People.

No federal 'positive law' regulation shall create a legal duty or liability for any citizen of these United States, unless and until the agency purporting to enforce such a regulation shall have established beyond reasonable doubt that said regulation is clearly and unambiguously authorized by the People in a specific section of the U.S. Constitution.

Congress hereby acknowledges that the government of these United States is a constitutional republic form of government under the Common Law as opposed to the positive law traditions of many foreign countries, notwithstanding the massive Deep State that has created an overwhelming burden of federal regulations produced by bureaucratic careerists at staggering cost to taxpayers.

Congress hereby further acknowledges that ultimate sovereignty in our republic is inherent in the American People rather than in a bureaucracy that propagates, promulgates and defends thousands of new 'positive law' regulations annually, which are too numerous and intentionally too complex for the average American to grasp or understand, much less to oversee or diminish.

The United States Code is the Code of Laws of the United States of America (also referred to as United States Code, U.S. Code, or U.S.C.) and is a compilation and codification of all the general and so-called 'permanent' federal laws of the republic. But no law in this republic can be repugnant to the specific words and spirit of the U.S. Constitution. Any federal law which is found to be in clear violation of, or repugnant to the plain language of the U.S. Constitution is and has been null and void since its enactment.

The U.S. Code does not include regulations issued by executive branch agencies, published in the Code of Federal Regulations (C.F.R.). Proposed and recently adopted regulations are posted in the Federal Register.

Congress shall make available online, at no cost to the user, the 51 titles of the United States Code as maintained by the U.S. House of Representatives Office of the Law Revision Counsel, and the cumulative supplements which are published annually.

Section 2. The Standing Committee to Defund Non-Enumerated Powers (SCDNEP) is hereby created in the U.S. House, to bind this body to obey the U.S. Constitution as actually written.

Section 3. Upon its formation, the SCDNEP shall appropriate adequate funding for a website and appurtenant support to serve and support the Citizens' Volunteer Research Service (CVRS) as described herein.

Section 4. In appropriating funds for CVRS website and support for citizen volunteers, Congress does not suggest that it, a federal servant, has authority to create such an oversight organ for the People themselves; only that Congress seeks hereby to provide for the People's oversight function to the extent that the People themselves require and employ it.

Section 5. Congress hereby acknowledges that the American People themselves, collectively, are sovereign in this and all other matters of federal government, as clearly and unambiguously stipulated in the Preamble, in Article I, Section 8 and especially in Amendment X of the U.S. Constitution, which sections only reiterate the People's original, God-given, organic, inherent, retained power to oversee all operations and budgets of their servants in federal government.

Congress hereby acknowledges that any CVRS Work Group or Supergroup casting its vote to de-fund and terminate any regulation issued by executive branch

agencies shall infer that the CVRS has determined that the regulation in question does usurp, undermine, or countermand the stipulations of the U.S. Constitution or the retained powers of the sovereign People as stipulated in Amendment X of the U.S. Constitution. Said regulation shall become null and void and of no effect, immediately upon said vote.

Section 7. Prior to being funded or observed for any future fiscal year, any federal budget request whether executive or legislative – whether submitted by an agency, bureau, department, office, power, program, code or regulatory body, service branch, or via executive order or treaty – shall be accompanied by a written demonstration that it falls within a specifically enumerated power in Article I Section 8 or Article II Section 2 of the U.S. Constitution or duly ratified Amendment thereto, or can be reasonably inferred by the American citizen of average intelligence to be a rational appurtenance thereto. Any budget request not so accompanied, shall cease to be funded at the end of the then-current fiscal year.

Section 8. Because the functions of federal government were enumerated so as to limit the reach and power of the federal servant, such that it should never be considered either the master or the provider of the People, any agency, bureau, department, office, power, program, code or regulation not specifically enumerated in the U.S. Constitution or being an unambiguously 'necessary and proper' adjunct to the powers enumerated, as can be reasonably inferred by the American citizen of average intelligence, unless proposed and ratified as a constitutional amendment adhering to Article V of the U.S. Constitution, shall be subject to CVRS review and closure.

Section 9. In light of the long history of federal legislative, executive and judicial malfeasance and treachery by stretching the 'interstate commerce', 'general welfare', and 'necessary and proper' clauses, no federal agency, bureau, department, office, power, program, statute, code or regulation shall be added to others in any omnibus bill or amendment. If not enumerated in Article I, Section 8 and requiring application of public funds, each proposed agency, bureau, department, office, power, program, statute, code or regulation shall be proposed as a discrete bill or constitutional amendment.

Section 10. To maintain the delineation between the jurisdiction of an authorizing committee and the House Appropriations Committee, House Rule XXI creates a point of order against unauthorized appropriations in general appropriations bills. While any appropriation in such a bill is out of order unless the expenditure is authorized by existing law, if the point of order is not raised or is waived and the bill is enacted, said unauthorized appropriation is treated as legitimate. This practice has been tantamount to embezzlement of public funds.

Language requiring or permitting government action carries an implicit authorization for money to be appropriated for that purpose. The 'authorization of appropriations' provision limits the authorization of a piece of legislation to the amount and/or to the fiscal years stated. Accordingly, any prior budget authorization appropriating "such sums as may be necessary", without specifying the amount, years, and specifically constitutional purpose for which such appropriations were authorized, shall receive no further funding after the date of enactment hereof.

Section 11. There is hereby authorized a national Citizens' Volunteer Research Service (CVRS) with five citizens per U.S. congressional district, comprising one CVRS Work Group, said citizens selected by each U.S. representative's staff at random from the legislator's congressional district tax and voter rolls.

No citizen selected at random to serve on a CVRS Work Group shall be compelled to serve. All CVRS members shall be volunteers, receiving no remuneration for their service to the public.

Section 12. As with a Grand Jury, all CVRS members selected shall remain anonymous, to protect the Members from lobbying pressure or threats, and from threats or retaliation by endangered government employees.

Section 13. The deliberations of each and every CVRS Work Group shall remain completely confidential within the Work Group. Divulging the name of a CVRS member or divulging in advance of publication on the 'More Constitutional Government' website, any decision of a Work Group to retain or de-fund a federal budget item – whether an agency, bureau, project, code section, regulation or project – shall be a felony.

Section 14. Each CVRS Work Group shall review individual federal codes, regulations and regulatory bodies and associated federal budget line items. Each CVRS Work Group shall review at one time only a single, discrete federal budget line item unless the powers and functions of the agencies, bureaus, programs, code sections or regulations entail several or many similar functions or areas of endeavor appearing to violate the U.S. Constitution, being neither explicitly nor implicitly authorized therein.

Section 15. In such cases, an entire federal agency, bureau or regulatory entity shall be reviewed and voted on for defunding and closure by a CVRS Supergroup, which shall consist of twelve (12) CVRS Work Groups located in twelve (12) states, with two Work Groups from each region (Northeast, South-east, Midwest, South Central, Southwest, Northwest).

Such draconian action by a 'mere' 60 citizens compares favorably to countless coercive actions impacting over 320 million citizens yet imposed by a single federal judge or at most by five justices of the U.S. supreme Court. As set out in the U.S. Constitution, the collective sovereignty of the American People is superior in authority to that of the People's servants, be they legislative, executive or judiciary, particularly when servants have violated the Constitution or occupy an office nowhere authorized by the People through that supreme Law.

Section 16. Each CVRS Work Group shall have 60 days to research, assess, and recommend de-funding and terminating a federal code section or regulation or its associated agency or office. At the conclusion of its deliberations, the CVRS Work Group shall submit the code section, regulation, agency, program or bureau selected for de-funding and termination, to the manager of the CVRS website, for posting.

Within 30 days after said posting, each recommended defunding and termination measure shall be voted on by each and every CVRS Work Group. Each Work Group shall cast one vote, representing the majority vote of that Work Group's members casting a vote on that item.

Section 17. Each Work Group's vote shall be the vote of the U.S. congressman who represents that district. No member of Congress shall influence, counter-mand, veto, or otherwise interfere with final decisions of a CVRS Work Group or Supergroup.

No member of Congress shall recruit, entice, hire, contract, coerce or otherwise obtain the services of any staff member, agent or intermediary to influence or otherwise interfere with a final decision of any CVRS Work Group or Supergroup.

Section 18. De-funding and termination of any federal code section or regulation shall occur within 180 days of a vote having been cast with a simple majority of all votes cast, in favor of de-funding and termination.

Each such vote shall be posted on the dedicated secure CVRS website server for public access within 72 hours after the vote is cast, on the CVRS 'More Constitutional Government' portal.

Section 19. Pursuant to this legislation, the SCDNEP shall provide adequate funding and staffing to maintain a comprehensive database of each and every federal agency, bureau, code and regulation under review including date of commencement of review and effective date for de-funding and termination..

Section 20. No member of Congress or staff of any member of Congress shall interfere with any CVRS Work Group, other than each legislator's staff randomly selecting from voter registration or tax rolls, the citizens to serve on a CVRS Work Group.

Section 21. A CVRS member must serve a minimum of 90 days, and may serve on a Work Group for four consecutive years. No CVRS member shall serve for more than eight years in aggregate, with a minimum of two years intervening between periods of service.

Work Group members shall provide 30 days' notice prior to resigning or retiring from service.

Every CVRS member rendered incapable of service due to death or disability shall be immediately replaced with the next name in the service queue in that district and said replacement shall be summoned to begin service within 10 calendar days.

Section 22. No person shall serve on a CVRS Work Group if (s)he is presently employed by any agency of government or has been so employed within the preceding three years.

Section 23. Any current or former CVRS member receiving a financial benefit of more than $100 by virtue of his/her positive decision to retain a federal code section, regulation, agency, bureau, program or project shall be guilty of a federal felony.

4) The **Clean Bill Act**, stipulating:

Section 1. No omnibus bill shall be permitted. All bills passing out of any committee in Congress shall treat only the subject found in the title of the bill, and shall not exceed 50 pages, single-sided, double-spaced, 12-point type.

Section 2. No committee shall add any amendment, rider, or earmark or authorize any agency, bureau, department, expenditure, office, power, program or regulation that cannot be demonstrated is directly entailed in the subject and title of the bill.

Section 3. All bills when filed shall list the names and contact information of every private-sector individual and entity who initiated and/or proposed or suggested elements of said legislation.

5) The **Secure Borders Act**, stipulating:

Section 1. Each citizen of these United States has an in-alienable right to defend his own life, liberty, and property.

Section 2. Attending that right is the duty stipulated in Article I, Section 8, Clause 15 of the U.S. Constitution, for Citizen Militia to "execute the Laws of the Union, suppress Insurrections, and repel Invasions".

Section 3. Congress hereby acknowledges each border State's legislature's special right and duty stipulated in Article I, Section 8, Clause 16, to appoint the officers and train the Militia of that State.

Section 4. To aid in its duty per Clause 15, Congress shall provide for immediately finish constructing a secure border barrier, with reasonable alternatives employed for riverine sections of the U.S.-Mexico border, and Congress shall waive environmental, regulatory, and bureaucratic requirements such that the border fence project shall avoid the time and cost overruns common to federal government projects.

Section 5. Congress shall provide for an increase in border federal troop strength, airborne assets, and electronic detection as to furnish a demonstrably effective impediment to illegal crossing by any means.

Section 6. Congress shall coordinate this effort with the legislatures and their duly authorized Citizen Militia (where applicable) of the sovereign States of California, Arizona, New Mexico, and Texas, and shall accept all reasonable aid and alliance with said legislatures along their own sovereign borders, to timely construct said wall and/or fence.

Section 7. Congress shall immediately discontinue and de-fund all agencies, bureaus, policies and programs that encourage, facilitate, or support illegal immigration.

Section 8. As the Islamic belief system is well established and self-described as a militant organization and an exclusive, invasive law-code, Congress will assure that any individual shall be barred from immigration into this republic who is reasonably believed to adhere to sharia law, regardless of whether the aspiring immigrant's domicile of origin is an officially Islamic state.

Section 9. As stipulated in Article I, Section 8, Clause 15 of the U.S. Constitution, the several States retain the power to enforce this legislation by appropriate State legislation and duly authorized Citizen Militia enforcement within their respective jurisdictions.

6) **Senate Joint Resolution 6** of the 111th Congress, ending the illegal alien 'anchor baby' practice.

7) The **Congressional Anti-Corruption Act**, stipulating:

Section 1. SEC insider trading rules shall apply to members of Congress. It shall be a federal crime for a member of Congress, directly or through proxies, trusts, or other entities, to purchase or sell stock in any company materially affected by legislation of which the member of Congress may be reasonably expected to have knowledge.

Section 2. No incumbent or former member of Congress may lobby Congress on behalf of any domestic interest for a period of five years after leaving Congress, or on behalf of any foreign interest, for life.

Section 3. For any member of Congress to require any member to raise money as a prerequisite to being considered for or offered a seat or leadership role on any committee of Congress, shall be a federal felony.

Section 4. As stipulated in Article I, Section 8, Clause 15 of the U.S. Constitution, the several States retain the power to enforce this legislation by appropriate State legislation and duly authorized Citizen Militia enforcement within their respective jurisdictions.

8) The **Citizens' Privacy and Liberty Act**, stipulating:

Section 1. The American people's own persons, houses, papers, telephone, email, and other communications, vehicles and effects shall be free from any and all government surveillance, collection, seizure, storage, or detainment unless preceded by issuance of a specific, bona fide judicial warrant issued upon probable cause, as stipulated in the Fourth Amendment to the U.S. Constitution.

Section 2. With the benefit of the doubt accruing to the citizen, any portion of the FISA, RFPA, USA Patriot Act, NDAA, and Intelligence Authorization Act of 2004 or any similar legislation presently in effect that violates the Fourth Amendment, are hereby repealed.

Section 3. Congress shall bear responsibility and accountability to the American People to assure that any operations of the FBI, NSA, CIA, or any other federal intelligence agency, or any major U.S.-based technology provider shall scrupulously refrain from infringing on the privacy, or on the freedom of speech and expression of any American citizen, whether residing in any of the 50 sovereign States or residing temporarily overseas.

Section 4. It shall be a federal felony for any individual, corporation, or federal entity to engage in any optical, electronic, airborne, or satellite surveillance, collection, seizure, storage, detainment, tracing, or tracking of any American citizen, his property, or his communications, whether by means of traditional devices and methods or by 'nanobots', mini-drones, sniffer aircraft, satellite, concealed cameras or sensors, or any other means, unless the citizen has requested such 'service', or until a judicial or Grand Jury warrant is issued upon probable cause, supported by oath or affirmation and particularly describing place, items, or data to be searched and persons or things to be seized.

152

Section 5. No visa of an American citizen seeking to return to one of the 50 sovereign States, shall be revoked without due process of law.

Section 6. As stipulated in Article I, Section 8, Clause 15 of the U.S. Constitution, the several States retain the power to enforce this legislation by appropriate State legislation and duly authorized Citizen Militia enforcement within their respective jurisdictions.

9) The **Religious Treason Act,** outlawing religious laws or seditious activities in the name of any foreign religion, state, or legal system operating within these United States, stipulating as follows:

Preamble. As explained in hundreds of passages in the Quran itself as well as in precise detail in the book The Quranic Concept of War by Pakistani General S.K. Malik, the belief system established by Mohammed in the 7th century is full theocracy; a system of law and government. Islam demands adherence by all, obedience by all Muslims, and payment of a dhimmi's tax by all non-Muslims.

As Europe reels under a new Muslim invasion, we are prudent to recall the words of U.S. supreme Court Justice Joseph Story, who wrote in his massive work on the Constitution, "The real object of the First Amendment was not to countenance, much less to advance Mohammedanism, or Judaism, or infidelity, by prostrating Christianity, but only to exclude all rivalry among Christian sects and to prevent any national ecclesiastical establishment."

Ending immigration of potential enemies of America and our Constitution is neither the establishment of religion or impeding the free exercise of religion; rather, it is within Congress' responsibility to support the U.S. Constitution and the security of the sovereign States of this republic.

Section 1. Because Islam is <u>a means of warfare against all rivals</u>, and given the common tactic known as taqiyya which instructs Muslims to deceive in the interest of furthering Mohammed's system of law and government, the United States shall not allow immigration of any foreign national who adheres to Islam.

Section 2. For the same reason, adherence or allegiance to Islam shall disqualify any American citizen from taking public office at school district, city, county, state or national level.

Section 3. It shall be a federal offense for any elected or appointed U.S. federal public servant to travel to a foreign country with such travel funded by a foreign government or by a foreign or domestic private foundation or lobbying organization on behalf of any foreign country, people, or religion.

Section 4. Every lobbying group for any foreign country or religious cause – specifically any lobbying organization for Israel or any Islamic state – is required to register within

180 days of passage of this legislation, under the Foreign Agents Registration Act of 1938.

Section 5. Every applicant for U.S. naturalization shall be required to swear under oath his or her full allegiance to these United States of America and their laws. Any reasonably suspected of adherence to Islam or any other faith that calls for or sanctions in its established doctrines forcible conversion, supplanting American Law, or substantive discrimination against other faiths, shall be required to make an unambiguous public, videotaped renunciation of that faith.

Section 6. It shall be a federal offense for any educational or religious institution, public or private, to promote or incite violence, war, or a foreign code of law on the basis of any religious teaching, tradition, law, or on any other basis than the liberty and security of these United States of America.

Section 7. All individuals including American nationals, immigrants, resident aliens, and foreign diplomats, and all institutions within these United States found in violation of this law shall receive a warning and fine for the first infraction. A second offense shall warrant forfeiture of the individual's U.S. visa, indictment for treason or sedition, and seizure of assets held within these United States.

Section 8. Upon the first instance in any of these United States of attempted murder by conventional explosive or mass attack (three or more victims) by any individual or group associated with, or on behalf of, a religious belief or legal system, using any potentially lethal object (firearm, knife or vehicle) there shall issue a nationwide warning of a ban on all gatherings in, or use of, any and all facilities affiliated with said religious belief system within these United States.

Section 9. Upon the second instance described in Section 8, there shall issue a ban throughout these United States on all gatherings in, or use of, any and all facilities affiliated with said religious system within these United States.

Section 10. Upon the third instance described in Section 8, all property and other assets held by or in favor of, said religious system within these United States shall be seized and where applicable destroyed, and willful adherence to said system of belief or law within these United States shall thereafter be classified as sedition and if sufficiently egregious, treason.

Section 11. Upon the first instance of an individual or group associated with a foreign religious or legal system, discharging in any of these United States a nuclear, chemical, or biological device capable of inflicting mass casualties: all U.S.-based land, buildings, training facilities, bank accounts, and other assets of said religious or legal system shall be seized and where applicable, destroyed.

154

Section 12. As stipulated in Article I, Section 8, Clause 15 of the U.S. Constitution, the several States retain the power to enforce this legislation by appropriate State legislation and duly authorized Citizen Militia enforcement within their respective jurisdictions.

10) The **Internet Liberty Act**, stipulating:

Section 1. It shall be a federal felony for any individual or group within federal government or within any major technology service provider who – unilaterally or with other individuals, groups, organizations, or governments – disables or censors any citizen's access to the Internet so that it becomes inaccessible to the average computer or other Internet device in these sovereign States.

Section 2. As stipulated in Article I, Section 8, Clause 15 of the U.S. Constitution, the several States retain the power to enforce this legislation by appropriate State legislation and duly authorized Citizen Militia enforcement within their respective jurisdictions.

11) The **Constitutional Supremacy Act**, assuring the sovereignty of the American People and States, stipulating:

Section 1. No provision of a treaty or agreement, public or secret, conflicting with this Constitution or not made in pursuance thereof, shall be the supreme Law of the Land or be of general force or effect.

Section 2. No provision of a treaty or other international agreement shall become effective as internal law in the United States until it is enacted through legislation in Congress acting within its constitutionally enumerated powers.

Section 3. No Continuity of Government (COG) order may contravene, suspend or violate the U.S. Constitution in any particular.

Section 4. Per Article III, Section 2, Clause 2 of the U.S. Constitution, Congress hereby stipulates as an Exception that no federal court shall have jurisdiction in any matter arising under this Act.

Section 5. Any vote regarding advice and consent to ratification of a treaty shall be determined by yeas and nays and names of all persons voting for and against shall be entered in the Journal of the Senate.

Section 6. It shall be a federal felony for any individual or group to engage in or to materially support actions that threaten the legal or financial sovereignty of any of the sovereign States of America without the knowledge and consent of the legislature of each and every State whose citizens would be affected, regardless whether such action may formally constitute treason.

Section 7. Within 12 months from passage of this Act, Congress shall cease all foreign aid of a military nature to any government, regime, entity, or individual.

Section 8. Within 24 months from passage of this Act, Congress shall cease all foreign aid of a non-military nature to any government, regime, entity, or individual. Said aid shall be immediately reduced by 33% for the first 12 months and by 66% for the second 12 months.

12) The **American Sovereignty Restoration Act** of 2017 (HR193) of the 115th Congress, and stipulating:

Section 1. This bill repeals the United Nations Participation Act of 1945 and other specified related laws.

Section 2. The President shall terminate U.S. membership in the United Nations (U.N.), including any organ, specialized agency, commission, or other formally affiliated body.

Section 3. The President shall close the U.S. Mission to the United Nations.

Section 4. The following shall hereafter be unlawful: a) Any funds for the U.S. assessed or voluntary contribution to the U.N.; b) Any authorization of funds for any U.S. contribution to any U.N. military or peacekeeping operation; c) Expenditure of funds to support the participation of U.S. Armed Forces as part of any U.N. military or peacekeeping operation; d) U.S. armed forces serving under U.N. com-mand; and d) diplomatic immunity for U.N. officers or employees.

13) The **Lawful Wars Act**, reiterating Congress' duty to declare wars, repealing the War Powers Resolution of 1973 and barring any administration from initiating foreign hostilities or mobilizing U.S. military in foreign lands without a Declaration of War; requiring Congress to assure that such mobilization or hostilities are necessary to defend against a demonstrable threat to these United States.

14) The **Federal Pork Sunset Act,** stipulating:

In Fiscal Year 2019, federal government doled out over $700 billion in illicit funds to the States, counties, and cities across our republic. The long tradition of such 'pork' projects with strings attached has perverted the citizen's view of his place atop the Constitution's hierarchy and allowed Washington D.C. organized crime to assume the role of benevolent master, with the sovereign States and cities as so many piglets at sow-teats. This criminogenic arrangement has rendered our local, county and State public servants willing to do whatever they must, to receive their share of funds (originating from the people themselves) from countless unaccountable, largely invisible federal agencies. This criminal activity must end.

Section 1. For three (3) fiscal years after passage of this Act, all revenues sent by federal government as grants to States and their subdivisions shall be remitted as a single block grant to each State, with no federal conditions attached, i.e., the States having liberty to determine all uses of said funds.

Section 2. Commencing on the first day of the fourth fiscal year after the date of passage of this Act, any federal grant to a State or subdivision thereof shall be a federal felony.

15) The **Minuteman Act**, pursuant to Congress's power to "provide for…arming…the Militia" contained in the U.S. Constitution, stipulating:

Section 1. The National Firearms Act of 1934, Omnibus Crime Control and Safe Streets Act of 1968, the Gun Control Act of 1968, the Firearm Owners Protection Act of 1986, and the Brady Handgun Violation Prevention Act of 1993 are hereby repealed.

Section 2. No statute, regulation, executive order, or other directive with the purported force of law of federal government, present or future, or that of any State or subdivision thereof, shall infringe on or burden the right of any citizen of, or legal resident alien in, any State who is eligible for membership in that State's Militia to purchase, own, possess, transport, or sell, whether interstate or intrastate, any firearm, ammunition, or related accoutrements suitable for service in a Militia as that term is used in the U.S. Constitution.

Section 3. No statute, regulation, executive order, or other directive with the purported force of law of federal government, present or future, shall infringe on or burden, except on the same terms as apply to any other business, the right of any person to engage in the commercial design, manufacture, repair, sale and distribution, or other trade or occupation involving firearms, ammunition, and Militia accoutrements.

Section 4. As stipulated in Article I, Section 8, Clause 15 of the U.S. Constitution, the several States retain the power to enforce this legislation by appropriate State legislation and duly authorized Citizen Militia enforcement within their respective jurisdictions and subdivisions.

16) The **Non-Conscription Act**, stipulating:

Section 1. Neither Congress nor any president or federal court has the power to conscript Americans of any age into involuntary national service or servitude of any kind.

Section 2. As stipulated in Article I, Section 8, Clause 15 of the U.S. Constitution, the several States retain the power to enforce this legislation by appropriate State legislation and duly authorized Citizen Militia enforcement within their respective jurisdictions.

17) The **Return of Sovereign Lands Act**, stipulating:

Section 1. Upon acceptance as a sovereign State of these United States, all lands and resources within said State become the sovereign property of the American People living within said State, and the individual right to private property is no more sacred than the collective right of sovereign property for every sovereign government on earth. The federal government has no lawful authority or claim of sovereignty over – or claim to minerals or other natural resources in, on or under – any land on earth, except as stipulated in Article I, Section 8, Clause 17 of the U.S. Constitution.

Section 2. No sale of any land or resource within any of the sovereign States shall be made by the U.S. government or any entity thereof on behalf of said government, effective immediately, except such surface land as stipulated in Article I, Section 8, Clause 17 of the U.S. Constitution.

Section 3. The United States government shall, within 24 months of the passage of this Act, relinquish all claims to, or jurisdiction in, all sovereign places other than those lands specifically stipulated in Article I, Section 8, Clause 17 of the U.S. Constitution as being within the exclusive legislative domain of Congress.

Section 4. The federal government has no constitutional authority to **seize** *private or State sovereign land, water, timber, oil, gas, minerals, or other natural resources in, on, or under such land in any State, for any reason, under any conditions.*

Section 5. Other than purchases from the States for military installations, federal government has no constitutional authority to **accept** *lands or resources via a State constitution or legislative act.*

Section 6. As to purchases from the sovereign States for military installations, federal government has constitutional authority to purchase lands in a State only with "Consent of the Legislature of the State in which the Same shall be". Said consent of the State Legislature must be accompanied by a majority-vote approval of the People of that State via single-issue referendum or plebiscite.

Section 7. All present federally claimed, held, or controlled lands and any minerals, water, forests and timber, or any other resource within each sovereign State shall revert within 24 months to full control and ownership of the State in which it is located, to be managed and controlled as the People of that State shall determine. The costs of transferring control of formerly federally-claimed lands and natural resources shall be borne by the State in which said lands and resources are located.

Section 8. All federal land-use regulations, national forest and park acts, and like federal controls, restrictions, and prohibitions that deprive private owners of the full use and enjoyment of their private properties pursuant to the laws of the several States, shall be repealed within 12 months of passage of this Act.

Section 9. As reparations for the past federal use and control of sovereign State lands, all federal government improvements, fixtures, facilities, equipment, vehicles and other appurtenances located within each sovereign State (except on military installations) shall become the property of that State, effective immediately. The legal transfer of all said public property located within each State shall be administered by the government of that State, and shall include executive, legislative and judicial branches and Citizen Militia as applicable.

Section 10. Congress shall provide to the sovereign People of the United States, within 12 months of passage of this Act, its detailed plan to relinquish control of all foreign military bases and to cease funding for, and operations of, all foreign land-based military and civil government operations, transferring foreign civil governance to the governments or people of those sovereign lands, within 36 months of the passage of this Act.

Section 11. Irrespective of any local independence movements within sovereign foreign lands outside the 48 contiguous and United States, all noncontiguous, foreign, and/or 'U.S. possession' claims shall revert to the full, un-fettered control of the peoples of those sovereign lands (including Hawaii and Alaska, neither of which People ever applied for statehood but were instead invaded and claimed by Washington D.C.) at their own expense and with no additional expense borne by American citizens after 24 months from passage of this Act.

18) The **Lawful United States Money and Banking Act** which will contain elements of, but be more comprehensive than H.R. 459, 833, 1094, 1095, 1098, 1496 and 2768 and SB 202, stipulating:

Section 1. The American people have delegated the power to 'coin Money' only to Congress, and have delegated to Congress only the power to 'coin' Money.

Section 2. Congress lacks any authority to delegate or to fail, neglect, or refuse to exercise this power.

Section 3. The Legal Tender Act of 1862, the Federal Reserve Act of 1913, and all subsequent amendments of those acts, have been unconstitutional since their enactment.

Section 4. The special privileges now attaching to Federal Reserve Notes— that such notes shall be redeemed in lawful money by the United States Department of the Treasury, shall be receivable for all taxes and other public dues, and shall be legal tender for all debts, public and private—have since enactment been in violation of our Supreme Law.

Section 5. As remedies for these violations of the Constitution, Congress shall establish as an alternative to the Federal Reserve System and notes, a system of official money consisting solely of gold and silver, with silver coins valued in 'dollars' at the prevailing exchange rate between silver and gold in the free market.

Section 6. This new, lawful U.S. money shall be produced through immediate free coinage of whatever gold and silver may be brought to the United States Mints; including sale of the existing national gold stocks, replaced by silver stock if the gold-silver ratio suggests silver as preferable for the initial coinage.

Section 7. Said reserves and coinage and/or fully-convertible paper or electronic receipts for physical gold and silver, shall be substituted for Federal Reserve Notes as rapidly as maintenance of stability throughout America's economy will permit, in all financial transactions of the general government.

Section 8. The Federal Reserve Act of 1913 (as amended) shall be further amended such that: a) after the effective date of such legislation, the Federal Reserve System shall have no official relationship to the general government, and b) Federal Reserve regional banks shall obtain new charters from the States consistent with the laws thereof or cease doing business as of the date on which the Secretary of the Treasury shall certify that all financial transactions of federal government are being conducted solely in gold and silver or fully-convertible paper or electronic receipts for physical gold and silver.

Section 9. The States have always enjoyed the right as sovereign governments and a duty pursuant to Article I, Section 10 of the Constitution to employ gold and silver coin or fully-convertible paper or electronic receipts for physical gold and silver, to the exclusion of any other currency as the medium of exchange in their functions. Neither Congress, nor the president, nor any court, nor any international or supra-national body, nor any private parties have any authority to require a State to employ anything other than gold and silver coin or fully-convertible paper or electronic receipts for physical gold and silver, for such purposes.

Section 10. The practice of fractional reserve banking is to be ended within 12 months of passage of this legislation, and all American financial institutions shall be required to maintain in their vaults 100% reserves against loans made. Any financial institution accepting deposits, that is unable to pay on demand all such deposits in gold and/or silver or fully-convertible paper or electronic receipts for physical gold and silver, the directors, officers, shareholders, partners, trustees, or other owners and managers of said institution shall be personally liable (their own personal assets subject to seizure) to satisfy unpaid deposit balances under the laws of the State in which the demand for payment of such balances is made.

Section 11. It shall be a federal felony for any person to enact or enforce any tax or financial burden on: a) any exchange of one form of United States money for another form of money thereof, notwithstanding that the nominal value of one form may be different than the nominal value of the other form involved in the transaction; or b) the movement of privately-owned United States money by any private citizen, to or from the United States to or from any other domicile that said private citizen may desire, provided

160

said funds are not being demonstrably used in, or do not demonstrably result from, illegal activity.

Section 12. This legislation shall apply to Federal Reserve Notes, base-metallic and debased silver coinage, and all paper currencies of the United States until the date on which the Secretary of the Treasury shall certify that all federal financial transactions are being conducted solely in gold and silver or fully-convertible paper or electronic receipts for physical gold and silver, and thereafter only as Congress deems necessary.

19) The **Intelligent Republic Act**, a reform law based loosely on the Smart Nation Act, sponsored by Congressman Rob Simmons (R-CT), must provide for orderly dismantling of all secret intelligence operations of federal government as recommended by former CIA officers Kevin Shipp and Robert Steele.

The National Security Act of 1947 created the CIA and the National Security Council, which is accountable only to presidents. *Congress, which represents the People and the States, allowed itself no oversight of the NSC.* That criminal act of legislation never defined or limited what the CIA can do or cannot do, but also clearly cannot and must not authorize, allow, or fund covert operations closed to congressional oversight.

Even if the House Permanent Select Committee on Intelligence and the Senate Select Committee on Intelligence attempted to de-fund the most egregious crimes of this criminal agency, the CIA makes this impossible. First, it makes all of its budget line items and appropriations classified, keeping its operations secret from Congress thus making it impossible to de-fund the agency in part.

Second, the CIA maintains blackmail dossiers on all members of Congress so that no legislator would dare reduce that criminal organization's programs or funding. Thus, this criminal operation as well as the deeply corrupt FBI, must be dismantled, outlawed, and de-funded *in full*.

With illicit funding generated by foreign drug operations, these criminal agencies give themselves vast, unconstitutional powers over the American People and even over American elections and those of foreign countries.

Secret agencies unaccountable to the American people are unconstitutional and have increasingly destructive impact on American security, liberty, and public morale. It is clearly unconstitutional for federal government to create foreign operating agencies, fund private offshore contractors, or create alliances with foreign countries, whether for

161

intelligence or supposed 'defense'. Such corrupt traditions violate the Constitution by usurping the authority of Congress and the Militia.

The Constitution stipulates that the Citizen Militia shall *"execute the Laws of the Union, suppress Insurrections, and repel Invasions"*. Thus, all networks, cells, and offices for intelligence in the American republic *must* operate under the local aegis of the Citizen Militia and are ultimately the duty and authority of the American People themselves. Each unit of Citizen Militia, according to the Constitution, is to follow *"the discipline prescribed by Congress"*, with officers appointed by and training, equipment, logistics supplied by its State legislature.

~~~

We The People reserve the right to revise and extend the list of federal government arrogations, violations, and usurpations brought to our attention for remediation by AmericaAgain! members via our State courts and through reform legislation. Notwithstanding the long tradition of congressional corruption and arrogation warned against by James Madison, the numerous retained powers of We the People includes power to allow *no implication beyond the powers specifically enumerated* to our federal servant; for our benefit, not theirs. As members of AmericaAgain! and its TACTICAL CIVICS™ chapter network, we resolve to enforce the Law of the Land under Amendment X; the People and States retain all powers not specifically enumerated to federal government.

For many generations, Washington D.C. has arrogated to itself powers nowhere granted to federal government by the sovereign People or States. We The People shall now put the shoe on the other foot, exercising our almost limitless retained powers as clearly stipulated in Amendment X, but only to enforce the U.S. Constitution and its limitations on our federal servants. We intend to thus tighten the chains of the Constitution via our Indictment Engine™ and the Grand Juries of our States to criminally indict members of Congress and State legislatures whose violation of the supreme law and our liberty are found to coincide with felonies in their State criminal statutes.

We shall bring our members of Congress home from doing the bidding of powerful individuals in party machines behind the scenes – to now work beside us and under our watchful eyes in their own home districts which shall now be smaller and more difficult for powerful interests to corrupt.

Violations of State criminal statutes are exclusive original and appellate jurisdiction of the courts of the State in which the parties reside. No State

162

being a party to these actions, nothing in the Constitution or federal law can be construed to allow federal courts to steal jurisdiction and exonerate such perpetrators.

AmericaAgain!, through its Tactical Civics™ chapter network, seeks to rekindle the lawful, pre-constitutional Grand Juries and Militias in each County, for we share the founders' concerns about government – now including many State governments – seeking to disarm the People, their sovereign and violating the U.S. Constitution and their state constitutions with impunity. It is the duty of all citizens, as codified in the Fourth, Fifth, and Sixth Amendments to the U.S. Constitution, to serve in their county Grand Jury to check and superintend their servants in county and municipal government, and any other servant, whether in state or federal office who lives and works in the county, to investigate any credible complaint or presentment of potential criminal behavior by said officers.

And it is also the duty of all citizens who are physically and mentally fit for the duty, to be armed and trained to fulfill the Citizen Militia functions in Article I, Section 8, Clause 15 of the Constitution. Per Clause 16, it is the duty of the States to provide officers and training for Citizen Militias, yet no State legislature has yet fully performed such duty. Until the State legislatures do so, it is the People's express and retained power as well as our God-given right, to have our County governments fill the void, or even to defend ourselves. We seek to be better stewards of the natural resources that God has entrusted to us – rather than allowing our government in our name, to help corporations plunder foreign countries.

A Christian Organization

This organization is explicitly, unashamedly Christian. It will *perpetually* hold to, support, and defend the Christian doctrines contained in Scripture. Although this be a perpetual trust, should it ever fail to glorify Jesus Christ and defend the faith and norms thereof, *it shall be dissolved.*

In our membership and operations we seek no theocracy; but the American civilization was founded as a Christian commonwealth. No other belief system has produced equally efficacious or humane law, economics, or social practices. Although some Founding Fathers were not orthodox Christians, the vast majority were. A survey of America's original colonial documents of government, law, economics, and social life demonstrates that America is founded on Christianity and no other belief system. But we only exclude Muslims because that is a *system of government and law* at war with ours; not merely a religion.

Public Employees and Elected Servants Not Allowed

Marx's pitch for communism was that everyone is equal because it is fair, and government controls everything because it is efficient. Both are false. The reality is that government jobs are easier, you're never fired for failure to produce, average pay is higher, and as in Europe, the pension system makes the productive sector unattractive. With over 20 million public employees in America, we can only imagine what's ahead when "social justice warriors" begin taking government jobs. This bedrock principle in our mission is based on Biblical ethics, conflict of interests, basic logic, hard experience, and our ballooning public employee army making us more 'European' by the month. To those who say, *"but my friend/relative the secretary, bus driver, or teacher wants to help from the inside!"*, nonsense. They want to continue receiving checks and benefits and *cannot* help the productive sector. The only thing they can do to reduce the blob is, work in the productive sector. This graphic depicts our system of government. The highest office, 'We The People', is Americans who care enough to oversee the servants and enforce the limits we put on them in the Constitution.

164

The People's Only Counter-Organization

We elect and we pay public servants and office-holders to work within the limits that we set for them, but they manage to take for themselves whatever they can get away with. School districts running parents out of the room they pay for...city and county employees treating their taxpayer employers like dirt...state legislators and their staffs doing basically anything they can sneak by the People...mayors and governors making lawless edicts and declaring sanctuary from rule of law: all are evidence of total breakdown of our system of government. And as the infographic illustrates, *only the People* can restore government by enforcing the law!

In the *land of the free and home of the brave*, We The People can no longer own private property! If we fail to pay taxes to the school district, city, or county we lose our home, farm, or shop when the sheriff sells it on the courthouse steps, even if we paid off the note. We cannot own property because by Marx's definition, *American Communism* exists in our school districts, towns, counties, and states. The takers are numerous, *and they are organized*.

The websites below are only the tip of the iceberg of unions that program, train, and support America's public employees to lord it over the People, extracting more money and 'compliance' from us. Click on each link to witness how polished and organized the predators' and parasites' unions have become, *all funded by our tax dollars*. And this is only a *partial* list:

- **National Association of School Boards**

- **National Education Association**

- **AASA The School Superintendents' Association**

- **National League of Cities**

- **United States Conference of Mayors**

- **National Association of Counties**

- **County Judges & Commissioners' Association**

- **National Conference of State Legislatures**

- **American Federation of Government Employees**

Is there a similar union for congress, presidents, and federal judges? Yes; Washington, D.C.: the most powerful, ruthless, unaccountable, predatory, independent city-state in human history.

165

With all those unions and their staffs training, briefing, and supporting over 20 million public employees you may wonder, how can Tactical Civics™ fight all of that? As the first full-spectrum action solution for the People, our mission is inspired by, and serves at the pleasure of, *the Creator of the Universe.* Our job is only to repent and do our part.

In building, reinforcing, promoting, refining and organizing our Tactical Civics™ chapter network, we refuse to operate in any unlawful, seditious, riotous, rebellious, paranoid, or terroristic manner. We also refuse to allow this tactical mission of We the People to be co-opted, overseen, or infested by politicians, lobbyists, or operatives from any government or political party, foreign or domestic. And we will not accept any current employee or elected servant in government at any level.

We will organize and operate locally as free citizens in the privacy of our homes, businesses, and churches – or in public parks and any venue that suits us as owners and residents of such places – expecting to have no government infiltration, or coercion as is common to tyrant regimes.

Should our member of congress, state legislator, or governor refuse to cease violating the law; should he prevaricate and bloviate as politicians do, or conspire anew with like-minded scoundrels and oligarchs who purchased his first allegiance – we will seek his criminal conviction in State Court; the longest possible State Penitentiary term; and as actual and punitive damages for massive fraud and conspiracy, we will seek to have our State Court seize all assets held under any structure, in any jurisdiction, inuring to his benefit or that of his family or descendants.

To any state or county prosecutor, district attorney, judge, constable, sheriff or other public servant who refuses to oversee justice as your oath of office demands, We The People will see that your complicity in potential high crimes is included in a separate felony presentment to your Grand Jury, jointly deployed with our community or county Militia.

No defendant in Congress can plead ignorance of the U.S. Constitution or ignorance of federal laws over which he is responsible – even those for which he voted without reading. Ignorance of the law is no defense for public servants who swear an oath to support the U.S. Constitution, only to violate it daily, as was done in the 'COVID-19' and Election Steal 2020 gaslighting scandals.

We the People will offer immunity from indictment to a member of Congress only if that defendant, in writing with notarized witnesses from among our membership, agrees to withdraw support for or cease

166

acquiescence in the crime(s) for which we seek his indictment; sponsor or co-sponsor legislation outlined above, drafted by citizens; and refrain from supporting any amendment thereto.

AmericaAgain! and its Tactical Civics™ chapter network is an effort conceived by free, productive citizens of these sovereign States of America who believe that by God's grace, a diligent minority can restore liberty, private property, rule of law, honest elections, and the collective sovereignty of We the People that we guarantee ourselves in the U.S. Constitution.

Each public servant leaves a public record in history. Their response to their sovereign now enforcing the Constitution will demonstrate either their repentant fidelity or their ignominious corruption.

We give thanks to God in the name of Jesus Christ His Son, and ask His blessing on this formerly godly republic, that we may be AmericaAgain!

We The People of the united States of America

National Day of Thanksgiving

Original, November 22, 2012

Revision 113 (12 April 2022…the day in 1861 that Lincoln sparked the War to Enslave the States.)

Tactical Civics™ Declaration

The charter members of Tactical Civics™ are, for the first time in mankind's history, forging a responsible, repentant Remnant into an educated, organized, lawful force of Popular Constitutionalism, and helping our Congress become history's first distributed legislature. *That is no small feat.*

What Obama and the Dragon Brought

Hatched in the Lincoln administration, we began witnessing the kicking, screaming, clawing, biting death of 150-year-old American Communism when Hussein Obama removed Communism's mask and the Chinese dragon took 'Resident' Biden's invitation and removed its mask as well. Now, the CCP is helping to transform Washington DC into a brazen, arrogant, clinically insane Communist stronghold. *The Russiagate, Shampeachment, BLAntifa riots, Plandemic masking and jabbing operation, and Election Steal 2020 are the attempted overthrow of America.*

At least 100 million normal, productive Americans in the heartland will never stand for this. As the criminal, ruthless 10-by-10-mile city state on the Potomac has finally shown the world its true colors in 2015-2022, it's awakening America's Heartland. Until Tactical Civics™, We The People did not know what to do about it. *Most still don't.*

What America's Going to Do About It

But now, we in the repentant remnant *do* know what to do...

First, we are turning off Washington DC; watching and listening to organized crime as it sinks into its final pathetic years as a world power. We're increasingly tuning it out. For us normal folks, watching this idiocy in the federal, state, county, local, and school district palaces is like sitting in an insane asylum. We're outta there, and taking our money, too (more on that, below).

Second, We The People are walking away from Google, Facebook, Twitter, all mainstream media, Hollywood, and any tech company that decides to de-platform or ban us. Fantastic; you're dead to us, too. We'll find alternatives. *You won't.*

Third, We The People will pay no more attention to the sociopath political machines of Atlanta, Baltimore, Chicago, Dallas, Detroit, Houston, Los Angeles, Phoenix, Minneapolis, New York City, Philadelphia, and a couple of dozen other feral hellholes. In America's 31,000 small towns and all the rural homesteads in between, we intend to take control back, and *not* by the rigged game called politics. We're going to live our lives as normal, God-fearing, God-glorifying Americans. We refuse to give another minute to the sick values of God-hating, collapsing urban sewers. Hey, big cities: that's why your real estate values and tax bases are plummeting. Get a clue.

Fourth, We The People are restoring our Grand Jury and constitutional Militia in every one of the 3,141 counties, boroughs, and parishes in these sovereign States.

Fifth, We The People working on the app development team at Tactical Civics™ plan to develop, refine, and launch the Indictment Engine™ mobile app to scan every proposed state or federal bill before it becomes legislation, and if it violates the Constitution, generate felony presentments to be sent to the Grand Jury of the counties of every sponsor and co-sponsor (conspirator and co-conspirator of the attempted felony) in each perpetrator's State Judicial District.

Sixth, We The People intend to force 27 more State legislatures to ratify the original First Right in the Bill of Rights, requiring that no US congressional district exceed 50,000 persons; the only subject on which George Washington felt strongly enough about to address during the four-month constitutional convention in 1787. America's 31,000 small towns and millions of rural Americans will have representation in the U.S. House and Electoral College for the first time in a century.

Seventh, We The People intend to then bring Congress home to work under *our* watchful eye, as they obviously have not 'checked and balanced' one another in generations. In Article I, Section 8, Clause 17, we grant that Congress shall have 'exclusive legislative jurisdiction' in that 10-by-10-mile plot of land on the Potomac. So once we bring them home and have normal American statesmen filling those seats, we will take control of the agencies and bureaucracies that fill that ruthless, criminal city-state that plunders and threatens the whole earth, beginning with its own sovereigns, enriching the few thousand wealthiest and most ruthless humans on earth.

Eighth, through 6600+ Citizens Volunteer Research Service (CVRS) teams created by our Non-Enumerated Powers Sunset Act (NEPSA), We

170

The People will review, red-line, de-fund, and outlaw ('sunset') every agency, bureau, department, office, program, and regulation that We The People did not *specifically* authorize in our Constitution and have no need for. This review will be *at the People's sole discretion,* with each member of the U.S. House *required* to sign off to his/her CVRS team's decisions. When a majority of CVRS teams has red-lined an agency, program, or regulatory line item, it is de-funded, shut down, and outlawed. *Period.*

We The People are serious about organized crime. Any congressman found to have interfered with or attempted to change any CVRS team's decision will have committed a felony, as will be stipulated in NEPSA and similar State statutes.

Ninth, We The People intend to immediately de-fund the US Department of Education (Indoctrination) and assure that no public, private, or religious school shall have any nexus with federal government, except as stipulated in our proposed *Religious Treason Act,* outlawing religious laws or seditious activities in the name of any foreign religion, state, or legal system operating within these United States, stipulating,

"As explained in hundreds of passages in the Quran itself as well as in precise detail in the book The Quranic Concept of War by Pakistani General S.K. Malik, the belief system established by Mohammed in the 7th century is theocracy; a system of law and government. Islam demands adherence by all, obedience by all Muslims, and payment of a dhimmi's tax by all non-Muslims".

Any such 'school' is seditious and destructive to America's rule of law. We The People are shutting down jihad.

Tenth, We The People intend to start keeping what we earn. As explained in the book, *A Tax Honesty Primer,* without a dollar of individual income taxes needed, the combination of corporate tax revenues, federal excises, imposts, and import duties are *more* than sufficient to fund what We The People authorize government to do.

Note on Parental Choice in Child-Rearing

We will support other efforts that are not included in our formal mission's trust deed; especially every state reform law providing parental school choice vouchers, beginning with tax credits and equal to 100% of state per-pupil expenditure, no strings attached, for each student who is homeschooled or enrolled in a private school. Liberating American minds from the propaganda and counter-factual American history programmed into us for the past century is vitally important.

Note on Private Property in this Republic

The same is true of ending *ad valorem* property taxes in this Republic. The rapacious state legislatures in their palaces, in the name of bureaucrats have *outlawed* private property in America, in favor of wasteful, bloated pork programs and bureaucratic empires over which the owners of homes, farms, and shops have no control or voice, yet by which predators, parasites, and their sheriffs and collections lawyers hold us hostage for life, as the people of every Communist country. This practice of a monarch holding the People hostage for life to the crown began with William the Conqueror in 1066 A.D. and was exported to the American colonies by King James, along with chattel and indentured slavery.

It is time for this cruel, despotic practice of feudalism to end in this Republic! When an American has paid in full for a piece of property, that property should be the free, clear property of its owner, with no level of government having its hooks (and its collections lawyers' and sheriffs' hooks) in that private property. It's always been a fundamental tenet of American self-government that the People be truly self-governing; that a grasping, communistic majority cannot seize the property of the minority against the minority's will or hold that minority in lifelong servitude to cover growing expenses of lawless bureaucrats.

But the huge state has led to an increasing number of Americans opting for careers in the lawless, limitless 'public sector', which at this point is closer to Karl Marx's system than to that of our Founding Fathers.

Preparing For Your Chapter

We The People are now rising up and reporting for duty in our own counties from coast to coast, to create and maintain a 3,141-county *permanent* law enforcement against organized crime and corrupt arrogations from our federal, state, county, city, and school district palaces. *Enough is enough!*

There are 19 sweeping reform laws in the AmericaAgain! Declaration that Tactical Civics™ chapters will be pushing in decades to come. But no population has ever done anything like this before. Yes, it's just what's in our Constitution. Yes, the Internet and social media makes it a no-brainer. But by God's grace and the counsel of the Holy Spirit over more than a decade in the lives of 44 volunteers, Tactical Civics™ is the first organization to finally put all the pieces together.

The 'Great Reset' seems to be destroying America; but today, every corrupt careerist in government is thinking like *the cantina scene in A Bug's Life* when Hopper tells the other grasshoppers that their lives of leisure are over. This is *the Great We-Set!* The sleeping giant is waking up, and our mission is the point of the spear: lawful, full-spectrum, and long-term.

So far, we are like infants in a crib, just figuring out our shapes, colors, and letters. So until you know the materials, don't hold your first formal meeting. First, gather with one or two or a handful of new acquaintances to show them the new way of life that lies ahead for the responsible remnant, even as you join in your statewide Tactical Civics™ meetings to learn the materials.

We cannot adequately stress that your first task is: join as a dues-paying member in the Training Center, follow the step-by-step instructions, and *learn the mission!*

Before You Have County Chapter Meetings

Introductory online meetings are being held weekly (several times per week). Before even thinking about constitutional Militia you must read our book, *Time to Start Over, America: Introducing American Militia 2.0™, Restoring Our Founding Fathers' Law Enforcement, Riot & Border Control, and Social Glue*

America's 50-year-old 'militia movement' *is not constitutional Militia*. While a minority of the movement is comprised of honorable men, the majority are not serious and many are downright dangerous. This is why that movement has stigmatized the word 'militia', killing the desire in able-bodied American men to serve in constitutional Militia.

Of course we will work with sincere leaders in that movement who will push through our County Militia Ordinance and work closely with their county Tactical Civics™ chapter. But if you deal with 'the movement', you will meet Alpha Male private militant group leaders who think their group belongs to them. In truth, it does; every existing armed group using the label 'militia' today is a *private club,* not the public function that the Founding Fathers stipulate in the Constitution.

To any well-meaning American claiming their 'militia' is a legitimate civil function: *show it to me in the Constitution.* We do not mean to antagonize, but we also will not be intimidated by men who are essentially working for FBI, Antifa, and others who keep Militia from ever being restored in our land. That may not be their intention, but the Constitution is the only test. Any group leader who is sincere, will work with his county chapter of

173

Tactical Civics™. He will work to get our Militia Ordinance passed in your county government's public meeting right after we get our Grand Jury Ordinance passed.

If he refuses or conveniently 'forgets' or drags his feet week after week in that one good faith action, you will know that the well is poisoned. Move on. That leader has no interest in properly executed, constitutional Militia and will eventually destroy the unit or at least waste a great deal of time and your chapter morale before you grasp the problem.

We recommend to any potential Militia leader: if you can start with a clean sheet, *do it*. Recruit men who are tough, smart men of their word, who will show up for training and muster; who are godly, rational, and respectful. We call our program American Militia 2.0™ because too many 'militia' groups are like false flag Antifa cells hidden among America's frustrated, honorable men who want to do their duty but can never seem to find a group with a real plan.

Regarding Pastors

Men of God need to start acting the part. We have several pastors in our number, all the same kind of man: they don't march to the tune of a franchise and they don't lead a flock for a salary, house, and benefits.

In general, America's pastors are even more stiff-necked than 'threeper' Alpha Males. That's why George Barna reported over a decade ago in his book *Revolution,* that 25 million Christians had walked away from church buildings and back to Jesus. The number is surely much larger now. On both sides of the Atlantic, pastors have a great deal to repent.

The local church can be every bit as vital as the local gun dealer, shooting range, or Militia unit. Repairing these ruins without pastors makes no sense. Our 7-week Crash course is a book called *Mission to America,* and is perfect for church small groups, and *Tactical Civics™ For Church Leaders* was written for American pastors to stop avoiding our civic duties while making the excuse, "we don't do politics". *Our Romans 13 duty over the Constitution and rule of law is not politics!*

What a Massive Job Ahead!

Well, yes; that's true. And what a zoo all around us, predators and parasites threatening to outnumber the honest and productive if we, like Europeans, continue to avoid our duties.

Tactical Civics™ is full-spectrum and long-term, and it looks extremely difficult. But those who go through our Training Center step by step will learn that this mission is designed for the newbie. We break this new way of life down into simple steps and individual study units and action projects. It will be much easier for the next generation, and even easier for the one after that.

But for now, we repeat the old aphorism...

People who say that it cannot be done should not interrupt those who are doing it.

Declaration of Independence

The Declaration of Independence as finally edited by Congress from Thomas Jefferson's draft, appeared on July 8, 1776 in The Pennsylvania Packet, a weekly newspaper.

The Unanimous Declaration of the Thirteen United States of America

When, in the course of human events, it becomes necessary for one people to dissolve the political bands which have connected them with another, and to assume among the powers of the earth, the separate and equal station to which the laws of nature and of nature's God entitle them, a decent respect to the opinions of mankind requires that they should declare the causes which impel them to the separation.

We hold these truths to be self-evident, that all men are created equal, that they are endowed by their Creator with certain unalienable rights, that among these are life, liberty and the pursuit of happiness. That to secure these rights, governments are instituted among men, deriving their just powers from the consent of the governed. That whenever any form of government becomes destructive to these ends, it is the right of the people to alter or to abolish it, and to institute new government, laying its foundation on such principles and organizing its powers in such form, as to them shall seem most likely to effect their safety and happiness.

Prudence, indeed, will dictate that governments long established should not be changed for light and transient causes; and accordingly all experience hath shown that mankind are more disposed to suffer, while evils are sufferable, than to right themselves by abolishing the forms to which they are accustomed. But when a long train of abuses and usurpations, pursuing invariably the same object evinces a design to reduce them under absolute despotism, it is their right, it is their duty, to throw off such government, and to provide new guards for their future security. –Such has been the patient sufferance of these colonies; and such is now the necessity which constrains them to alter their former systems of government. The history of the present King of Great Britain is a history of repeated injuries and usurpations, all having in direct object the establishment of an absolute tyranny over these states. To prove this, let facts be submitted to a candid world.

He has refused his assent to laws, the most wholesome and necessary for the public good.

He has forbidden his governors to pass laws of immediate and pressing importance, unless suspended in their operation till his assent should be obtained; and when so suspended, he has utterly neglected to attend to them.

He has refused to pass other laws for the accommodation of large districts of people, unless those people would relinquish the right of representation in the legislature, a right inestimable to them and formidable to tyrants only.

He has called together legislative bodies at places unusual, uncomfortable, and distant from the depository of their public records, for the sole purpose of fatiguing them into compliance with his measures.

He has dissolved representative houses repeatedly, for opposing with manly firmness his invasions on the rights of the people.

He has refused for a long time, after such dissolutions, to cause others to be elected; whereby the legislative powers, incapable of annihilation, have returned to the people at large for their exercise; the state remaining in the meantime exposed to all the dangers of invasion from without, and convulsions within.

He has endeavored to prevent the population of these states; for that purpose obstructing the laws for naturalization of foreigners; refusing to pass others to encourage their migration hither, and raising the conditions of new appropriations of lands.

He has obstructed the administration of justice, by refusing his assent to laws for establishing judiciary powers.

He has made judges dependent on his will alone, for the tenure of their offices, and the amount and payment of their salaries.

He has erected a multitude of new offices, and sent hither swarms of officers to harass our people, and eat out their substance.

He has kept among us, in times of peace, standing armies without the consent of our legislature.

He has affected to render the military independent of and superior to civil power.

He has combined with others to subject us to a jurisdiction foreign to our constitution, and unacknowledged by our laws; giving his assent to their acts of pretended legislation:

For quartering large bodies of armed troops among us:

For protecting them, by mock trial, from punishment for any murders which they should commit on the inhabitants of these states:

For cutting off our trade with all parts of the world:

For imposing taxes on us without our consent:

For depriving us in many cases, of the benefits of trial by jury:

For transporting us beyond seas to be tried for pretended offenses:

For abolishing the free system of English laws in a neigh-boring province, establishing therein an arbitrary government, and enlarging its boundaries so as to render it at once an example and fit instrument for introducing the same absolute rule in these colonies:

For taking away our charters, abolishing our most valuable laws, and altering fundamentally the forms of our governments:

For suspending our own legislatures, and declaring them-selves invested with power to legislate for us in all cases whatsoever.

He has abdicated government here, by declaring us out of his protection and waging war against us.

He has plundered our seas, ravaged our coasts, burned our towns, and destroyed the lives of our people.

He is at this time transporting large armies of foreign mercenaries to complete the works of death, desolation and tyranny, already begun with circumstances of cruelty and perfidy scarcely paralleled in the most barbarous ages, and totally unworthy the head of a civilized nation.

He has constrained our fellow citizens taken captive on the high seas to bear arms against their country, to become the executioners of their friends and brethren, or to fall themselves by their hands.

He has excited domestic insurrections amongst us, and has endeavored to bring on the inhabitants of our frontiers, the merciless Indian savages, whose known rule of warfare, is undistinguished destruction of all ages, sexes and conditions.

In every stage of these oppressions we have petitioned for redress in the most humble terms: our repeated petitions have been answered only by repeated injury. A prince, whose character is thus marked by every act which may define a tyrant, is unfit to be the ruler of a free people.

Nor have we been wanting in attention to our British brethren. We have warned them from time to time of attempts by their legislature to extend an unwarrantable jurisdiction over us. We have reminded them of the circumstances of our emigration and settlement here. We have appealed to their native justice and magnanimity, and we have conjured them by the ties of our common kindred to disavow these usurpations, which, would inevitably interrupt our connections and correspondence. They too have been deaf to the voice of justice and of consanguinity. We must, therefore, acquiesce in the necessity, which denounces our separation, and hold them, as we hold the rest of mankind, enemies in war, in peace friends.

We, therefore, the representatives of the United States of America, in General Congress, assembled, appealing to the Supreme Judge of the world for the rectitude of our intentions, do, in the name, and by the authority of the good people of these colonies, solemnly publish and declare, that these united colonies are, and of right ought to be free and independent states; that they are absolved from all allegiance to the British Crown, and that all political connection between them and the state of Great Britain, is and ought to be totally dissolved; and that as free and independent states, they have full power to levy war, conclude peace, contract alliances, establish commerce, and to do all other acts and things which independent states may of right do. And for the support of this declaration, with a firm reliance on the protection of Divine Providence, we mutually pledge to each other our lives, our fortunes and our sacred honor.

New Hampshire: Josiah Bartlett, William Whipple, Matthew Thornton

Massachusetts: John Hancock, Samuel Adams, John Adams, Robert Treat Paine, Elbridge Gerry

Rhode Island: Stephen Hopkins, William Ellery

Connecticut: Roger Sherman, Samuel Huntington, William Williams, Oliver Wolcott

New York: William Floyd, Philip Livingston, Francis Lewis, Lewis Morris

New Jersey: Richard Stockton, John Witherspoon, Francis Hopkinson, John Hart, Abraham Clark

Pennsylvania: Robert Morris, Benjamin Rush, Benjamin Franklin, John Morton, George Clymer, James Smith, George Taylor, James Wilson, George Ross

Delaware: Caesar Rodney, George Read, Thomas McKean

Maryland: Samuel Chase, William Paca, Thomas Stone, Charles Carroll of Carrollton

Virginia: George Wythe, Richard Henry Lee, Thomas Jefferson, Benjamin Harrison, Thomas Nelson, Jr., Francis Lightfoot Lee, Carter Braxton

North Carolina: William Hooper, Joseph Hewes, John Penn

South Carolina: Edward Rutledge, Thomas Heyward, Jr., Thomas Lynch, Jr., Arthur Middleton

Georgia: Button Gwinnett, Lyman Hall, George Walton

— APPENDIX I —

U.S. Constitution

*This edition of the Constitution contains the exact language of the original, including archaic spellings. For ease of reference, we have added an indexing system, appearing before each clause in bold numerals. For instance, Article I, Section 8, Clause 15 reads, "**1.8.15** To provide for calling forth the Militia to execute the Laws of the Union, suppress Insurrections and repel Invasions". This system allows the citizen to quickly reference and more easily memorize the Constitution.*

We the People of the United States, in Order to form a more perfect Union, establish Justice, insure domestic Tranquility, provide for the common defence, promote the general Welfare, and secure the Blessings of Liberty to ourselves and our Posterity, do ordain and establish this Constitution for the United States of America.

Article I

Section 1

All legislative Powers herein granted shall be vested in a Congress of the United States, which shall consist of a Senate and House of Representatives.

Section 2

1.2.1 The House of Representatives shall be composed of Members chosen every second Year by the People of the

several States, and the Electors in each State shall have the Qualifications requisite for Electors of the most numerous Branch of the State Legislature.

1.2.2 No Person shall be a Representative who shall not have attained to the Age of twenty five Years, and been seven Years a Citizen of the United States, and who shall not, when elected, be an Inhabitant of that State in which he shall be chosen.

1.2.3 Representatives and direct Taxes shall be apportioned among the several States which may be included within this Union, according to their respective Numbers, which shall be determined by adding to the whole

Number of free Persons, including those bound to Service for a Term of Years, and excluding Indians not taxed, three fifths of all other Persons.

1.2.4 The actual Enumeration shall be made within three Years after the first Meeting of the Congress of the United States, and within every subsequent Term of ten Years, in such Manner as they shall by Law direct. The Number of Representatives shall not exceed one for every thirty Thousand, but each State shall have at Least one Representative; and until such enumeration shall be made, the State of New Hampshire shall be entitled to chuse three, Massachusetts eight, Rhode-Island and Providence Plantations one, Connecticut five, New-York six, New Jersey four, Pennsylvania eight, Delaware one, Maryland six, Virginia ten, North Carolina five, South Carolina five, and Georgia three.

1.2.5 When vacancies happen in the Representation from any State, the Executive Authority thereof shall issue Writs of Election to fill such Vacancies.

1.2.6 The House of Representatives shall chuse their Speaker and other Officers; and shall have the sole Power of Impeachment.

Section 3

1.3.1 The Senate of the United States shall be composed of two Senators from each State, chosen by the Legislature thereof, for six Years; and each Senator shall have one Vote.

1.3.2 Immediately after they shall be assembled in Consequence of the first Election, they shall be divided as equally as may be into three Classes. The Seats of the Senators of the first Class shall be vacated at the Expiration of the second Year, of the second Class at the Expiration of the fourth Year, and of the third Class at the Expiration of the sixth Year, so that one third may be chosen every second Year;

1.3.3 and if Vacancies happen by Resignation, or otherwise, during the Recess of the Legislature of any State, the Executive thereof may make temporary Appointments until the next Meeting of the Legislature, which shall then fill such Vacancies.

1.3.4 No Person shall be a Senator who shall not have attained to the Age of thirty Years, and been nine Years a Citizen of the United States, and who shall not, when elected, be an Inhabitant of that State for which he shall be chosen.

1.3.5 The Vice President of the United States shall be President of the Senate, but shall have no Vote, unless they be equally divided.

1.3.6 The Senate shall chuse their other Officers, and also a President pro tempore, in the Absence of the Vice President, or when he shall exercise the Office of President of the United States.

1.3.7 The Senate shall have the sole Power to try all Impeachments. When sitting for that Purpose, they shall be on Oath or Affirmation. When the President of the United States is tried, the Chief Justice shall preside: And no Person shall be convicted without the Concurrence of two thirds of the Members present.

1.3.8 Judgment in Cases of Impeachment shall not extend further than to removal from Office, and disqualification to hold and enjoy any Office of honor, Trust or Profit under the United States: but the Party convicted shall nevertheless be liable and subject to Indictment, Trial, Judgment and Punishment, according to Law.

Section 4

1.4.1 The Times, Places and Manner of holding Elections for Senators and Representatives, shall be prescribed in each State by the Legislature thereof; but the Congress may at any time by Law make or alter such Regulations, except as to the Places of chusing Senators.

1.4.2 The Congress shall assemble at least once in every Year, and such Meeting shall be on the first Monday in December, unless they shall by Law appoint a different Day. [Changed; see 20th Amendment.]

Section 5

1.5.1 Each House shall be the Judge of the Elections, Returns and Qualifications of its own Members, and a Majority of each shall constitute a Quorum to do Business; but a smaller Number may adjourn from day to day, and may be authorized to compel the Attendance of absent Members, in such Manner, and under such Penalties as each House may provide.

1.5.2 Each House may determine the Rules of its Proceedings, punish its Members for disorderly Behaviour, and, with the Concurrence of two thirds, expel a Member.

1.5.3 Each House shall keep a Journal of its Proceedings, and from time to time publish the same, excepting such Parts as may in their Judgment require Secrecy; and the Yeas and Nays of the Members of either House on any question shall, at the Desire of one fifth of those Present, be entered on the Journal.

1.5.4   Neither House, during the Session of Congress, shall, without the Consent of the other, adjourn for more than three days, nor to any other Place than that in which the two Houses shall be sitting.

Section 6

1.6.1   The Senators and Representatives shall receive a Compensation for their Services, to be ascertained by Law, and paid out of the Treasury of the United States.

1.6.2   They shall in all Cases, except Treason, Felony and Breach of the Peace, be privileged from Arrest during their Attendance at the Session of their respective Houses, and in going to and returning from the same; and for any Speech or Debate in either House, they shall not be questioned in any other Place.

1.6.3   No Senator or Representative shall, during the Time for which he was elected, be appointed to any civil Office under the Authority of the United States, which shall have been created, or the Emoluments whereof shall have been encreased during such time; and no Person holding any Office under the United States, shall be a Member of either House during his Continuance in Office.

Section 7

1.7.1   All Bills for raising Revenue shall originate in the House of Representatives; but the Senate may propose or concur with Amendments as on other Bills.

1.7.2   Every Bill which shall have passed the House of Representatives and the Senate, shall, before it become a Law, be presented to the President of the United States; If he approve he shall sign it, but if not he shall return it, with his Objections to that House in which it shall have originated, who shall enter the Objections at large on their Journal, and proceed to reconsider it.

1.7.3   If after such Reconsideration two thirds of that House shall agree to pass the Bill, it shall be sent, together with the Objections, to the other House, by which it shall likewise be reconsidered, and if approved by two thirds of that House, it shall become a Law.

1.7.4   But in all such Cases the Votes of both Houses shall be determined by yeas and Nays, and the Names of the Persons voting for and against the Bill shall be entered on the Journal of each House respectively. If any Bill shall not be returned by the President within ten Days (Sundays excepted) after it shall have been presented to him, the Same shall be a

Law, in like Manner as if he had signed it, unless the Congress by their Adjournment prevent its Return, in which Case it shall not be a Law.

1.7.5 Every Order, Resolution, or Vote to which the Concurrence of the Senate and House of Representatives may be necessary (except on a question of Adjournment) shall be presented to the President of the United States; and before the Same shall take Effect, shall be approved by him, or being disapproved by him, shall be repassed by two thirds of the Senate and House of Representatives, according to the Rules and Limitations prescribed in the Case of a Bill.

Section 8

1.8.1 The Congress shall have Power To lay and collect Taxes, Duties, Imposts and Excises, to pay the Debts and provide for the common Defence and general Welfare of the United States; but all Duties, Imposts and Excises shall be uniform throughout the United States;

1.8.2 To borrow Money on the credit of the United States;

1.8.3 To regulate Commerce with foreign Nations, and among the several States, and with the Indian Tribes;

1.8.4 To establish an uniform Rule of Naturalization, and uniform Laws on the subject of Bankruptcies throughout the United States;

1.8.5 To coin Money, regulate the Value thereof, and of foreign Coin, and fix the Standard of Weights and Measures;

1.8.6 To provide for the Punishment of counterfeiting the Securities and current Coin of the United States;

1.8.7 To establish Post Offices and post Roads;

1.8.8 To promote the Progress of Science and useful Arts, by securing for limited Times to Authors and Inventors the exclusive Right to their respective Writings and Discoveries;

1.8.9 To constitute Tribunals inferior to the supreme Court;

1.8.10 To define and punish Piracies and Felonies committed on the high Seas, and Offences against the Law of Nations;

1.8.11 To declare War, grant Letters of Marque and Reprisal, and make Rules concerning Captures on Land and Water;

1.8.12 To raise and support Armies, but no Appropriation of Money to that Use shall be for a longer Term than two Years;

1.8.13 To provide and maintain a Navy;

1.8.14 To make Rules for the Government and Regulation of the land and naval Forces;

1.8.15 To provide for calling forth the Militia to execute the Laws of the Union, suppress Insurrections and repel Invasions;

1.8.16 To provide for organizing, arming, and disciplining, the Militia, and for governing such Part of them as may be employed in the Service of the United States, reserving to the States respectively, the Appointment of the Officers, and the Authority of training the Militia according to the discipline prescribed by Congress;

1.8.17 To exercise exclusive Legislation in all Cases whatsoever, over such District (not exceeding ten Miles square) as may, by Cession of particular States, and the Acceptance of Congress, become the Seat of the Government of the United States, and to exercise like Authority over all Places purchased by the Consent of the Legislature of the State in which the Same shall be, for the Erection of Forts, Magazines, Arsenals, dock-Yards, and other needful Buildings;—And

1.8.18 To make all Laws which shall be necessary and proper for carrying into Execution the foregoing Powers, and all other Powers vested by this Constitution in the Government of the United States, or in any Department or Officer thereof.

Section 9

1.9.1 The Migration or Importation of such Persons as any of the States now existing shall think proper to admit, shall not be prohibited by the Congress prior to the Year one thousand eight hundred and eight, but a Tax or duty may be imposed on such Importation, not exceeding ten dollars for each Person. [Nullified; now obsolete.]

1.9.2 The Privilege of the Writ of Habeas Corpus shall not be suspended, unless when in Cases of Rebellion or Invasion the public Safety may require it.

1.9.3 No Bill of Attainder or ex post facto Law shall be passed.

1.9.4 No Capitation, or other direct, Tax shall be laid, unless in Proportion to the Census or enumeration herein before directed to be taken.

1.9.5 No Tax or Duty shall be laid on Articles exported from any State.

1.9.6 No Preference shall be given by any Regulation of Commerce or Revenue to the Ports of one State over those of another: nor shall Vessels bound to, or from, one State, be obliged to enter, clear, or pay Duties in another.

1.9.7 No Money shall be drawn from the Treasury, but in Consequence of Appropriations made by Law; and a regular Statement and Account of the Receipts and Expenditures of all public Money shall be published from time to time.

1.9.8 No Title of Nobility shall be granted by the United States: And no Person holding any Office of Profit or Trust under them, shall, without the Consent of the Congress, accept of any present, Emolument, Office, or Title, of any kind whatever, from any King, Prince, or foreign State.

Section 10

1.10.1 No State shall enter into any Treaty, Alliance, or Confederation; grant Letters of Marque and Reprisal;

1.10.2 coin Money; emit Bills of Credit; make any Thing but gold and silver Coin a Tender in Payment of Debts;

1.10.3 pass any Bill of Attainder, ex post facto Law,

1.10.4 or Law impairing the Obligation of Contracts, or grant any Title of Nobility.

1.10.5 No State shall, without the Consent of the Congress, lay any Imposts or Duties on Imports or Exports, except

what may be absolutely necessary for executing its inspection Laws: and the net Produce of all Duties and Imposts, laid by any State on Imports or Exports, shall be for the Use of the Treasury of the United States; and all such Laws shall be subject to the Revision and Controul of the Congress.

1.10.6 No State shall, without the Consent of Congress, lay any Duty of Tonnage, keep Troops, or Ships of War in time of Peace, enter into any Agreement or Compact with another State, or with a foreign Power, or engage in War, unless actually invaded, or in such imminent Danger as will not admit of delay.

Article II

Section 1

2.1.1 The executive Power shall be vested in a President of the United States of America. He shall hold his Office during the Term of four Years, and, together with the Vice President, chosen for the same Term, be elected, as follows

2.1.2   Each State shall appoint, in such Manner as the Legislature thereof may direct, a Number of Electors, equal to the whole Number of Senators and Representatives to which the State may be entitled in the Congress: but no Senator or Representative, or Person holding an Office of Trust or Profit under the United States, shall be appointed an Elector.

2.1.3   The Electors shall meet in their respective States, and vote by Ballot for two Persons, of whom one at least shall not be an Inhabitant of the same State with themselves.

2.1.4   And they shall make a List of all the Persons voted for, and of the Number of Votes for each; which List they shall sign and certify, and transmit sealed to the Seat of the Government of the United States, directed to the President of the Senate.

2.1.5   The President of the Senate shall, in the Presence of the Senate and House of Representatives, open all the Certificates, and the Votes shall then be counted. The Person having the greatest Number of Votes shall be the President, if such Number be a Majority of the whole Number of Electors appointed;

2.1.6   and if there be more than one who have such Majority, and have an equal Number of Votes, then the House of Representatives shall immediately chuse by Ballot one of them for President; and if no Person have a Majority, then from the five highest on the List the said House shall in like Manner chuse the President. But in chusing the President, the Votes shall be taken by States, the Representation from each State having one Vote; A quorum for this Purpose shall consist of a Member or Members from two thirds of the States, and a Majority of all the States shall be necessary to a Choice. [Changed; see 12th Amendment.]

2.1.7   [Removed; see 20th Amendment.]

2.1.8   [Removed by the 20th Amendment.]

2.1.9   In every Case, after the Choice of the President, the Person having the greatest Number of Votes of the Electors shall be the Vice President. But if there should remain two or more who have equal Votes, the Senate shall chuse from them by Ballot the Vice President.

[Changed; see 12th Amendment.]

2.1.10   The Congress may determine the Time of chusing the Electors, and the Day on which they shall give their Votes; which Day shall be the same throughout the United States.

2.1.11   No Person except a natural born Citizen, or a Citizen of the United States, at the time of the Adoption of this Constitution, shall be eligible to the Office of President; neither shall any Person be eligible to that Office who shall not have attained to the Age of thirty five Years, and been fourteen Years a Resident within the United States.

2.1.12   In Case of the Removal of the President from Office, or of his Death, Resignation, or Inability to discharge the Powers and Duties of the said Office, the Same shall devolve on the Vice President, [Changed; see 25ᵗʰ Amendment.]

2.1.13   [See 25ᵗʰ Amendment]

2.1.14   and the Congress may by Law provide for the Case of Removal, Death, Resignation or Inability, both of the President and Vice President, declaring what Officer shall then act as President, and such Officer shall act accordingly, until the Disability be removed, or a President shall be elected.

2.1.15-18   [See 25ᵗʰ Amendment]

2.1.19   The President shall, at stated Times, receive for his Services, a Compensation, which shall neither be encreased nor diminished during the Period for which he shall have been elected, and he shall not receive within that Period any other Emolument from the United States, or any of them.

2.1.20   Before he enter on the Execution of his Office, he shall take the following Oath or Affirmation:—"I do solemnly swear (or affirm) that I will faithfully execute the Office of President of the United States, and will to the best of my Ability, preserve, protect and defend the Constitution of the United States."

Section 2

2.2.1   The President shall be Commander in Chief of the Army and Navy of the United States, and of the Militia of the several States, when called into the actual Service of the United States; he may require the Opinion, in writing, of the principal Officer in each of the executive Departments, upon any Subject relating to the Duties of their respective Offices, and he shall have Power to grant Reprieves and Pardons for Offences against the United States, except in Cases of Impeachment.

2.2.2   He shall have Power, by and with the Advice and Consent of the Senate, to make Treaties, provided two thirds of the Senators present concur; and he shall nominate, and by and with the Advice and Consent of the Senate, shall appoint Ambassadors, other public Ministers and Consuls, Judges of the supreme Court, and all other Officers of the United States, whose Appointments are not herein otherwise provided for, and which shall be established by Law:

2.2.3   but the Congress may by Law vest the Appointment of such inferior Officers, as they think proper, in the President alone, in the Courts of Law, or in the Heads of Departments.

2.2.4   The President shall have Power to fill up all Vacancies that may happen during the Recess of the Senate, by granting Commissions which shall expire at the End of their next Session.

Section 3

2.3.1 He shall from time to time give to the Congress Information of the State of the Union, and recommend to their Consideration such Measures as he shall judge necessary and expedient;

2.3.2   he may, on extraordinary Occasions, convene both Houses, or either of them, and in Case of Disagreement between them, with Respect to the Time of Adjournment, he may adjourn them to such Time as he shall think proper;

2.3.3   he shall receive Ambassadors and other public Ministers; he shall take Care that the Laws be faithfully executed, and shall Commission all the Officers of the United States.

Section 4

The President, Vice President and all civil Officers of the United States, shall be removed from Office on Impeachment for, and Conviction of, Treason, Bribery, or other high Crimes and Misdemeanors.

Article III

Section 1

The judicial Power of the United States, shall be vested in one supreme Court, and in such inferior Courts as the Congress may from time to time ordain and establish. The Judges, both of the supreme and inferior Courts, shall hold their Offices during good Behaviour, and shall, at stated Times, receive for their Services, a Compensation, which shall not be diminished during their Continuance in Office.

Section 2

3.2.1 The judicial Power shall extend to all Cases, in Law and Equity, arising under this Constitution, the Laws of the United States, and Treaties made, or which shall be made, under their Authority;—to all Cases affecting Ambassadors, other public Ministers and Consuls;—to all Cases of admiralty and maritime Jurisdiction;—to Controversies to which the United States shall be a Party;—to Controversies between two or more States;— between a State and Citizens of another State,—between Citizens of different States,—between Citizens of the same State claiming Lands under Grants of different States, and between a State, or the Citizens thereof, and foreign States, Citizens or Subjects. [Changed by the 11th Amendment.]

3.2.2 In all Cases affecting Ambassadors, other public Ministers and Consuls, and those in which a State shall be Party, the supreme Court shall have original Jurisdiction. In all the other Cases before mentioned, the supreme Court shall have appellate Jurisdiction, both as to Law and Fact, with such Exceptions, and under such Regulations as the Congress shall make.

3.2.3 The Trial of all Crimes, except in Cases of Impeachment, shall be by Jury; and such Trial shall be held in the State where the said Crimes shall have been committed; but when not committed within any State, the Trial shall be at such Place or Places as the Congress may by Law have directed.

Section 3

3.3.1 Treason against the United States, shall consist only in levying War against them, or in adhering to their Enemies, giving them Aid and Comfort. No Person shall be convicted of Treason unless on the Testimony of two Witnesses to the same overt Act, or on Confession in open Court.

3.3.2 The Congress shall have Power to declare the Punishment of Treason, but no Attainder of Treason shall work Corruption of Blood, or Forfeiture except during the Life of the Person attainted.

Article IV

Section 1

Full Faith and Credit shall be given in each State to the public Acts, Records, and judicial Proceedings of every other State. And the Congress may by general Laws prescribe the Manner in which such Acts, Records and Proceedings shall be proved, and the Effect thereof.

Section 2

4.2.1 The Citizens of each State shall be entitled to all Privileges and Immunities of Citizens in the several States.

4.2.2 A Person charged in any State with Treason, Felony, or other Crime, who shall flee from Justice, and be found in another State, shall on Demand of the executive Authority of the State from which he fled, be delivered up, to be removed to the State having Jurisdiction of the Crime.

4.2.3 <u>No Person held to Service or Labour in one State, under the Laws thereof, escaping into another, shall, in Consequence of any Law or Regulation therein, be discharged from such Service or Labour, but shall be delivered up on Claim of the Party to whom such Service or Labour may be due.</u> [Made obsolete by the 13th Amendment.]

Section 3

4.3.1 New States may be admitted by the Congress into this Union; but no new State shall be formed or erected within the Jurisdiction of any other State; nor any State be formed by the Junction of two or more States, or Parts of States, without the Consent of the Legislatures of the States concerned as well as of the Congress.

4.3.2 The Congress shall have Power to dispose of and make all needful Rules and Regulations respecting the Territory or other Property belonging to the United States; and nothing in this Constitution shall be so construed as to Prejudice any Claims of the United States, or of any particular State.

Section 4

The United States shall guarantee to every State in this Union a Republican Form of Government, and shall protect each of them against Invasion; and on Application of the Legislature, or of the Executive (when the Legislature cannot be convened), against domestic Violence.

Article V

Section 1 The Congress, whenever two thirds of both Houses shall deem it necessary, shall propose Amendments to this Constitution, or, on the

Application of the Legislatures of two thirds of the several States, shall call a Convention for proposing Amendments,

Section 2   which, in either Case, shall be valid to all Intents and Purposes, as Part of this Constitution, when ratified by the Legislatures of three fourths of the several States, or by Conventions in three fourths thereof, as the one or the other Mode of Ratification may be proposed by the Congress;

Section 3   Provided that no Amendment which may be made prior to the Year One thousand eight hundred and eight shall in any Manner affect the first and fourth Clauses in the Ninth Section of the first Article; and that no State, without its Consent, shall be deprived of its equal Suffrage in the Senate.

Article VI

Section 1   All Debts contracted and Engagements entered into, before the Adoption of this Constitution, shall be as valid against the United States under this Constitution, as under the Confederation.

Section 2   This Constitution, and the Laws of the United States which shall be made in Pursuance thereof; and all Treaties made, or which shall be made, under the Authority of the United States, shall be the supreme Law of the Land; and the Judges in every State shall be bound thereby, any Thing in the Constitution or Laws of any State to the Contrary notwithstanding.

Section 3   The Senators and Representatives before mentioned, and the Members of the several State Legislatures, and all executive and judicial Officers, both of the United States and of the several States, shall be bound by Oath or Affirmation, to support this Constitution; but no religious Test shall ever be required as a Qualification to any Office or public Trust under the United States.

Article VII

The Ratification of the Conventions of nine States, shall be sufficient for the Establishment of this Constitution between the States so ratifying the Same.

Done in Convention by the Unanimous Consent of the States present the Seventeenth Day of September in the Year of our Lord one thousand seven hundred and Eighty seven and of the Independence of the United

States of America the Twelfth. In witness whereof We have hereunto subscribed our Names,

Go. WASHINGTON — Presidt. and deputy from Virginia

New Hampshire

JOHN LANGDON   NICHOLAS GILMAN

Massachusetts

NATHANIEL GORHAM   RUFUS KING

Connecticut

WM. SAML. JOHNSON   ROGER SHERMAN

New York

ALEXANDER HAMILTON

New Jersey

WIL: LIVINGSTON   DAVID BREARLEY
WM. PATERSON   JONA: DAYTON

Pennsylvania

B FRANKLIN   THOMAS MIFFLIN
ROBT MORRIS   GEO. CLYMER
THOS. FITZ SIMONS   JARED INGERSOLL
JAMES WILSON   GOUV MORRIS

Delaware

GEO: READ   GUNNING BEDFORD jun
JOHN DICKINSON   RICHARD BASSETT
JACO: BROOM

Maryland

JAMES MCHENRY   DAN OF ST THOS. JENIFER
DANL CARROLL

Virginia

JOHN BLAIR   JAMES MADISON jr

North Carolina

WM. BLOUNT   RICHD. DOBBS SPAIGHT
HU WILLIAMSON

South Carolina

J. RUTLEDGE   CHARLES COTESWORTH PINCKNEY
CHARLES PINCKNEY
PIERCE BUTLER

Georgia   WILLIAM FEW   ABR BALDWIN

In Convention Monday, September 17th, 1787.

Present: The States of New Hampshire, Massachusetts, Connecticut, MR. Hamilton from New York, New Jersey, Pennsylvania, Delaware, Maryland, Virginia, North Carolina, South Carolina and Georgia.

Resolved,

That the preceding Constitution be laid before the United States in Congress assembled, and that it is the Opinion of this Convention, that it should afterwards be submitted to a Convention of Delegates, chosen in each State by the People thereof, under the Recommendation of its Legislature, for their Assent and Ratification; and that each Convention assenting to, and ratifying the Same, should give Notice thereof to the United States in Congress assembled. Resolved, That it is the Opinion of this Convention, that as soon as the Conventions of nine States shall have ratified this Constitution, the United States in Congress assembled should fix a Day on which Electors should be appointed by the States which have ratified the same, and a Day on which the Electors should assemble to vote for the President, and the Time and Place for commencing Proceedings under this Constitution. That after such Publication the Electors should be appointed, and the Senators and Representatives elected: That the Electors should meet on the Day fixed for the Election of the President, and should transmit their Votes certified, signed, sealed and directed, as the Constitution requires, to the Secretary of the United States in Congress assembled, that the Senators and Representatives should convene at the Time and Place assigned; that the Senators should appoint a President of the Senate, for the sole purpose of receiving, opening and counting the Votes for President; and, that after he shall be chosen, the Congress, together with the President, should, without Delay, proceed to execute this Constitution.

By the Unanimous Order of the Convention

Go. WASHINGTON — Presidt.
W. JACKSON Secretary

Amendments to the Constitution

On September 25, 1789, the First Congress of the United States proposed the first 12 amendments to the Constitution. The original 'Bill of Rights', all 12 Articles, is displayed in the National Archives Museum. Ten of the proposed 12 amendments were ratified by three-fourths of the states by December 15, 1791. In 1992, over 200 years after the first states ratified it, Article 2 was ratified as the 27th Amendment. Article 1 has been ratified by 11 states; <u>Our First Right</u> is our effort to gain ratification by 27 more states required to make it the 28th Amendment: no U.S. congressional district shall contain more than 50,000 persons.

Congress of the United States begun and held at the City of New-York, on Wednesday the fourth of March, one thousand seven hundred and eighty nine.

THE Conventions of a number of the States, having at the time of their adopting the Constitution, expressed a desire, in order to prevent misconstruction or abuse of its powers, that further declaratory and restrictive clauses should be added: And as extending the ground of public confidence in the Government, will best ensure the beneficent ends of its institution.

RESOLVED by the Senate and House of Representatives of the United States of America, in Congress assembled, two thirds of both Houses concurring, that the following Articles be proposed to the Legislatures of the several States, as amendments to the Constitution of the United States, all, or any of which Articles, when ratified by three fourths of the said Legislatures, to be valid to all intents and purposes, as part of the said Constitution; viz.

ARTICLES in addition to, and Amendment of the Constitution of the United States of America, proposed by Congress, and ratified by the Legislatures of the several States, pursuant to the fifth Article of the original Constitution.

[The following is a transcription of the first ten amendments to the Constitution in their original form. Ratified December 15, 1791 they are restrictions on the servants, but are erroneously called 'Bill of Rights'.]

Amendment I

Congress shall make no law respecting an establishment of religion, or prohibiting the free exercise thereof; or abridging the freedom of speech, or of the press; or the right of the people peaceably to assemble, and to petition the Government for a redress of grievances.

Amendment II

A well regulated Militia, being necessary to the security of a free State, the right of the people to keep and bear Arms, shall not be infringed.

Amendment III

No Soldier shall, in time of peace be quartered in any house, without the consent of the Owner, nor in time of war, but in a manner to be prescribed by law.

Amendment IV

The right of the people to be secure in their persons, houses, papers, and effects, against unreasonable searches and seizures, shall not be violated, and no Warrants shall issue, but upon probable cause, supported by Oath or affirmation, and particularly describing the place to be searched, and the persons or things to be seized.

Amendment V

No person shall be held to answer for a capital, or otherwise infamous crime, unless on a presentment or indictment of a Grand Jury, except in cases arising in the land or naval forces, or in the Militia, when in actual service in time of War or public danger; nor shall any person be subject for the same offence to be twice put in jeopardy of life or limb; nor shall be compelled in any criminal case to be a witness against himself, nor be deprived of life, liberty, or property, without due process of law; nor shall private property be taken for public use, without just compensation.

Amendment VI

In all criminal prosecutions, the accused shall enjoy the right to a speedy and public trial, by an impartial jury of the State and district wherein the crime shall have been committed, which district shall have been previously ascertained by law, and to be informed of the nature and cause of the accusation; to be confronted with the witnesses against him; to have compulsory process for obtaining witnesses in his favor, and to have the Assistance of Counsel for his defence.

Amendment VII

In Suits at common law, where the value in controversy shall exceed twenty dollars, the right of trial by jury shall be preserved, and no fact tried by a jury, shall be otherwise re-examined in any Court of the United States, than according to the rules of the common law.

Amendment VIII

Excessive bail shall not be required, nor excessive fines imposed, nor cruel and unusual punishments inflicted.

Amendment IX

The enumeration in the Constitution, of certain rights, shall not be construed to deny or disparage others retained by the people.

Amendment X

The powers not delegated to the United States by the Constitution, nor prohibited by it to the States, are reserved to the States respectively, or to the people.

Amendment XI

Passed by Congress March 4, 1794. Ratified February 7, 1795.

Article III, section 2, of the Constitution was modified by amendment 11.

The Judicial power of the United States shall not be construed to extend to any suit in law or equity, commenced or prosecuted against one of the United States by Citizens of another State, or by Citizens or Subjects of any Foreign State.

Amendment XII

Passed by Congress December 9, 1803. Ratified June 15, 1804.

A portion of Article II, section 1 of the Constitution was superseded by the 12th amendment.

The Electors shall meet in their respective states and vote by ballot for President and Vice-President, one of whom, at least, shall not be an inhabitant of the same state with themselves; they shall name in their ballots the person voted for as President, and in distinct ballots the person voted for as Vice-President, and they shall make distinct lists of all persons voted for as President, and of all persons voted for as Vice-President, and of the number of votes for each, which lists they shall sign and certify, and transmit sealed to the seat of the government of the United States, directed to the President of the Senate; — the President of the Senate shall, in the presence of the Senate and House of Representatives, open all the certificates and the votes shall then be counted; — The person having the greatest number of votes for President, shall be the President, if such number be a majority of the whole number of Electors appointed; and if no person have such majority, then from the persons having the highest numbers not exceeding three on the list of those voted for as President, the House of Representatives shall choose immediately, by ballot, the President. But in choosing the President, the votes shall be taken by states, the representation from each state having one vote; a quorum for this purpose shall consist of a member or members from two-thirds of the states, and a majority of all the states shall be necessary to a choice. [And if the House of Representatives shall not choose a President whenever the right of choice shall devolve upon them, before the fourth day of March next following, then the Vice-President shall act as President, as in case of the death or other constitutional disability of the President. –]* The person having the greatest number of votes as Vice-President, shall be the Vice-President, if such number be a majority of the whole number of Electors appointed, and if no person have a majority, then from the two highest numbers on the list, the Senate shall choose the Vice-

President; a quorum for the purpose shall consist of two-thirds of the whole number of Senators, and a majority of the whole number shall be necessary to a choice. But no person constitutionally ineligible to the office of President shall be eligible to that of Vice-President of the United States.

*Superseded by section 3 of the 20th amendment.

Amendment XIII

Passed by Congress January 31, 1865. Ratified December 6, 1865.

A portion of Article IV, section 2, of the Constitution was superseded by the 13th amendment.

Section 1.

Neither slavery nor involuntary servitude, except as a punishment for crime whereof the party shall have been duly convicted, shall exist within the United States, or any place subject to their jurisdiction.

Section 2.

Congress shall have power to enforce this article by appropriate legislation.

Amendment XIV

Passed by Congress June 13, 1866. Ratified July 9, 1868.

Article I, section 2, of the Constitution was modified by section 2 of the 14th amendment.

Section 1.

All persons born or naturalized in the United States, and subject to the jurisdiction thereof, are citizens of the United States and of the State wherein they reside. No State shall make or enforce any law which shall abridge the privileges or immunities of citizens of the United States; nor shall any State deprive any person of life, liberty, or property, without due process of law; nor deny to any person within its jurisdiction the equal protection of the laws.

Section 2.

Representatives shall be apportioned among the several States according to their respective numbers, counting the whole number of persons in each State, excluding Indians not taxed. But when the right to vote at any election for the choice of electors for President and Vice-President of the United States, Representatives in Congress, the Executive and Judicial officers of a State, or the members of the Legislature thereof, is denied to any of the male inhabitants of such State, being twenty-one years of age,* and citizens of the United States, or in any way abridged, except for participation in rebellion, or other crime, the basis of representation therein shall be reduced in the proportion which the number of such male citizens shall bear to the whole number of male citizens twenty-one years of age in such State.

Section 3.

No person shall be a Senator or Representative in Congress, or elector of President and Vice-President, or hold any office, civil or military, under the United States, or under any State, who, having previously taken an oath, as a member of Congress, or as an officer of the United States, or as a member of any State legislature, or as an executive or judicial officer of any State, to support the Constitution of the United States, shall have engaged in insurrection or rebellion against the same, or given aid or comfort to the enemies thereof. But Congress may by a vote of two-thirds of each House, remove such disability.

Section 4.

The validity of the public debt of the United States, authorized by law, including debts incurred for payment of pensions and bounties for services in suppressing insurrection or rebellion, shall not be questioned. But neither the United States nor any State shall assume or pay any debt or obligation incurred in aid of insurrection or rebellion against the United States, or any claim for the loss or emancipation of any slave; but all such debts, obligations and claims shall be held illegal and void.

Section 5.

The Congress shall have the power to enforce, by appropriate legislation, the provisions of this article.

Changed by section 1 of the 26th amendment.

Amendment XV

Passed by Congress February 26, 1869. Ratified February 3, 1870.

Section 1.

The right of citizens of the United States to vote shall not be denied or abridged by the United States or by any State on account of race, color, or previous condition of servitude.

Section 2.

The Congress shall have the power to enforce this article by appropriate legislation.

Amendment XVI

Passed by Congress July 2, 1909. Ratified February 3, 1913.

Article I, section 9 of the Constitution was supposedly (arguably) modified by amendment 16.

The Congress shall have power to lay and collect taxes on incomes, from whatever source derived, without apportionment among the several States, and without regard to any census or enumeration.

Amendment XVII

Passed by Congress May 13, 1912. Ratified April 8, 1913.

Article I, section 3, of the Constitution was modified by the 17th amendment.

The Senate of the United States shall be composed of two Senators from each State, elected by the people thereof, for six years; and each Senator shall have one vote. The electors in each State shall have the qualifications requisite for electors of the most numerous branch of the State legislatures.

When vacancies happen in the representation of any State in the Senate, the executive authority of such State shall issue writs of election to fill such vacancies: *Provided*, That the legislature of any State may empower the executive thereof to make temporary appointments until the people fill the vacancies by election as the legislature may direct.

This amendment shall not be so construed as to affect the election or term of any Senator chosen before it becomes valid as part of the Constitution.

Amendment XVIII

Passed by Congress December 18, 1917. Ratified January 16, 1919. Repealed by amendment 21.

Section 1.

After one year from the ratification of this article the manufacture, sale, or transportation of intoxicating liquors within, the importation thereof into, or the exportation thereof from the United States and all territory subject to the jurisdiction thereof for beverage purposes is hereby prohibited.

Section 2.

The Congress and the several States shall have concurrent power to enforce this article by appropriate legislation.

Section 3.

This article shall be inoperative unless it shall have been ratified as an amendment to the Constitution by the legislatures of the several States, as provided in the Constitution, within seven years from the date of the submission hereof to the States by the Congress.

Amendment XIX

Passed by Congress June 4, 1919. Ratified August 18, 1920.

The right of citizens of the United States to vote shall not be denied or abridged by the United States or by any State on account of sex.

Congress shall have power to enforce this article by appropriate legislation.

Amendment XX

Passed by Congress March 2, 1932. Ratified January 23, 1933.

Article I, section 4, of the Constitution was modified by section 2 of this amendment. In addition, a portion of the 12th amendment was superseded by section 3.

Section 1.

The terms of the President and the Vice President shall end at noon on the 20th day of January, and the terms of Senators and Representatives at noon on the 3d day of January, of the years in which such terms would have ended if this article had not been ratified; and the terms of their successors shall then begin.

Section 2.

The Congress shall assemble at least once in every year, and such meeting shall begin at noon on the 3d day of January, unless they shall by law appoint a different day.

Section 3.

If, at the time fixed for the beginning of the term of the President, the President elect shall have died, the Vice President elect shall become President. If a President shall not have been chosen before the time fixed for the beginning of his term, or if the President elect shall have failed to qualify, then the Vice

President elect shall act as President until a President shall have qualified; and the Congress may by law provide for the case wherein neither a President elect nor a Vice President elect shall have qualified, declaring who shall then act as President, or the manner in which one who is to act shall be selected, and such person shall act accordingly until a President or Vice President shall have qualified.

Section 4.

The Congress may by law provide for the case of the death of any of the persons from whom the House of Representatives may choose a President whenever the right of choice shall have devolved upon them, and for the case of the death of any of the persons from whom the Senate may choose a Vice President whenever the right of choice shall have devolved upon them.

Section 5.

Sections 1 and 2 shall take effect on the 15th day of October following the ratification of this article.

Section 6.

This article shall be inoperative unless it shall have been ratified as an amendment to the Constitution by the legislatures of three-fourths of the several States within seven years from the date of its submission.

Amendment XXI

Passed by Congress February 20, 1933. Ratified December 5, 1933.

Section 1.

The eighteenth article of amendment to the Constitution of the United States is hereby repealed.

Section 2.

The transportation or importation into any State, Territory, or possession of the United States for delivery or use therein of intoxicating liquors, in violation of the laws thereof, is hereby prohibited.

Section 3.

This article shall be inoperative unless it shall have been

ratified as an amendment to the Constitution by conventions in the several States, as provided in the Constitution, within seven years from the date of the submission hereof to the States by the Congress.

Amendment XXII

Passed by Congress March 21, 1947. Ratified February 27, 1951.

Section 1.

No person shall be elected to the office of the President more than twice, and no person who has held the office of President, or acted as President, for more than two years of a term to which some other person was elected President shall be elected to the office of the President more than once. But this Article shall not apply to any person holding the office of President when this Article was proposed by the Congress, and shall not prevent any person who may be holding the office of President, or acting as President, during the term within which this Article becomes operative from holding the office of President or acting as President during the remainder of such term.

Section 2.

This article shall be inoperative unless it shall have been ratified as an amendment to the Constitution by the legislatures of three-fourths of the several States within seven years from the date of its submission to the States by the Congress.

Amendment XXIII

Passed by Congress June 16, 1960. Ratified March 29, 1961.

Section 1.

The District constituting the seat of Government of the United States shall appoint in such manner as the Congress may direct: A number of electors of President and Vice President equal to the whole number of Senators and Representatives in Congress to which the District would be entitled if it were a State, but in no event more than the least populous State; they shall be in addition to those appointed by the States, but they shall be considered, for the purposes of the election of President and Vice President, to be electors appointed by a State; and they shall meet in the District and perform such duties as provided by the twelfth article of amendment.

Section 2.

The Congress shall have power to enforce this article by appropriate legislation.

Amendment XXIV

Passed by Congress August 27, 1962. Ratified January 23, 1964.

Section 1.

The right of citizens of the United States to vote in any primary or other election for President or Vice President, for electors for President or Vice President, or for Senator or Representative in Congress, shall not be denied or abridged by the United States or any State by reason of failure to pay any poll tax or other tax.

Section 2.

The Congress shall have power to enforce this article by appropriate legislation.

Amendment XXV

Passed by Congress July 6, 1965. Ratified February 10, 1967.

Article II, section 1, of the Constitution was affected by the 25th amendment.

Section 1.

In case of the removal of the President from office or of his death or resignation, the Vice President shall become President.

Section 2.

Whenever there is a vacancy in the office of the Vice President, the President shall nominate a Vice President who shall take office upon confirmation by a majority vote of both Houses of Congress.

Section 3.

Whenever the President transmits to the President pro tempore of the Senate and the Speaker of the House of Representatives his written declaration that he is unable to discharge the powers and duties of his office, and until he transmits to them a written declaration to the contrary, such powers and duties shall be discharged by the Vice President as Acting President.

Section 4.

Whenever the Vice President and a majority of either the principal officers of the executive departments or of such other body as Congress may by law provide, transmit to the President pro tempore of the Senate and the Speaker of the House of Representatives their written declaration that the President is unable to discharge the powers and duties of his office, the Vice President shall immediately assume the powers and duties of the office as Acting President.

Thereafter, when the President transmits to the President pro tempore of the Senate and the Speaker of the House of Representatives his written declaration that no inability exists, he shall resume the powers and duties of his office unless the Vice President and a majority of either the principal officers of the executive department or of such other body as Congress may by law provide, transmit within four days to the President pro tempore of the Senate and the Speaker of the House of Representatives their written declaration that the President is unable to discharge the powers and duties of his office. Thereupon Congress shall decide the issue, assembling within forty-eight hours for that purpose if not in session. If the Congress, within twenty-one days after receipt of the latter written declaration, or, if Congress is not in session, within twenty-one days after Congress is required to assemble, determines by two-thirds vote of both Houses that the President is unable to discharge the powers and duties of his office, the Vice President shall continue to discharge the same as Acting President; otherwise, the President shall resume the powers and duties of his office.

Amendment XXVI

Passed by Congress March 23, 1971. Ratified July 1, 1971.

Amendment 14, section 2, of the Constitution was modified by section 1 of the 26th amendment.

Section 1.

The right of citizens of the United States, who are eighteen years of age or older, to vote shall not be denied or abridged by the United States or by any State on account of age.

Section 2.

The Congress shall have power to enforce this article by appropriate legislation.

Amendment XXVII

Passed by Congress Sept. 25, 1789. Ratified May 7, 1992.

No law, varying the compensation for the services of the Senators and Representatives, shall take effect, until an election of Representatives shall have intervened.

Recommended Reading
(A Liberty Library)

When asked, *"Can you give me an essential reading list for Christians and other Tactical Civics™ members?"*, our staff could list several hundred books. But we will be selective and explain a little about books that I call 'vital titles'.

Besides obvious bedrock – the Bible, Shakespeare's Works, *Pilgrim's Progress,* C.S. Lewis's *Chronicles of Narnia* and other great novels, this Liberty Library introduces 72 works that transformed my thinking; that shocked me at the lies I had believed all my life. This is a great reading compendium for anyone who wants the equivalent of an undergraduate Liberal Arts and a Political Science degree.

Edmund Burke's dictum, *"(t)he only thing necessary for the triumph of evil is that good men do nothing"*, keeps repeating itself because as philosopher George Santayana said, *"Those who refuse to learn the lessons of history are doomed to repeat them."* With our civilization crumbling at every turn, where will it all end? Our members know my dictum, *The tombstone of a civilization can be laid at that point where truth is no longer defended, because it cannot be known.*

The U.S. Constitution is the Supreme Law of the Land, yet D.C. organized crime considers itself untouchable. Much of the world hates us, and we can't figure out why. The rich get richer, and the productive American increasingly joins the ranks of the poor and unemployed.

In this book, you learned how the Deep Axis has run our republic for at least six generations, with complete secrecy, _regardless of elections_. To restore America, We The People must take informed, coordinated tactical action. That means first we need basic education – such as this book! This is no longer available in most schools or colleges. But we need more; we need to expose the lies on which the 'culture war' is being waged, because truth _can_ be known.

This reading list makes an excellent reading program for an intensive 3-year regimen or a more leisurely 5-7 year pace. Reading the classics is fine; but our times call for more practical education. Having read all of the books listed here, an American will be in the top one-tenth of 1% of our population in American history, ethics, economics, geopolitics, political economy and more. *The Harvard Classics can't do that.*

During the 20th century, our republic was transformed into a plundering empire populated by historically clueless 'voters' who commute to their jobs every day to pay the bills, their apathy granting legitimacy to staggering international crimes.

Since most people will not read 72 works over the next few years, I list the 16 most vital works first (15 books and an online pamphlet and white paper). Pick the work that most intrigues you, and read it with highlighter in hand; when you finish that one, read another. Move at your own pace and you will find these great books growing on you.

As you later review highlighted passages, life lessons emerge and a pattern comes together as you begin to see through media propaganda and grasp the lies that steer American policy – especially Washington DC organized crime and its wars.

Given the duty before us, these 72 works will vault you over walls of ignorance about our history and Constitution; about money, credit, and banking; about how Israel and the Deep State used the boogeyman of communism and Islamic jihad to run America from behind the scenes with the help of mega-church pastors. You will begin to clearly see the fallen state of our Republic and the gullible, powerless Christian church. These books won't make you a pencil-necked geek; *they will impart real wisdom.*

If you believe that the Internet is all we need because it is opening minds and threatening tyrants all over the world, Egyptian dictator Mubarak proved in 2011 that government can shut down a country's Internet access. It has not happened fully yet in America, but see how far Big Tech has gone in that direction already! As Tim Wu explains in the book *Master Switch*, Big Tech can go much further still. As the movie *The Book of Eli* suggests, when civilization falls, printed books will become our most valuable treasures.

For less than the cost of two college courses, this Liberty Library will place you among that rare species: *the informed, self-governing American.*

The 15 Most Vital Books (and Two Online Resources)

The American Deep State is Peter Dale Scott's best book yet, of over 40 books published over 40+ years, exposing the Deep State. The author has spent his adult life laying a trail of primary-source evidence for the shocking, revealing assertions in his books. The Deep State refers to the banking, war, and oil industries together with the 'intelligence' industry in all its secret agencies. Every foreign war the USA has fought has been instigated by, and directly benefited, the Deep State. This shadow government is unelected, unaccountable, invisible to productive Americans, and ruthless. It first sought to hijack the Constitution through Hamilton and Clay, finally succeeding with Lincoln and ever since. *If you read only one book on the list, make it this one.*

The Sovereign Individual by James Davidson & Lord William Rees-Mogg explains the shake-up of nations introduced by the Internet, much like the impact that the movable-type printing press had in medieval times. Even now, 18 years after the first edition of this book, the world's institutions have not come to grips with the Internet. But the news is daily illustrating the acceleration of revolution against wicked and bloated industries, institutions, and governments. As institutions attempt to deal with newly-liberated humanity, the authors posit that informed individuals and small businesses will win, and fascism (big governments plus industry) will lose. AmericaAgain! Trust agrees with this assessment, and the TACTICAL CIVICS™ Training Center is our antidote to anything the evil ones can throw at our civilization.

I will here clarify that we do not subscribe to the anarchist school of thought touting 'sovereign citizen' nonsense. We The People are only collectively the sovereign of this republic, and only as we operate within the stipulated bounds that we ourselves set in the U.S. Constitution.

Hamilton's Curse: How Jefferson's Arch Enemy Betrayed the American Revolution – and What it Means for Americans Today by Thomas J. DiLorenzo (2009) is a long-overdue correction of the record about Alexander Hamilton. Although a courageous hero of our War for Independence, Hamilton was a wily tactician in laying the foundation for America's corrupt banking industry, and perhaps the most destructive 'founding father'. DiLorenzo debunks the long-held legends that deify Hamilton, exposing the man for what he was: a conniving, self-absorbed con artist. In the final chapter, *Ending the Curse,* I find nothing upon which to disagree with the author except that, like most authors offering reform proposals, he fails to offer a mechanism to *enact* his solutions.

The Problem With Lincoln by Thomas J. DiLorenzo debunks the legends offered as reasons for Lincoln's war. The author exposes why Lincoln suspended *habeas corpus,* why he imprisoned thousands of Northern war dissenters, and why he shut down hundreds of opposition newspapers. He also exposes Lincoln's real economic agenda. If you wonder why schools don't teach this, understand that the uber-wealthy love their riches more than God, and are as ruthless as they are treacherous, smiles and all.

Lincoln's Marxists: Marxism in the Civil War by Walter D. Kennedy and Al Benson, Jr. is another of those books that convinced me that I was cheated even in my expensive private education. The book exposes Union army generals that were Marxists, and the Marxist ideas that informed the Lincoln administration. I voted GOP for 25 years because I thought the GOP was the party that would conserve the Constitution. How little I knew about the history of the GOP's founding and its Red Roots! Rather than the party of individual liberty, it has always been the power center for American mercantilists and bankers.

A Century of War by John Denson; an exhaustively-documented account of how Lincoln deliberately suckered the South into war at the behest of Northern mercantilists, directly against the unanimous counsel of his cabinet. Denson omits the crucial Spanish American War – where America was transformed into a world empire – but *The War Lovers* (see below) offers that vital story.

Overthrow: America's Century of Regime Change from Hawaii to Iraq by veteran news correspondent Stephen Kinzer is the best single-volume historical survey I can find covering the U.S. government's attempts at empire. This fast-moving little book is a series of vignettes of U.S. government takeovers of Hawaii, Guam, the Philippines, Puerto Rico and countless others including botched invasions of Mexico, Venezuela, Panama, and sweet spots around the globe, all long before the present invasion of Iraq and Afghanistan. Bottom line: for 125 years, small nations and islands of the world have been mere real estate assets for American corporations and military, violating our Constitution every time.

Drugs, Oil and War by Peter Dale Scott is a more narrowly-focused explanation of how the Deep State planned and executed American foreign policy and wars since World War II. Many Americans on the left and right are finally realizing that the bankers and war industry are joined at the hip. But in this book, Scott adds the missing pieces, demonstrating how the oil industry and CIA-spawned drug cartels from Latin America to Southeast Asia, and then the Middle East, made the trap complete.

The New American Militarism: How Americans Are Seduced by War is unlike 'anti-war' books, which I do not generally care for. Andrew Bacevich is a former U.S. Army colonel, Vietnam veteran, West Point professor of history and international relations. This Christian offers a logical,

214

historically accurate analysis of what President Eisenhower dubbed the Military-Industrial Complex. Patriotic Christians, especially active military or veterans, can discover that while the U.S. military industry outspends all other militaries on earth combined, it also opposes the positions of Washington, Jefferson, and Madison. Bottom line: veterans and civilians need to reconsider what they were taught; the Deep State programs America's military subculture to violate our Supreme Law as it directs the foreign policy of our republic.

Against Our Better Judgment by Alison Weir is only 93 pages of body text, followed by 107 pages of endnotes. With most professional academics being paid shills of the Deep State and its private foundations, a reader should not look for truth and authors' credentials to necessarily jibe. This book is copiously documented, with almost 375 references. Does Israel control Washington DC? Read, and decide.

JFK-9/11: 50 Years of the Deep State I disagree with his dismissal of Old Testament Scripture, but Frenchman Laurent Guyenot is a Renaissance man with degrees in engineering and Medieval Studies who worked in the arms industry and also authored a study on the psychological and social damage of mass pornography. In this book, Guyenot offers an even better analysis of 9/11 than Ruppert's book, in that he demonstrates the Deep State sponsorship of both the JFK assassination and the 9/11 attacks. Bottom line: the smoking gun of both Deep State actions leads to the Israeli Mossad and the CIA.

The Fourth Turning: What the Cycles of History Tell Us About America's Next Rendezvous With Destiny by William Strauss and Neil Howe is a smaller, more exciting 1998 follow-up to their 1991 book _Generations: The History of America's Future._ In this national bestseller, Strauss and Howe illustrate the historical 80- to 100-year cycle called a _saecula,_ further divided into five 20-year periods/generations. The authors call each transition between these generations, a _turning._ Thus in 1998, the authors accurately predicted the fourth turning of our saecula; a crisis period from 2005-2015.

This was partially fulfilled in the Ron Paul Revolution, TEA Party movement, 'Great Recession', staggering collapse of the U.S. Dollar, and increasing mistrust of institutions leading to the election of Trump. Tracing 'heroic' generations back to pre-colonial times, the authors conclude that by 2015, Americans in the 'Baby Boomer' and 'Thirteener' generations would step up to meet the crisis. They thought they did, by electing Trump, but didn't know enough civics to realize that presidents can't do the People's job. The bottom line of this book is still correct:

today's Chicken Little refrain is dead wrong, and we believe that Tactical Civics™ is the most likely contender for the major, long-term return to responsibility that Strauss & Howe predicted.

The Lost World of Genesis One: Ancient Cosmology and the Origins Debate by John H. Walton, who has a PhD in Hebrew and is a professor of Old Testament Theology at Wheaton, is one of the most liberating books I have ever read! I mean this sincerely. This book smashes the Young-Old Earth Creation debate; smashes it flat, into irrelevance, for begging the question of material origins. His thesis consists of a series of propositions, culminating in the hypothesis that the creation account in Genesis is a description of the universe's construction as a temple of God, not as material 'stuff'. A few high points...

First: There is no reason that God would have communicated 'scientifically-correct' data about His creation to simple, ancient people. In other words, no statement in the Bible conveys scientific truth that the biblical writers would not have already known.

Second: Some statements in the Bible convey cosmological and physiological notions that do not comport with science; for instance, 'domed' cosmology has no scientific merit but it worked well for primitive ancients. Some of the words translated as 'mind' in English actually mean 'entrails' in the Hebrew; people in those days (and for centuries after) believed that emotions and feelings derived from the guts. Walton suggests that God didn't correct them; there was no point, in their place and time. We would not waste our time today trying to argue that our guts are the seat of our thoughts and emotions, yet that is how Young Earth creationists and Intelligent Design apologists defend the creation account!

Third: Walton explains how the ontology of the creation account is not material but *functional*. To illustrate, he compares a chair to a corporation; a chair is 'created' by the nature of its *material* status, but a corporation is 'created' by its *functional* status; on pg. 26: *"In a functional ontology, to bring something into existence would require giving it a function or a role in an ordered system, rather than giving it material property."* Because the entities created in the Genesis account are material entities, we presume that Genesis must be a material ontology. This is a senseless assumption, as Walton explains with contextual evidence of many ancient Near Eastern creation accounts and analyzing Hebrew words like *bara*. Bottom line: the whole Origins debate is a false dilemma.

Constitutional Income: Do You have Any? by former Idaho state representative and structural engineer Phil Hart is the meticulously-documented story of how from 1909-1913, Congress conspired to create the largest, longest-running financial crime in history. Featuring facsimile copies of congressional floor debate, private memoranda, and newspaper articles of the period, this book will make every Taxpayer furious, and give ammunition to every law-abiding Nontaxpayer among today's estimated 67 million non-filers. Bottom line: all of that corruption and pork isn't magic; follow the money.

A Tax Honesty Primer is my little book on congress' check-skimming operation. Having read the Internal Revenue Code, countless court rulings and cases, seven books on Tax Honesty, and dozens of websites over two years, I then became a law-abiding Nontaxpayer in 1994. I couldn't find in one place enough information to take action and expose the corruption, so I created _A Tax Honesty Primer_ as the first step in Taxpayer due diligence, so that others can avoid years of wading through tax protester theories. The book is not my opinion or 'position'; it's a compendium of easily verifiable facts, court rulings, Tax Code sections, federal regulations, jury verdicts, IRS commissioner and IRS employee statements, and well-settled law. I was confronted 14 times by IRS over the first decade as a law-abiding Nontaxpayer, and all 14 times, they went home empty-handed and have left me alone for the 18 years since.

Tax Honesty is wonderful defense for the self-employed (it's all but impossible if you work for someone else, especially a large company); but playing defense will never arrest Congress' crimes. Until our Indictment Engine™ becomes our permanent citizen mechanism to arrest organized crime in Congress, at least Tax Honesty offers short-term relief; like household secession from Congress' corruption.

The Official Counterfeiter is a 36-page free cartoon booklet created in 1969 by Vic Lockman; the clearest explanation I've ever read, of Congress' money and banking crimes on behalf of the corrupt banking industry.

http://scripturalscrutinydotcom.files.wordpress.com/2012/01/the-official-counterfeiter-biblical-economics.pdf

War, Oil, Drugs, Banking, and The Deep State

The Devil's Chessboard by David Talbot is the story of the Dulles brothers (Allen and John Foster), creators and evil masterminds of the CIA. As Talbot exposes the characters of these two sociopath brothers and their evil, world-shifting chicanery, you begin each chapter asking yourself how the American People failed to stop these criminals. But you cannot stop what you do not see. You begin to understand that the very existence of the CIA – like the FBI, DOJ, NSA, DIA and others – is criminal. Nowhere authorized in the Constitution, and in fact, a 'shadow government', as described in countless whistleblower books exposing the criminality of these agencies.

Gold Warriors by Sterling and Peggy Seagraves is one of the most fascinating books I have ever read. After years and years of painstaking journalistic investigations and collecting scores of first-person testimony and actual photographs of the caves filled with gold bars and crates upon crates of gold bonds, the intrepid couple present the story of the most fascinating story in history of gold and war.

After World War II, the DC government captured and seized 288,000 metric tons of gold, plundered from Europe and China by Japan and Germany, called 'Yamashita's Gold' and 'Black Eagle Gold', respectively. How was it located, and by whom? How was it transported, and to what location? What happened to this astounding hoard of gold after the DC cabal seized it? What have congresses done about it, since this is the constitutional purview of Congress? A fascinating detective story, illustrating that Washington DC is truly the most ruthless, lawless city-state in modern world history.

The Transparent Cabal: The Neoconservative Agenda, War in the Middle East, and the National Interest of Israel by Stephen Sniegoski, is a more detailed dive into the American war industry's operations in the Middle East. If you first read Alison Weir's book, _Against Our Better Judgment_ (see above), you will understand who created the modern political state of Israel, that also created a domestic PR campaign in thousands of American churches, twisting Scripture to make the case that the anti-Christian -- indeed atheistic -- political state of our day in Israel, is actually the remnant of God described in the New Testament.

Sniegoski goes much deeper into mechanics of geopolitical crime, and the DC cabal's operations. If you want to understand how and why powerful pro-Israel neoconservatives in the U.S. misled Americans and used the complicit Dubya Bush (of the Bush oil family!) to order the U.S. invasion of Iraq in 2003, and how they persuaded the U.S. Congress to give Dubya the (supposed) authority to order the invasion, read this outstanding book. Prepare to be very angry...but as with dozens of the books on this list: once you know the players and discover their massive financial motivation, the history of America's foreign wars (ALL of them) turns out to be just a series of pirate stories.

Myths, Lies and Oil Wars by William Engdahl is probably the best book if you want to learn about the theory of 'Abyssal Abiotic Petroleum Origins' (i.e., petroleum doesn't come from dead plants and dinosaurs – so-called 'fossil fuel' – but from deep in the earth and is practically limitless) and to grasp U.S. military industry geopolitics in the Middle East, Russia and China over the past few decades.

The Deep, Hot Biosphere: The Myth of Fossil Fuels by Dr. Thomas Gold was plagiarized from the Russian-Ukrainian theory of Abyssal Abiotic Petroleum Origins – the theory that there exists an enormous store of hydrocarbons upwelling from deep within the earth that can provide us with gas and petroleum for as long as man lives on Earth. In this 1999 book, Dr. Gold copied the original work of the Ukrainian and Russian pioneers to debunk the myth that petroleum had its genesis in dinosaurs and old plants. The theory is thus called the theory of 'abiotic oil' and includes three controversial, potentially earth-shattering positions:

First: Below the surface of the earth is a biosphere of greater mass and volume than the sum of all living things on all continents and in all oceans.

Second: The inhabitants of this subterranean biosphere are not plants or animals but heat-loving bacteria that survive on hydrocarbons (natural gas & petroleum).

Third: Most hydrocarbons on Earth are not the byproduct of biological debris ('fossil fuels'), but were a common constituent of the materials from which Earth itself was formed.

If all of these scientists are correct, the implications are astounding, and disastrous for the oil industry. This would also explode the environmentalist so-called 'Peak Oil' theory – which went the way of the dinosaurs in 2012 with the GAO reported that the Green River Formation alone contains more recoverable petroleum than the entire previously-known world oil reserves.

Further down in this list, I link to a white paper by J.F. Kenney, senior geologist at Gas Resources Corporation in Houston, listing most of the Russian and Ukrainian scientists that hypothesized abyssal abiotic petroleum origins' long before Dr. Gold plagiarized their work to claim in the American scientific media that it was his own. Besides the Ukrainian and Russian originators of the theory, a growing body of supporting

219

evidence is being produced by American scientists like Jean Whelan at Woods Hole Oceanographic Institute; Mahlon Kennicutt, Professor of Chemical Oceanography at Texas A&M; Giora Proskurowski, professor of Oceanography at University of Washington, and others.

Crossing the Rubicon: The Decline of the American Empire at the End of the Age of Oil by Michael Ruppert is the only 9/11 book I include, and this will be a long synopsis because the 9/11 debacle is important – not for the tragedy itself, but because of the major shift in government and media propaganda that took place over the 20 years since that 'New Pearl Harbor'.

Erasmus of Rotterdam said, *"In the land of the blind, the one-eyed man is king".* We needn't know everything about the 911 debacle; what we do know is more than sufficient to know it was a massive government fraud on the American people.

A fifth grader in possession of the facts grasps this general concept: powerful men and institutions have influenced governments throughout history. The 160-year pattern in America since Fort Sumter is: first we experience a catalyst attack either of unexplained origin or out of proportion to the war that follows. Next, federal government and its industry allies ratchet their power; government gains new ground against its own population, then holds the new ground to gain further illicit powers. This is the one-way advance of tyranny.

Ruppert's book is the most credible of twenty-two books and three videos I reviewed over nine years relating to the 9/11 debacle. I no longer spend time on this issue; as I said above, I only include this book because that hoax catalyzed American domestic and foreign policy for the foreseeable future. The government's official story and its media hacks must be hooted off the stage!

We did a podcast 11/11/18, *Collateral Damage (Beyond Treason)* discussing a report by E.P. Heidner, the only surviving member of the Office of Naval Intelligence task force that was investigating George Bush Senior's shady deal with Russian oligarchs that Heidner shows was the most likely reason for the 9/11 operation. Heidner's ONI task force's offices just happened to be located precisely where that cruise missile hit the Pentagon on 9/11. Just coincidence!

Yet it's pointless to argue about 9/11 itself; TACTICAL CIVICS™ can empower the American people to beat the predator-parasite horde at last: self-governing citizens and resurgent sovereign States can *enforce* the Constitution and arrest the long pattern of government-corporate-military corruption using a legal choke-collar on each individual member of Congress. As we work on a new long-term arrest mechanism, there's no sense arguing about one of the criminals' last in a 120-year series of frauds, since 9/11 was followed by the Russiagate-Shampeachment-BLAntifa-Chinavirus-Election Steal overthrow of anything even *resembling* legitimate government. Those who still don't get it are beyond help.

Whoever our domestic enemies are, they use Congress for financing and legislative enablement. The typical globalist player's goal is always to become insanely wealthy, and Congress is their key. After every war, they get us arguing among ourselves for decades about who caused the fire so we won't stop to think about trapping the kingpins who hired the arsonist.

I am one of several hundred engineers, scientists, and architects who signed on at *Architects and Engineers for 911 Truth* not because I care to argue about this latest in a long pattern of war-sparking hoaxes, but because the official story is so preposterous in structural forensics, physics, and materials science. As a professional engineer having performed structural design for 28 years, I became interested in the story when I witnessed video of the collapses of WTC 1 and 2 and especially WTC Building 7, that day. To assert that the first three instances in history of fire-induced collapse of steel multistory buildings occurred in one city, in one day (one of them with no aircraft collision) is ludicrous. Of countless raging fires in steel structures around the world, some have lasted far longer than the WTC fires, yet none led to plastic collapse, much less to the pulverizing (pyroclastic-style) destruction and free-fall-velocity collapse seen thrice on 9/11 but never seen before or since. *Except in every controlled demolition.*

Occam's Razor holds that the simplest explanation is most likely; put another way, if evidence contradicts an explanation that adds a pile of unlikely assumptions, that explanation is likely not true. On the morning of July 28, 1945, a fully-fueled B-25 Mitchell *bomber* lost in fog over Manhattan slammed into the 79th floor of the *Empire State Building*. *The* structure sustained no lasting damage, much less did it collapse in the free-fall-velocity, symmetrical implosion failure seen in steel structures *only* in controlled demolition.

Geopolitical forces in play in the world's mega-events need phenomenal amounts of money, logistics, and coordination that only major financial players enjoy. The idea that 9/11 was done by a handful of Muslims with the U.S. defense system fully engaged, is preposterous. It is one thing to believe legends about 'Honest Abe' because you were indoctrinated in school; it is another thing to believe a ludicrous story that defies logic and evidence simply because a few in the 'truther' camp happen to be eccentric. Just listen to the analysis we did in our November 11, 2018 podcast, read Heidner's report, and apply Occam's Razor.

Bottom line: from the assassination of JFK in 1963 to the 9/11 debacle, Russiagate, Shampeachment, the Chinavirus shutdown of America, and Election Steal 2020 – the Deep State will continue to destroy our economy, flood our borders with illegals, commit murders of presidents or of thousands of civilians foreign and domestic until We The People learn to focus on _our_ target: their power source and puppet institution, _congress_.

Churchill's Folly: How Winston Churchill created modern Iraq by Chris Catherwood, is the story of Britain's dissection of the Persian Empire into the petrodollar bloodbath we've seen ever since. Ralph Raico's _Rethinking Churchill_ chapter in the book _Reassessing the Presidency_ removed my blinders about the old Bulldog whose clever turns of phrase had always captured me. Bottom line: this book will teach you just what a scheming monster Churchill actually was.

Considerations About Recent Predictions of Impending Shortages of Petroleum Evaluated From the Perspective of Modern Petroleum Science by J. F. Kenney, is an online white paper that smashes the unfounded 'Peak Oil' scare trotted out along with the equally unsupported 'anthropogenic Climate Change' theory. These false prophets, ironically, helped drive oil prices through the roof for years; without a shred of evidence from petroleum science, they are useful puppets for Big Oil. The old 'fossil fuels' hypothesis originated in the 18th century; it held that petroleum miraculously evolves from decayed biological material – plants and animals – which would mean it is limited. The fossil fuels hypothesis has been replaced over the past four decades by the Russian-Ukrainian theory of 'Abyssal Abiotic Petroleum Origins' which establishes that petroleum is a primordial material that erupts from great depth and is practically unlimited in abundance, only depending on extraction technology and exploration competence. http://www.csun.edu/~vcgeo005/Energy.html

It's the Crude, Dude: Greed, Gas, War, and the American Way by Linda McQuaig is a well-documented history of America's role in the game played first by the British and French in the sands of Araby. She lists individual deals, companies, sheikhs, and contracts over the past century. As bloody as we think Mohammedans are, this book proves that the Deep State, using _both_ sides, causes these wars. Bottom line: we should feel sorry for any Middle East population as long as the Deep State owns Congress.

Reassessing the Presidency: The Rise of the Executive State and the Decline of Freedom is a 791-page lesson about how American history has been steered by our presidents; edited by John V. Denson. Each chapter can be read on its own to grasp a particular presidency or period. Bottom line is the book's recurring theme: as Madison and Jefferson, both presidents themselves, constantly reminded us that presidents are not to be trusted; the People must stay in control and remain always vigilant.

The Costs of War: America's Pyrrhic Victories is another compendium edited by John Denson. A treasure-trove for those who want to learn why our wars were fought. The book is worth buying for Raico's *Rethinking Churchill* chapter alone; it finally puts the butcherous Bulldog of Britain in the hall of infamy alongside Lincoln, Teddy Roosevelt, and FDR. But read Denson's *A Century of War* first.

War is a Racket is the small, powerful classic by the most-decorated officer in the history of the US Marine Corps, General Smedley Butler. He describes how the military industry – all the branches – conditions young minds to do its will, right or wrong; how he, as a decorated officer, did the bidding of banks, oil companies, sugar companies and military contractors, plundering foreign countries. General Butler spent many years after leaving the military, trying to warn America just as former 5-star general President Dwight Eisenhower did 25 years later in his farewell address when he coined the term 'Military Industrial Complex'. Bottom line: top military brass exposed the Deep State 80 years ago!

Truth is a Lonely Warrior by James Perloff is something like a Cliff's Notes version of half a dozen of the books I mention here. For lots of American history in one small book, this one is a winner.

The War Lovers: Roosevelt, Lodge, Hearst and the Rush to Empire, 1898 by Evan Thomas is the amazing story of how America was transformed from a non-interventionist economic giant into the world's foremost military plundering and invading power, knocking England from its hegemonic throne. Teddy Roosevelt was a romantic fraud; a sickly child who overcompensated by bullying the world. With his best friend, powerful warmonger Henry Cabot Lodge – and the timely help of America's most powerful newspaper man of the time – these men literally *created* the Spanish-American War to plunder the Philippines, Guam, Puerto Rico and others. Bottom line: as the Deep State used Lincoln to hijack our Constitution and occupy America, they used Teddy Roosevelt to spawn the worldwide Military-Industrial Complex that plagues the whole world to this day.

Wilson's War: How Woodrow Wilson's Great Blunder led to Hitler, Lenin, Stalin & World War II by Jim Powell is an excellent primer on Tom 'Woodrow' Wilson, highlighting the milquetoast do-gooder's colossal blunders from Mexico to Venezuela to America joining Europe's two world wars for huge military industry profits. Reading this account of presidential incompetence that many other presidents have since displayed, I finally understood that Wilson's chief weakness wasn't incompetence so much as useful wickedness. Bottom line: how Wilson knowingly dragged America into Europe's mega-wars.

FDR's Folly: How Roosevelt and his New Deal prolonged the Great Depression is the second primer on America's world-war presidents by historian Jim Powell. As he does with Wilson, the author illustrates how mendacious, bungling and evil FDR was. The hero of my parents' generation was also a good friend of Stalin, who killed 20 million of his own people. Another Deep State tool.

Roosevelt's Secret War: FDR & World War II Espionage is the story of FDR's creation of America's intelligence industry. Author Joseph Persico says, *"Few leaders were better adapted temperamentally to espionage than FDR; (he) compartmentalized information, misled associates, manipulated people, conducted intrigues, used private lines of communication, scattered responsibility, duplicated assignments, provoked rivalries, held the cards while showing few, and left few fingerprints."* And this from an author who *likes* FDR, referring to him as a principled Machiavellian who hoped to achieve clear ends (getting America into WWII) although most Americans wanted nothing to do with it.

Day of Deceit: The Truth about FDR and Pearl Harbor is Robert B. Stinnett's copious proof showing that Pearl Harbor was no surprise to FDR, just the 9/11 that the devious president needed to prime a multi-billion-dollar war machine on both sides of the ocean. *Millions of new jobs! What's a few tens of thousands dead?* Like Persico, Stinnett is still supportive of FDR; yet by simply reporting what he found, Stinnett's smoking guns expose FDR as a puppet of the Deep State 30 years before Eisenhower coined the term 'military-industrial complex'.

The Great Oil Conspiracy: How the U.S. Government Hid the Nazi Discovery of Abiotic Oil from the American People by Dr. Jerome Corsi is much like Thomas Gold's book, building on the Ukrainian and Russian theory of Abyssal Abiotic Petroleum Origins without giving due credit to the Ukrainian and Russian scientists that developed the theory long before the rise of a German variation of the theory.

Reset: Iran, Turkey, and America's Future is another master work by Stephen Kinzer. It is likely that 99.99% of Americans have never heard of the popular revolutions against Islamic rule by the people of Iran and Turkey a century ago. The 'Young Turks' – led by Mustafa Kemal Ataturk – succeeded, while the Persian (Iranian) people were enslaved in Mohammed's system. _Fascinating_ read.

Unrestricted Warfare by Qiao Liang and Wang Xiangsui can be readily found in book form, but look it up online and you will find it in PDF format, over 200 pages, a 1999 publication by two Chinese politicians and military officers. Those who do not see the bigger picture (God's dealing with mankind on earth) often worry these days that China will conquer the world. Perhaps this is understandable...

First, because this 22-year-old book perfectly explains the Chinese bioweapon created and released, with funding and direction for gain-of-function viability research from bats to humans, by the diabolical Anthony Fauci. Late in 2019, the virus was allowed to infect a number of Chinese, who carried it from the laboratory in Wuhan province. The Chinese Communist Party took prophylactic precautions in China while allowing a few virus carriers to travel to Europe and America as human bioweapons. A demonic strategy, perfectly fitting the thesis of _Unrestricted Warfare._

Secondly, Americans should be afraid because of the sheer intellectual and strategic prowess of the two authors. A reader cannot fault the impressive and extensive knowledge of western history and culture displayed by these two Chinese military men. To read this 1999 treatise and compare it to anything published by any American author – especially an American politician or military officer – the reader chillingly understands that those Chicoms are not the boorish robots we believe they are. One wonders: how many such brilliant minds exist in the Chinese Communist Party?

Read the book. I read it for my own education and edification, and learned a great deal of military history, East and West, and strategic thinking, besides. All I can say is: the CCP is here already, in force, especially in our universities and corporations. They are brilliant, godless, and ruthless; with that unnerving smile and superficial graciousness that puts the target at ease before they slip the stiletto under your ribs.

The New Empire of Debt by Bill Bonner and Addison Wiggin is the second edition of a work that traces America's past 120 years of world conquest, measuring blood and money with a mix of humor and morose fact that keeps you turning the pages to find out how stupid we can get before

Congress' Deep State puppeteers bankrupt us entirely. Bottom line: illustrates exactly how America has become so hated around the world, and so bankrupt as well.

Two More on Lincoln, America's First Deep State Puppet

Forced Into Glory: Abraham Lincoln's White Dream is a 662-page shocker by Black author and history scholar Lerone Bennett Jr. This is from the back cover of this courageous African-American's book: _"Every American schoolchild knows the story of "The Great Emancipator" who freed Negroes with the stroke of a pen out of the kindness of his heart. (But) Lincoln wasn't the great emancipator...(he) was a conservative politician who said repeatedly that he believed in White supremacy. Not only that, he believed Blacks and Whites would be better off separated, preferably by the Atlantic Ocean...(his) Emancipation Proclamation...freed few if any of the slaves, and he called for the deportation of African-Americans and the creation of an all-White country."_

Bennett's scholarship is impeccable, his indictment of Lincoln, withering. Are all men created equal, as the Declaration of Independence holds? Not according to Lincoln, Bennett writes on page 315: _"Large chunks of Lincoln's debate speeches...are taken from Henry Clay's mouth...Lincoln said he had never tried to apply the principles of the Declaration of Independence to slavery or the political rights of Blacks in America. On at least fifteen occasions, he said publicly that the principles of the Declaration didn't require him or anybody else to do anything about slavery in the South and Jim Crow in the North."_

Bottom line: A racist monster was the best salesman ever in the White House.

America's Caesar: The Decline and Fall of Republican Government in the United States of America by Greg L. Durand probes more deeply than does DiLorenzo into the personal and religious aspects of Lincoln's character, using primary-sources to prove that Lincoln was a cross between Bill Clinton and Saddam Hussein: a godless butcher with a slick public persona. After you read these quotes from his friends, contemporaries, and Lincoln's own pen, you'll know that we all had a _propagandist_ education.

Studies in the U.S. Constitution

The Tactical Civics™ Ready Constitution is a spiral-bound, super-handy desk copy of the U.S. Constitution with a unique design. It features Mike Holler's numbering system for each clause in the Constitution, making it easy to start memorizing where your favorite clauses are. Amendments are integrated in context where they affect the law. You can buy this handy spiral-bound edition in our Training Center. I use it every day.

Free, Sovereign, and Independent States: The Intended Meaning of the American Constitution by John Remington Graham explains the U.S. Constitution clause by clause, tracing legislative history from the kings' courts and parliaments of Great Britain to our Constitutional Convention. This ready reference on every clause in the Constitution is a masterful briefing on the origins of America's Supreme Law. Bottom line: this is the concise, historically complete explanation of every sentence in the U.S. Constitution.

The Founders' Constitution by editors Kurland and Lerner is a 5-volume massive reference set offering a more in-depth treatment than Graham's. It includes extracts from leading works of political theory, history, law, and constitutional argument that the Framers and their contemporaries used and produced. Available in paperback and CD-ROM, I find the electronic edition considerably handier. Bottom line: this is a far more in-depth background on the U.S. Constitution than Graham's book above, but Graham's work is more comprehensive regarding the provenance (legal roots) of every clause.

The People Themselves: Popular Constitutionalism and Judicial Review by Larry D. Kramer, former dean of Stanford Law School, is no dry tome filled with legal jargon. It is a refreshing look at why We The People have more lawful power than the U.S. Supreme Court. Dean Kramer discusses why it is critical that We The People begin to exercise that power peacefully and lawfully – or we will lose that power, and rule of law with it. Unfortunately, Dr. Kramer is now the president of a very liberal Silicon Valley foundation, but his thesis in this work still holds true. Bottom line: We the People have more power and authority than any U.S. supreme Court; we just never took advantage of it. *Until now!*

Founding Fathers and Roots of Our Condition

The First American Republic 1774-1789 by Thomas Chorlton is similar to an out of print book called *President Who?: Forgotten Founders* by Stanley Klos. George Washington called Payton Randolph "the Father of our country" because Randolph was the first President of the United States in Congress Assembled, and 14 presidential administrations existed prior to George Washington's! Read this one and you'll agree that most of us were cheated in our education.

The Republic of Letters: The Correspondence Between Jefferson and Madison 1776-1826 a 3-volume compendium of 50 years' correspondence between the two giants among America's founding fathers. Series editor James Smith makes segues from their correspondence to their historical context, helping the reader grasp these founders' development over their lifetimes. I learned more about Madison from these letters than from seven Madison biographies. To grasp a man's mind, read his letters.

Democracy in America by Alexis deTocqueville is a classic work of economics, sociology, and political science. Although the young Frenchman did not grasp the republican form of government guaranteed in our Constitution, he was prescient about *democracy* in America. Our founders created a representative constitutional republic of sovereign States specifically to *avoid* democracy, majority rule that always degenerates into warring mobs, grabbing for goodies from the all-knowing Nanny State.

From his limited view as a foreigner, Tocqueville accurately predicted that democracy in America would degenerate into soft despotism and 'tyranny of the majority' as Madison predicted 50 years earlier. Tocqueville said that majoritarian tyranny would spring from the confluence of two corrupting factors: dependence on government for material security, and the growing prejudices of an increasingly ignorant mass, against one another's factions and groups.

He was correct. After 150 years of government education, most Americans are European socialists, unfit to rule our passions and unwilling to oversee our servant government; instead, making it their master by begging security and provision from it.

Hull's Wall Chart of World History

Technically this is not a book, but a very long, folded pictographic chart of incredible intricacy. First published in the Victorian era, Edward Hull's superb *Wall Chart of World History: From Earliest Times to the Present* (the Dorset Press Edition if you can find it, dated 1989) is one of the most fascinating and entertaining resources I've ever used. I have bought half a dozen of them over the past 20 years, and only have one remaining. Several went to my children and grandchildren.

This wall chart is perhaps 18-20 feet long, but it folds up so that it can be read as a (large) book on your lap or table top. It's more fun to lay it out on the floor as I've done with children; you can spend hours teaching and learning world history. It is a jam-packed compendium of key people, facts, and dates in a whole new way of seeing them...as a visual flow of 'roots' from one generation to the next.

It covers all the major civilizations in the world, arranged chronologically. So you can easily see, for instance, what was happening in England, France, Germany, China, Italy, Egypt, et al, when Henry VIII was on the throne. Most people think of Henry VIII as the fellow who launched the 'Protestant' Church; but of course Martin Luther was turning the Vatican on its head at the same time and the first 'Protestant' Council took place in Augsburg.

Simultaneously, you can see that during Henry's reign, Ivan the Terrible was marauding, Michelangelo was creating his sublime works to edify mankind, the Vatican seated six successive popes, and Suleiman 'the Magnificent' had plundered and ravaged to carry the Ottoman Empire to new heights. Meanwhile, you see that Portugal had begun plundering and colonizing India, while Charles I of Spain became king...of Germany!...as China rumbled on in isolation under the Ming Dynasty.

I have never found a more powerful teaching and learning tool for world history. Buy one if you can find the Dorset 1989 edition. _Do not_ buy secular, revisionist imitations of Hull's priceless gem. There are knockoffs, but they leave out many important people and events, and add many unimportant trifles.

Economics, Money and Banking

Economics in One Lesson by Henry Hazlitt is a classic economics primer for people who would never read economics subjects but want to know how labor, money, government and credit operate in society to cause wars, inflation, depressions, and such.

The Mystery of Banking by Murray N. Rothbard, a student of Ludwig von Mises, a founder of 'Austrian School' classical economics. Rothbard shows where the bodies were buried as bankers and D.C. debased and despoiled our currency and engage daily in fraud, theft, and counterfeiting. More importantly, on pages 262-268 the author provides a concise plan to restore lawful currency and banking in America that, together with the work of Professor Huerta de Soto (see below), Tactical Civics™ is using to draft our Lawful United States Money and Banking Act.

Blood Money: The Civil War and the Federal Reserve by John Remington Graham is a little booklet explaining that the Federal Reserve scam actually began generations before the Jekyll Island gang and Congress teamed up in 1910-13.

Barbara Villiers or, A History of Monetary Crimes by Alexander del Mar is a tiny book with a misleading name. Villiers was a favored mistress of an English king, for whose personal benefit coinage laws were passed. If you think this bizarre, read Rothbard's history, cited above; American monetary legislation since Lincoln's time has been the same kind of deals but with many 'mistresses'.

The Case Against the Fed by Murray Rothbard is a small book with a practical goal: to show how to shut down history's longest-running counterfeiting scam. This work forms the basic guide for the design of our proposed reform legislation, the *Lawful American Money and Banking Act*.

Money, Bank Credit, and Economic Cycles in the second English edition (2009) by Professor Jesus Huerta de Soto is the finest single volume in print on practical economics. Like the late Murray Rothbard, this author also explains the criminal nature of the fractional reserve banking scam throughout history; how all business boom-and-bust cycles have been created by the Federal Reserve crime families. Like Joseph Salerno is his book *Money: Sound & Unsound*, the author explains how the theories of Keynes and Marx are still used by central banks and the banking industry generally to defraud us. In his final chapter, Professor de Soto offers a simple, powerful plan to restore honest money and banking.

Pieces of Eight: The Monetary Powers and Disabilities of the United States Constitution by Edwin Vieira, Jr. is the definitive explanation of lawful U.S. money as stipulated in our Supreme Law, and also the definitive history of the U.S. Dollar. Out of print for about a decade, the huge two-volume hardbound set (over 1,700 pages) is available again through Amazon.com and at $200 is a bargain if you need definitive legal citations regarding U.S. money.

Unaccountable: How the accounting profession forfeited a public trust by Mike Brewster takes you from ancient clay tablets in Sumeria up to the breakup of the Big Eight, in a fast-moving tale of deceit and unprofessionalism, making 'the dismal profession' a riveting read.

For background on how deeply Congress has been involved in financial crimes this century, *AmericaAgain! – The Movie* is the best start. But here are a few good resources regarding banking:

The Best Way to Rob a Bank is to Own One by UMKC Law professor and former federal bank regulator William Black explains how at the end of last century the S&L crisis was a tremor of things to come. Many more recent books expose the grifters' games today; three good ones are:

It Takes a Pillage: Behind the Bailouts, Bonuses and Backroom Deals From Washington to Wall Street by Nomi Prins

The Great American Stickup: Greedy Bankers and the Politicians Who Love Them by Robert Scheer

Griftopia: A Story of Bankers, Politicians, and the Most Audacious Power Grab in History by Matt Taibbi

If you're not much of a reader, learn how staggeringly corrupt the banking industry is (and how it controls Congress and presidents) by watching the Academy-Award winning documentary *Inside Job*. You'll never feel the same walking into your bank.

Crumbling and Corrupt Civilization

Ideas Have Consequences by Richard M. Weaver is a little classic which proposes that language, virtue, maleness, femaleness, and ancient mores have almost gone out of our world. I disagree with Weaver's somber note at the end, but this book caused me to think about truth, goodness, and beauty outside my religious categories.

Amusing Ourselves to Death by Neil Postman is the most trenchant, helpful guidebook for ridding your home of television. Written in 1985, Postman's work is in many ways an extension of the thoughts of Walter Ong in his classic *Orality and Literacy*. There are clear reasons why the American mind degenerated as it has; to know why these things happened and how they are happening still, read Postman. Then sell your televisions and start buying good books; you'll be wealthier in spirit.

The Beast on the East River: The U.N. Threat to America's Sovereignty and Security by Nathan Tabor, the founder of The ConservativeVoice.com, is the best analysis of the U.N. threat that I have read. We used this work to draft the sections of the AmericaAgain! Declaration that deal with ending our U.N. debacle.

The Master Switch by Columbia University professor Tim Wu explains several things that I had always wondered about. How did the big radio corporations of the early 20th century become big television and media empires by the end of the century? How do media content empires fit together with the distribution empires to determine what Americans see and hear? Is the Internet really the open sea of information for everyone to dip into as we imagine, or do certain entities control what we can get access to, and how it's presented? We've seen Facebook and Twitter answer that question! And of course, what about Microsoft, Apple, and Google, the 800-pound gorilla on the block, whose motto was "don't be evil"? Each corporation is more powerful than most governments on earth; we now see them working with corrupt government to be evil; controlling the content of what we think is the Internet world. The author probes all this, and more.

The Mechanical Bride by Marshall McLuhan, is a useful book on *noetics* (knowing how we know), orality, and the impact of the written word on a world lit only by fire. This revolution of writing vs. speaking was far more fundamental to the human spirit than the modern reader might imagine. McLuhan gets a bit weighty and also more than a bit flighty at times; but if you stay with him, I think it pays off in the end.

Christians, Muslims, and Jews

A Wind in the House of Islam by David Garrison is the story of the nine geocultural variants of Islam around the world – what the author calls 'rooms in the House of Islam' – and how the Wind of God's Spirit is blowing through every one of them. Garrison spent three years travelling 250,000 miles through every corner of the Muslim world to investigate reports of Muslims turning to faith in Christ.

The researcher collected the stories of over 1,000 formerly-Muslim Christians, asking them the question: "What did God use to bring you to faith in Jesus Christ? Tell me your story." The result is an unprecedented look into the greatest turning of Muslims to Christ in history; stories of men and women who have sacrificed everything – home, family, even their lives – to follow Jesus. You hear from men and women from Africa to Indonesia and everywhere in between; how God is at work through answered prayers, and through dreams and visions and through technology (Internet, satellite television, video and audio tools). The reader gains insight into each of the nine geo–cultural 'rooms' within Islam and, most importantly, learns how we can be part of the greatest turning of Muslims to Christ in history, both overseas and in our own communities.

The three main takeaways: 1) Christianity is growing today as never before on earth; 2) There is a great need for sound Biblical teaching among new converts; syncretism and pseudo-Christianity are always a danger; and 3) Most importantly, conservative Americans need to lose our hatred of all Muslims.

Similar books surveying the sudden growth of Christianity in the Middle East today are such books as *Jesus in Iran* by Eugene Bach; *Too Many to Jail: The Story of Iran's New Christians* by Mark Bradley; *Muslims, Christians and Jesus* by Carl Medearis; *The Coming Fall of Islam in Iran* by Reza Safa; *Seeking Allah, Finding Jesus* by Nabeel Qureshi and many others.

The Next Christendom by Philip Jenkins, Penn State University professor, suggests that the rapid growth of primitive and Pentecostal Christianity – both within and alongside existing traditions – is reshaping the world. 'Southern Christianity', Jenkins proposes, is Pentecostal, evangelical, and politically and morally conservative, pushing aside the cosmopolitan, unbelieving northern sensibilities that marked the senescence of European and American mainline denominations that now dismiss the basic teachings of the Bible in favor of enlightened, metrosexual life. (One caveat: Chapters 3&4 are his statistical and demographic thesis; slow, dry reading! I recommend reading the first two chapters, then jump to Chapter 5.)

Even as politically correct popes regurgitate Communism and Hollywood political correctness, the Next Christendom is draining the dying European denominations; for instance, openly challenging Anglicanism's apostasy. Jenkins posits that geopolitics, too, will be shaped by new Christians. 'Northern Christianity' and its secular political ideals are dying, as the opposite is happening in the southern hemisphere. With the gospel no longer shaped by a Eurocentric ethos and historical memory, the prophets of the 'post-Christian' world are wrong...*the Church is as alive as ever.*

Martyrs Mirror by Thielemann vanBraght is a hardbound compendium of 16 centuries of martyrs for the faith, from Christ's apostles through the 'Reformation', when believers who refused to sprinkle their babies and call it baptism were ruined, run out of town, jailed indefinitely and left to starve, drowned, or burned to death by Roman Catholics, Lutherans, and Calvinists. The purpose of reviewing these murders is to see that: a) Christians have been as savage as Muslims, for religion; b) the 'Reformation' was a *political* movement; and c) 'Reformed' folk run from these facts as Catholics run from the Inquisition. Ask me how I know this.

The Untold Story of the New Testament Church by Frank Viola explains how trying to read the Bible in the order we have it today is like re-arranging all the chapters of a novel, binding it back together, then trying to make sense of the story. Fascinating book.

Finding Organic Church: A Comprehensive Guide to Starting and Sustaining Authentic Christian Communities also by Frank Viola is a sequel to the amazing book, _Pagan Christianity?_ – explaining how to gather with other believers in an organic fellowship without repeating the 501c3 lunacy of Christianity, Inc. or the opposite lunacy of most short-lived house church startups. Viola brings many years of hard experiences, as he has become a major figure in modern reformation.

The Great Christian Revolution by Otto Scott demonstrates that no matter how they may balk, even the most heathen anti-Christian in the West benefits from centuries of Christian foundation in every area of human endeavor.

Dismissing God by D. Bruce Lockerbie exposes the lives and work of the most influential writers of Abraham Lincoln's and subsequent generations. He explains how these angry humanists kicked out our moral underpinnings: Emily Dickinson, Walt Whitman, Ralph Waldo Emerson, Nathaniel Hawthorne, Herman Melville, Mark Twain, William Blake, Percy Bysshe Shelley, John Keats, John Ruskin, William Morris, William Butler Yeats, James Joyce, D.H Lawrence, Oscar Wilde, F. Scott Fitzgerald, Hemingway; the full lineup of perpetrators used by schools to _destroy_ our Christian civilization.

About the Author

David M. Zuniga is a graduate of the University of Texas (BS, Architectural Engineering) and was for 28 years a professional engineer designing schools, churches, industrial, and commercial buildings and their structural, plumbing, HVAC, electrical, and site civil systems. He has also been a cattleman, custom homebuilder, commercial contractor, SCUBA instructor, cross-culture church planter, missionary pilot, land surveyor, and subdivision designer/developer.

Having founded four classical Christian K-12 schools in three states, he designed a curriculum with Latin, Logic, Rhetoric, and the Great Books of Western Civilization.

Shocked at the government fraud of 9/11, beginning in 2006 he spent 14 months in monastic seclusion, prayer and study of 110 key books. He wrote the first draft of the *AmericaAgain! Declaration* and refined the document with help of many fine Americans including constitutional radio show host Mike Church and constitutional scholar and author Edwin Vieira Jr.

Establishing AmericaAgain! Trust with his brother in 2009, David wrote his first book *This Bloodless Liberty* in 2010 to convey his vision. In 2015 he published *Fear The People,* introducing a full-spectrum action plan to restore popular sovereignty and rule of law. In 2018, he began writing the 5-volume Tactical Civics™ series and several other standalone books to break this new way of life into brief books for action. With his co-founders, in January 2021 David helped launch the Tactical Civics™ Training Center. By early 2022, Americans had launched over 200 county chapters.

David has been a guest on Infowars Nightly News and is a recurring guest on radio shows across the republic. His published articles have appeared on many blogs, forums, and alternative media.

David has two children and six grandchildren. They live in the Hill Country of Texas where they serve no king but King Jesus.

Made in United States
North Haven, CT
11 March 2023

33927586R00135